Corporate Social Investing

Corporate
Social
Investing

THE BREAKTHROUGH STRATEGY
FOR GIVING AND GETTING
CORPORATE CONTRIBUTIONS

CURT WEEDEN

FOREWORDS BY PAUL NEWMAN & PETER LYNCH

Berrett-Koehler Publishers, Inc.
San Francisco

Berrett-Koehler Publishers, Inc.
450 Sansome Street, Suite 1200
San Francisco, CA 94111-3320
Tel: (415) 288-0260   Fax: (415) 362-2512

Ordering Information

Individual sales. Berrett-Koehler publications are available through most bookstores. They can also be ordered direct from Berrett-Koehler at the address above.

Quantity sales. Special discounts are available on quantity purchases by corporations, associations, and others. For details, contact the "Special Sales Department" at the Berrett-Koehler address above.

Orders for college textbook/course adoption use. Please contact Berrett-Koehler Publishers at the address above.

Orders by U.S. trade bookstores and wholesalers. Please contact Publishers Group West, 1700 Fourth St., Berkeley, CA 94710. Tel: (510) 528–1444; Fax: (510) 528-3444.

Printed in the United States of America

 Printed on acid-free and recycled paper that is composed of 85% recovered fiber, including 15% postconsumer waste.

Library of Congress Cataloging-in-Publication Data

Weeden, Curt, 1942–
    Corporate social investing: the breakthrough strategy for giving and getting corporate contributions / Curt Weeden.
        p. cm.
    Includes bibliographical references and index.
    ISBN 1-57675-045-0 (alk. paper)
    1. Investments—Social aspects—United States. 2. Corporations—Charitable contributions—United States. 3. Social responsibility of business—United States. I. Title.
HG4910.W362   1998
361.7'65—dc21   98-27274
                                  CIP

First Edition
01 00 99 98   10 9 8 7 6 5 4 3 2 1

Copyediting: Sandra Beris
Proofreading: PeopleSpeak
Interior design and production: Joel Friedlander, Marin Bookworks
Indexing: Rachel Rice

To Marti—
with love and appreciation

Contents

Foreword by Paul Newman

In 1994, Paul Newman was awarded his second Oscar. While a previous Academy Award had recognized his performance as an actor, the second tribute acknowledged Newman's real-life role as a leading and ingenious philanthropist. In 1982, he founded Newman's Own, a food company that contributes 100 percent of its after-tax profits to charity. In the fifteen years since its founding, over $90 million has been donated by Newman's Own to charities around the world.

These charities include not only the seven international camps (the Hole in the Wall Gang Camp Association) that provide therapeutic camping experiences to children with serious and often life-threatening conditions but also hundreds of other charities in the United States and abroad. It is the policy of Newman's Own to donate the profits from its business to nonprofit organizations operating within the countries from which the profits are derived—a policy that not only sells products but also encourages the further development of the nonprofit sector.

In his life and philanthropy, Paul Newman acknowledges the role of luck—the generosity of it in his life and the absence of it in the lives of many others. He is quick to voice his respect for the hard work, ingenuity, and leadership that typify the American business executive, but he also reflects on the luck of being in the American business environment in which these talents can flourish. It is an environment that in no small measure flows from the extraordi-

nary partnership between business and the more than six hundred thousand organizations that make up the nonprofit sector.

A decade and a half ago, my friend A. E. Hotchner and I were both astounded and elated when we learned that people were actually buying Newman's Own vinaigrette. We had every reason to be surprised—this wasn't a business that was the fruition of an age-old dream or the product of some high-priced marketing study. It started as a kind of a joke, but it ended up giving back in satisfaction much more than we gave.

Our surprise over the success of our business has been dwarfed by something else—the discovery of what can happen when a line of food products is mixed with a hefty dose of creative marketing and then sprinkled on an assortment of social needs.

I am delighted that Newman's Own has found a niche in one of the toughest industries around, the grocery trade. I'm even more delighted that our products have generated over $90 million in donations to charities in the United States and other locations around the world. This business has taught me a lot of lessons but none more important than demonstrating how, with a little effort and imagination, commercial enterprise can have a powerful influence on society.

Newman's Own gives away every nickel that drops to the bottom line after taxes. I completely understand why most other companies cannot replicate our unusual economic business model. For publicly held corporations and most private enterprises, the profit motive is essential. However, here's the problem: *too many businesses are at the opposite extreme of the generosity continuum.*

Besides paying taxes, companies are inclined to set aside little or nothing at all to address issues and problems on the other side of the company property line. Giving money or product to a nonprofit is too often seen as an erosion of shareholder value. Contributing money has become, to many businesses, equivalent to giving an edge to a competitor that keeps its purse strings tightly knotted.

Along comes *Corporate Social Investing*. This is a book worth reading because it establishes important rules of the road for corporations. The ten-step plan described in the book creates a common denominator for every business, no matter how big or small.

The standards seem reasonable and appropriate for any company in any industry segment. The plan should go down easy, even for the most profit-driven businessperson in the country.

This book reminds us that corporate contributions when measured as a percent of profits have been on the decline for a long time. The concept of corporate social investing is the tide-turner. If companies buy into the plan (and they should), corporate social responsibility rises to a new level. Corporations have at their disposal a management plan that will enrich their own businesses and at the same time do a lot of good for people and places that need their help.

It is important to keep in mind that corporate social investing isn't just about how much cash and product companies strategically place with nonprofit institutions. In the end, it is also about leadership, social values, and the health and well-being of an extraordinary phenomenon called the nonprofit sector. From our great universities, cultural institutions, hospitals, and research centers, to local environmental groups, library committees, and homeless shelters, America (and increasingly other countries as well) is a nation of innovative and high-quality alternatives. Keeping in mind that the nonprofit sector has played no small part in sustaining one of the most favorable business environments in history, corporate leaders would do well to include its nurturing as an important strategic business objective.

Whether a company sells cars, airplanes, financial services—or salad dressing, it makes good business sense to preserve and enrich the nonprofit sector. Corporate social investing gives corporations an opportunity to take one more step in what is definitely a mutually beneficial direction.

Foreword by Peter Lynch

Peter Lynch is one of the world's most respected and admired investment experts. Under his leadership, Fidelity's Magellan Fund (the largest mutual fund in the United States) recorded an astonishing 28-fold increase per share between 1977 and 1990, when he left the fund. Now a lecturer and best-selling author (recent books include One Up on Wall Street: How to Use What You Already Know to Make Money in the Market; Beating the Street; *and* Learn to Earn: A Beginner's Guide to the Basics of Investing and Business, *all with John Rothchild), Peter Lynch is also prominent in the nonprofit world. He is on the board of several charitable and educational institutions.*

Finding both money and volunteers for thirteen nonprofit organizations is a high priority for me these days. These are not easy tasks, as anyone who has been asked to solicit donations or recruit people to donate their time will attest. *Corporate Social Investing* is a book that may make both of these usually unglamorous duties a little easier and more understandable.

The ten-step plan described in the following chapters offers corporations and nonprofit organizations a way to develop strategic relationships that yield a type of bilateral return on investment—that is, an "ROI" that benefits both the business and the nonprofit. This plan is at the heart of the corporate social investing concept and is an approach that should add value to any corporation or nonprofit that engages in the process.

A quick scan of the book may give a reader the erroneous impression that only businesses need to get a grip on how to apply the principles of corporate social investing. That simply is not the case. Any employee or volunteer in a nonprofit organization that gets—or is looking to get—private sector support needs to understand the notion of corporate social investing for at least two reasons.

First, corporate social investing opens up different fund-raising channels. It shakes off some of the constraints that come attached to traditional corporate philanthropy and allows companies and nonprofits to design creative partnerships that can result in mutually advantageous outcomes. There is a strong possibility that corporate social investing will motivate businesses to put more dollars and products on the table for nonprofit organizations—perhaps as much as $3 billion or more each year. Which nonprofits are likely to be first in line for these additional private-sector resources? In many cases, they will be those organizations that are able to grasp how corporate social investing works.

The second way in which corporate social investing could have a major impact on the nonprofit field happens to coincide with a strong personal interest of mine: volunteerism. When a business commits money to an organization, it is often accompanied by a commitment of employee time. As the number of business-nonprofit financial connections grows larger with corporate social investing, I predict that the opportunities for recruiting volunteers into the nonprofit field will also expand.

I am a strong believer in volunteerism. I have seen many organizations in which hours have proven more helpful than dollars. That is why I am disturbed by what is happening to volunteerism in the United States (and in other nations as well). I remain concerned in spite of the optimistic follow-up to the 1997 President's Summit for America's Future and a recent INDEPENDENT SECTOR report that showed a 4 percent increase in U.S. volunteerism from 1993 to 1995. And I have good reason. Although there has been a slight uptick in the number of volunteers in the past few years, America actually had five million fewer people donating their time in 1995 than seven years earlier! In other words, in the United States we have a ways to go just to get back to where we were in 1989. And if we look at the percentage of the U.S. population that is volunteering today as compared to the 1960s, it quickly becomes evident why seasoned nonprofit leaders exclaim that volunteer recruitment is a far more awesome challenge now than it was two or three decades ago.

What has led to this situation? The changes in the social fabric of the United States and many other developed nations have left their mark on volunteerism. There are over 10 percent more Americans in the workforce today than there were in 1970, and there are twice as many women employed outside the home now as in 1960. (In spite of the large number of women now in the workforce, women still represent a majority of volunteers in the United States, according to a Gallup Organization survey).

But even taking these changes into account, it is perplexing to me why businesses aren't doing more to encourage volunteerism among their employees. A 1996 INDEPENDENT SECTOR study shows how volunteering can be a factor in developing more well-rounded, fulfilled individuals who in turn tend to be more productive workers. Here are some of the personal benefits from volunteering that respondents mentioned to researchers:

Allows me to gain a new perspective on things	78 percent
Makes me feel needed	68 percent
Helps me deal with some of my personal problems	40 percent
Provides me with new contacts that help me with my business or career	23 percent

I have seen how these kinds of positive personal outcomes often translate into reduced absenteeism from work, less stress in the office, and an overall improvement in job performance. A three-year study carried out by The Conference Board backs up my observations with evidence. Researchers tracked employees in four hundred Target stores (part of the Dayton Hudson Company) who participated in Family Matters, an initiative sponsored by the Points of Light Foundation, a nonprofit organization founded in 1990 to engage more people in voluntary community service. The Conference Board released its findings in 1997, including an analysis of how volunteer leaders involved in the project thought volunteerism affected Target stores. Significant percentages of those leaders agreed or strongly agreed with the following statements:

Target's community image is improved	94 percent
Employee morale is improved	74 percent
Employee commitment to Target is stronger	74 percent
Guest/customer relations have improved	60 percent
New skills were brought to the company	51 percent

If the numbers are impressive, what the Target volunteer leaders had to say is even more so. The Conference Board reported these statements as part of its report:

On employee morale. "We attract better employees who are happier and more positive toward Target. Their attitudes show in their work."—Store team leader in Alton, Illinois/St. Louis

On improved productivity. "A happy team member at home and at work increases productivity—you get more than 100 percent."—Team relations leader in Bridgeton/St. Louis

On stronger commitment to the company. "I think team members take a sense of pride in knowing that their company is out there doing something good for the community; working for Target is more than just a job."—Good neighbor captain, Lancaster/Los Angeles

On new skill development. "You learn how to get along, who people are, and to respect diversity. It is so important in the workplace."—Store team leader, Sandy Springs, Georgia

Corporate social investing may not lead to an explosion of new company-motivated volunteer initiatives like Target's program. But it can bring volunteerism into focus and it should make an incremental difference. Just as important, it has the capacity to connect employee volunteers with the organizations that are wrestling with America's toughest social problems—the nonprofits that often have the hardest time attracting volunteers.

When experts paint a picture of volunteerism, especially in America, they tend to use a very broad brush. An estimated *twenty billion hours* were volunteered in 1995, we are told. However, when we put those hours under a microscope, we find that *less than 10 percent* were directed toward organizations that offer services to the needy. This has led to charges that volunteerism too frequently skirts "core problems" and rather is often reduced to activities that are not as vital to society. Is such criticism correct? After all, we need people to volunteer to run school bake sales, serve as museum docents, participate in hospital auxiliaries, and give time to organizations that generally round out the quality of life in our neighborhoods and communities. However, we also need to find ways to induce more people to tackle our most challenging social issues—for instance, tutoring at-risk children (today less than 4 percent of volunteers work with poor kids). This is where I feel corporate social investing can make an important difference.

One of the ten steps in the corporate social investing model says that there needs to be a significant business reason for any commitment a company makes to a nonprofit. That might suggest that most "human service" ventures (such as soup kitchens, homeless centers, neighborhood revitalization efforts, and so on) will not qualify as candidates for volunteer activities that a corporation would promote. Actually, these types of volunteer experiences have already been embraced by many companies and have proven themselves to be helpful in meeting business objectives. Some corporations use volunteer projects to hone management leadership skills, develop team cohesion, or strengthen employee morale. There appears to be business relevance in all the programs that won the Points of Light Foundation's Excellence in Corporate Community Service award in 1997. Here are a few examples of the winners:

▶ AT&T Wireless Services managers start each of their national meetings with a community service project.

▶ Chase Manhattan's Partners in the Community program helps three hundred communities through the morale-building volunteer efforts of over nine thousand of the bank's employees.

▶ The Gap has an aggressive volunteer program, including working with AIDS groups, that connects the company with communities in which it does business.

▶ UGI Utilities supports an Excellence in Education program that helps brings volunteers, books, and the corporation's name into schools and the community.

▶ Unitrode Corporation participates in the Salvation Army's Reach Out program, where employees and their spouses get recognized for the time they spend acting as role models for children.

These company programs help explain why a group of large businesses surveyed by The Conference Board and INDEPENDENT SECTOR gave volunteerism high marks. Eighty percent stated that volunteer activities improved employee retention and enhanced training. Nearly as many companies—77 percent—said that volunteer programs benefited their strategic business objectives.

If corporate social investing does lead to more business-inspired volunteerism, new programs are likely to take on very different characteristics. Some companies may be in a position to set up highly structured volunteer programs with staff members assigned to handle administration duties (H. B. Fuller Company and Frontier Corporation, for example, already have employees working full-time on volunteer program management). Other corporations may follow the lead of the Calvert Group (Bethesda, Maryland) and permit workers to do several days of community service volunteer work without any loss of pay.

It is likely that most companies won't feel they are in a position to offer employees paid time away from their jobs to volunteer. Fine—there are still many other cost-effective options open to businesses that are interested in helping employees find ways to volunteer on their own time. According to a 1992 survey conducted by The Conference Board for Points of Light, the methods companies use most frequently to encourage employee volunteerism are placing articles in internal and external publications, issuing personal letters of commendation; nominating employees for external awards, presenting certificates and plaques, organizing special events such as receptions with the company CEO, and recognizing increments of volunteer service with suitable gifts.

These are not difficult or expensive commitments. Nor are other strategies companies use to promote volunteerism or recognize employee volunteers. Putting up a list of volunteer openings in the company elevator or posting them on a computer or traditional bulletin board doesn't require much (if any) expense. Inviting nonprofit organizations into the corporate cafeteria to participate in an annual volunteer fair won't be considered an unwelcome intrusion by employees. Setting up a clearinghouse that matches workers with nonprofit organizations doesn't require much time and can make the process of looking for a volunteer opportunity much more efficient and effective for employees. (Some companies such as Johnson & Johnson run these employee-nonprofit matching services with the help of college interns.)

It comes down to this: companies that adopt corporate social investing as a management model shouldn't overlook volunteerism. The potential return on investment from a well-thought-out employee volunteer strategy is too significant to ignore. However, the same principles a company uses to make and monitor financial investment decisions need to be applied to a business-based volunteerism initiative. The purpose of the program needs to be defined up-front (Why is our company doing this?) and its outcomes regularly measured (Is this program achieving what we expected it to?). As with any investment portfolio, some volunteer programs won't make the grade. Those that don't meet expectations should be dropped and replaced with new, more promising opportunities. All corporate social investments—whether of cash, products, land or equipment, or employee time—should be held to these basic investing standards.

Corporate social investing holds much promise for redefining financial relationships between businesses and nonprofits. Expectations should be just as high for social investing to bring more of the private sector's people-power to bear on some of our most pressing social needs.

Preface

It would be unfortunate if *Corporate Social Investing* were to be categorized as just a business book. It is meant to be much more than that. It is a resource that can be used to improve the lives of millions of people by creating new and powerful connections between the private sector and thousands upon thousands of nonprofit organizations. Caught between the pages of this book is a plan that, if unleashed, *could pour at least another $3 billion a year* into causes and organizations that could uplift the quality of life not just in the United States but in other parts of the world as well.

Like the mythical genie in the bottle, the plan proposed in *Corporate Social Investing* isn't worth much unless someone releases it into the business and social mainstream. That "someone" could be any person who

- ▶ Works for a profit-making business
- ▶ Is an employee, board member, or active volunteer of a non-religious nonprofit organization
- ▶ Owns stock in a publicly traded corporation
- ▶ Is a faculty member or student in an undergraduate or graduate business school

Every money-making corporation and all nonprofit organizations that raise (or hope to raise) money from the private sector stand to benefit from the ideas presented in this book. However, not all business and nonprofit decision makers are going to pay close attention to *Corporate Social Investing* without some encouragement. Anyone who thinks the principles outlined in the following chapters make sense can free the genie by passing this book along to the "right" individual—possibly with a buck slip similar to one of those that follow:

Corporate employees (especially those who are also board members or active volunteers of nonprofit organizations)—in a memo to senior management: "Corporate social investing appears to be a plan that could have a positive impact on our bottom line and on employee morale as well. Is there anything that we as employees (particularly those of us who are involved with nonprofit causes) can do to help bring corporate social investing to our company?"

Nonprofit board members or volunteers—in a note to the executive director of a nonprofit organization: "I know how difficult it has been to raise corporate contributions. This notion of corporate social investing gives us a new way of partnering with companies. How can we take advantage of this opportunity?"

Shareholders—in a letter to a corporate CEO: "As a shareholder concerned about the continued success of our business, I am enclosing a copy of *Corporate Social Investing*. The prescription in this book should enable us to be profitable and socially responsible at the same time."

Business school faculty members—in an e-mail to the dean: "Students want to prepare themselves for business careers, but many are also looking for ways to make a difference in society. *Corporate Social Investing* addresses both these interests."

This book's mission is convey to any of these audiences a few reasonable, attainable standards that should make life in the corporate and nonprofit worlds a lot easier. In working to carry out that mission, *Corporate Social Investing*

▶ Tells a company specifically how much it should consider spending (at a minimum) each year for programs/activities involving nonprofit organizations

▶ Explains what a business should expect back in return for making these payments

▶ Gives shareholders a means of holding companies accountable for their nonprofit investments

▶ Arms nonprofit and public organizations with new ideas for attracting more corporate support

In addition, this book does something else: it erases the term *corporate philanthropy* from the private sector vocabulary. That term has always been something of an oxymoron. Now it's gone. In its place is a description of a new process that is at the core of this book: *corporate social investing*

Much of the book is a how-to-do-it manual that explains in detail what businesses can do to convert corporate philanthropy into a corporate social investing strategy that they can use to open markets, recruit employees, improve customer relations, and solve any number of business problems. Through a plan that any company has the capacity to implement, corporate philanthropy can be transformed into a resource that turns nonprofits from supplicants to potent business allies.

This book comes with two important disclaimers.

First, the concept of corporate social investing isn't new. There are businesses—not a lot of them, but some—that have adopted many of the principles described in this book. These companies may not use *corporate social investing* as the label to describe what they are doing. S*trategic giving. Focused philanthropy.* These are other terms sometimes applied to management practices that equate to social investing (or at least to segments of the plan).

Second, many of the component parts of the corporate social investment model have been "stolen" from companies where they have shown themselves to be effective. They have been plucked from businesses that have discovered savvy ways of coupling their interests with nonprofit programs and activities. Some corporations have been churning out these inventive relationships for a long time.

Please don't be misled—these disclaimers should not be interpreted to mean that corporate social investing has become a widespread phenomenon throughout the business world. Quite the contrary. Most corporations have yet to discover its benefits. An even smaller percentage of nonprofit organizations knows much about the concept. Getting businesses and nonprofits to rally around corporate social investing in a big way is the driving force behind this book.

The management plan proposed in *Corporate Social Investing* comes from my twenty years of working with business executives charged with administering corporate philanthropy and social responsibility programs. Having been responsible either directly or indirectly for over $1 billion in private sector gifts and grants, I have celebrated many successful alliances between businesses and nonprofit organizations. I have also mourned a good many disappointments and failures. The ten-step plan for corporate social investing that is presented in this book is a product of those experiences—a product that is a reflection of practical, achievable ideas and an avoidance of the pitfalls that abound in the corporate social responsibility field.

The strategies described in the upcoming pages are offered as a universal reference point for all businesses, but there is plenty of room for modification and fine-tuning. Corporate social investing (as will be noted in a later chapter) is a "one-size-fits-all" concept. Nevertheless, many businesses will want to go beyond the minimum standards of the plan and others will be inclined to "customize" its elements. Regardless of how it is ultimately configured, corporate social investing will be a success if it leads to a vigorous and more mutually beneficial union between business and society.

CURT WEEDEN
June 1998

Acknowledgments

A ny writer who attempts to mine new fields in the private and
nonprofit sectors quickly learns that this is a job that requires
a lot of help. I am most grateful to the battalion of people who
joined in the heavy lifting that has made this book possible.

I am especially beholden to Bob Campbell, retired vice chairman of Johnson & Johnson. He spent a vast amount of time reading and rereading different versions of *Corporate Social Investing*.
Much of the wisdom in this book can be traced back to Bob.

My other friends and colleagues at Johnson & Johnson have
also been invaluable allies in this project. Roger Fine, general
counsel, and Bill Nielsen, vice president for public affairs, kept this
book on track. Russell Deyo, vice president for administration,
understood the need to reform corporate philanthropy. Bill
Dearstyne, Jerry Ostrov, Andrea Alstrup, Wendy Logan, and the
other members of the extraordinary Johnson & Johnson
Corporate Contributions Committee helped shape the contents of
this book. John Heldrich continues to show me how to translate
philanthropy into meaningful results.

Michael Bzdak, Helen Hughes, and Conrad Person are staff
members in the Office of Corporate Contributions at Johnson &
Johnson. They, along with my assistant Alexis McKay and co-
workers Nancy Lane, Gary Gorran, Stan Stern, Elisabeth King, and
Fred Patterson, have provided me with a steady flow of ideas
steeped in common sense that have greatly enriched this book.

Perhaps no group of people has been more important in shaping the contents of *Corporate Social Investing* than the members of The Conference Board Contributions Council. Some of the private sector's most astute and caring managers sit on that council. People like Dr. Richard Mund, executive director of the Mobil Foundation; Pat Hoven, president of the Honeywell Foundation; and Kristin Swain, president of the Corning, Inc. Foundation, all took time they didn't have to read early versions of the book and help make it more practical and powerful. However, no one on the Council did more for *Corporate Social Investing* than David Ford, past president of the Chase Manhattan Foundation and newly appointed president of The Lucent Technologies Foundation. I am thankful that he has shared with me both his intelligence and his friendship.

There are others whose thoughts and concepts will be found within the pages of this book. My longtime friend Dr. Reed Whittle was, as usual, on the mark in his suggestions for improving *Corporate Social Investing.* Other cheerleaders like Ann and Vernon Jordan, United Way's Betty Beene, David Morgan at the Council for Aid to Education, and UCLA's Dr. Al Osborne all helped me get this book to the finish line. Bob Forrester, of Payne, Forrester & Olsson, has sharpened my thinking with penetrating questions and good old-fashioned horse sense.

I am indebted to my son, Ryan, for his support of this book and other related projects. His research and writing for the National Center for Employee Ownership have given me new perspectives that should make corporate social investing even more valuable to businesses and nonprofit organizations.

A note of thanks to Steve Piersanti and his competent staff at Berrett-Koehler. Their skillful hands helped hone a rough manuscript into a product worthy of the Berrett-Koehler label. To have *Corporate Social Investing* included on the Berrett-Koehler list is indeed an honor.

The Confused State of Corporate Philanthropy

E ach year, companies spend billions on something called *external relations,* and they frequently do so without enforcing the same kind of tough management standards that they usually apply to other aspects of their businesses. Stakeholders are often left scratching their heads about the true value of a hodgepodge of "soft" functions that encompass community and public affairs, corporate social responsibility, and—most of all—corporate philanthropy.

Mixed Impressions

Of all the activities that have been stuck into this curious corporate corner, perhaps nothing is more mystifying than the way businesses relate (or don't relate) to nonprofit organizations and government institutions. If the public is left with a schizophrenic impression about what's going on between the private sector and these outside audiences, it's understandable. Consider the following two prevalent if contradictory impressions.

IMPRESSION A: BUSINESSES ARE CHEAP

The evidence is indisputable that when it comes to supporting nonprofit organizations, corporations are getting parsimonious with both their fiscal and their human resources. Companies are donating less of their pretax earnings to nonprofits than they did only a few years ago. What's more, it's getting harder to squeeze employee volunteers out of significantly downsized corporations.

It seems that many American companies are not connecting to the world outside the workplace the way they could or should. They are pulling back into themselves, consumed with a passion for reorganization and restructuring as they chase the dream of becoming the leanest profit-making machines on the face of the globe. One consequence of this inward focus among corporations is that nonprofit organizations that rely (at least in part) on business donations and volunteers are being turned away at the company gate.

The amount of tax-deductible corporate contributions made each year has been and still is a good indicator of how businesses relate to social issues and needs. These cash, product, equipment, and land donations are the mercury in the social responsibility thermometer. The latest temperature reading inside many companies is unsettling as it becomes apparent that philanthropy isn't keeping pace with the rapid rise in annual profits. To put it another way, many businesses are more closefisted than in the past when deciding what size slice of their earnings they should carve out for grants and contributions to the nonprofit world. And this new attitude about philanthropy is causing aftershocks being felt in college quadrangles, museum galleries, soup kitchens, and community health centers all over the country.

Something else is perceived to be wrong, too. Some shareholders of publicly held companies have a growing concern that corporate contributions are being misused by senior management. The complaints center on gifts and grants going to nonprofits that are of *personal* interest to CEOs and other high-level executives, organizations that have little or no affinity to the corporation's business concerns.

This kind of business and executive self-centeredness may be disrupting an unusual and remarkable alliance in America.

Corporations, government, and hundreds of thousands of non-profit organizations have long been intertwined in a way that defines our quality of life in the United States. According to Impression A, this delicate coalition may be unraveling. Company leaders appear to be turning a blind eye toward nonprofit organizations at a time when government is trying to off-load more of its human service responsibilities onto these same institutions.

These days, the sounds coming from nonprofit organizations and agencies caught in the middle of this commotion are hardly screams of joy.

IMPRESSION B: BUSINESSES ARE SOCIALLY RESPONSIBLE

But something else is also happening between nonprofits and businesses. This action is largely offscreen—not usually captured on camera because it falls outside what has come to be defined as "traditional" philanthropy. Some businesses are putting up sizable amounts of cash to lure nonprofits into the private-sector circle where the main aim of the game is to make money.

Suddenly, nonprofits are in the business of *profit sharing*. They are splitting the take from cause-related marketing campaigns, endorsements, and sponsorships. New kinds of deals are being cut that rewrite the rules for corporate-nonprofit relationships. Here are some recent examples:

▸ PRIMESTAR paid the American Red Cross $10 for each new subscriber to its satellite television service and referenced the nonprofit organization as part of its $5 million ad campaign to entice potential customers to subscribe.

▸ HBO designed commercials featuring primate researcher Jane Goodall and a cast of chimpanzees—a deal that brought a year's worth of funding to the Jane Goodall Institute in Connecticut.

▸ The Walt Disney Company and the American Society for the Prevention of Cruelty to Animals worked out more than a hundred merchandising agreements that the ASPCA's management says "will be worth many millions."

3

▶ Denny's, Flagstar's restaurant chain, has become Save the Children's largest corporate supporter, raising $2.5 million over three years by selling special meals, scarves, and neckties—an arrangement that has proven financially beneficial to both partners.

▶ For each of five hundred thousand Rosie O'Dolls (sixteen-inch dolls modeled after television talk-show host Rosie O'Donnell) that Tyco sold in 1997, $10 went to the For All Kids Foundation.

Corporations usually consider these kinds of transactions as marketing expenses, not as charitable grants or gifts. The money handed over to outside organizations in this way rarely gets mentioned in any public statement the company makes about philanthropy or social responsibility.

As for the receiving team, the organizations that get cash from these corporate spigots aren't complaining. The dollars are just as green whether they are paid as part of a marketing arrangement or handed out as a donation.

A DUAL REALITY

So which impression is correct, A or B? The answer is, both.

On the one hand, corporations *have* become more miserly in recent years when carving out a percentage of their profits for traditional philanthropy. But at the same time, businesses are negotiating new, interesting, creative, and sometimes controversial relationships with nonprofit organizations.

The reality is that business connections to the "outside" world are not what they used to be. Some marketing and promotion executives are circumventing corporate contributions or community relations personnel in order to build their own bridges to nonprofit organizations. In at least a few companies, manufacturing departments are producing goods for charities without any coordination or oversight by managers in other parts of the firm. In this very unsettled atmosphere, many philanthropy, public affairs, and community relations staffers are struggling to figure out their roles and responsibilities. Because of all of this, the public gets a jumbled picture of where companies stand when it comes to these external activities.

Relations between the private sector and the nonprofit world started changing back in the early to mid-1980s. It was a time when corporations in the United States were getting *very* serious about losing weight—shedding excess baggage that was standing in the way of efficiency and improved profits. Wall Street hovered over businesses like Richard Simmons with an attitude, screaming at top management to sweat off every bump and lump in their organizations. The weigh-ins came every quarter, and if companies didn't look better than they had the day before, the Street tolerated no excuses.

Over the years, businesses impulsively grabbed any weight-loss plan that was put in front of them. These plans came with different names—reengineering, downsizing, rightsizing. In many instances, the crash diets actually worked. So much so that the corporate bottom line took on a very appealing shape, which investors greeted with wolf whistles. Slimmer, trimmer companies basked in the glow of their financial success. (See Figure 1.)

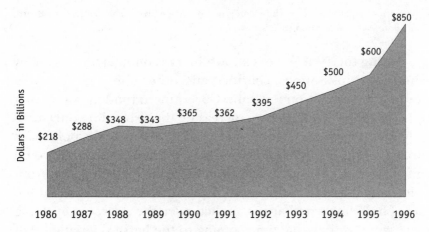

Fig. 1. Corporate Profits (Before Taxes), 1986–1996

Reprinted with permission by The Conference Board. Sources: The Conference Board, Council for Aid to Education (RAND)

As businesses became increasingly absorbed in their own appearance, their attitudes changed about what was going on outside the corporate walls. After a period when companies had been pumping up their philanthropy spending until it reached more than 2 percent of their pretax earnings, the private sector did an about-face. Businesses began assigning less importance to philanthropy. Year by year, corporate gifts and grants eroded until the percentage of profits set aside for philanthropy fell to nearly half of the spending levels in the mid-eighties. (See Figure 2.)

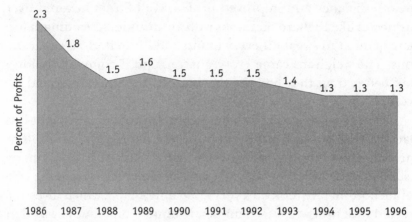

Fig. 2. Declining Rate of Corporate Giving (as Percent of Profits), 1986–1996

Reprinted with permission by The Conference Board. Sources: The Conference Board, Council for Aid to Education (RAND)

During the same era of extraordinary economic success, many educational institutions, charities, and other nonprofit organizations were taking it on the chin. Government funding was drying up, private foundations were increasing their spending only modestly, and personal donations were erratic. Meanwhile, politicians threatened to negotiate a new Contract with America that would shift more tax-funded human service activities to the nonprofit field—and a goodly number of corporate executives cheered the idea. Shell-shocked charities mulled over the prospect of doing more while at the same time coming to the harsh realization that their share of the corporate profit pie was steadily eroding.

Corporate Frugality

What has made the private sector turn so frugal? Here are a few reasons why many American corporations seem to have partially zipped up their wallets.

CEO DISINTEREST

Fifteen or twenty years ago, a few chief executives had a reputation for nudging social responsibility (mainly a do-it-for-the-country-or-community and don't-expect-anything-back-in-return way of thinking) to the front of the stove. People like John Filer (Aetna), Kenneth Dayton (Dayton Hudson), Fletcher Byrom (Koppers), Thomas Watson (IBM), and David Rockefeller (Chase Manhattan) weren't shy about getting on the stump to talk about why businesses needed to go beyond paying taxes to help solve critical social problems. Today's CEOs, with a handful of exceptions, aren't known for that kind of talk. Visionaries are hard to find when it comes to corporate social responsibility.

A SHIFT IN PHILOSOPHY

There have always been those within the business world who have held that corporations should not spend their resources or time worrying about matters that don't directly affect their ability to make money. The business of business is—*business!* Make a profit and provide jobs. That's a corporation's ultimate responsibility. Ever since the 1930s, when the IRS declared that corporations could consider charitable contributions as legitimate business expenses, executives and shareholders have debated how much of a company's profits or energies should be directed toward supporting nonprofit institutions. Although there are those who argue corporations have a moral obligation to assist outside causes and issues, the let's-keep-business-focused-on-business approach has gained ground in recent years.

HERDISM

There's something about straight-out corporate philanthropy that makes companies want to head for the middle of the pack. Corporations give (or don't give) based on what other businesses are thought to be giving (or not giving). Few companies dream about running ahead of the pack when it comes to spending money on contributions. Without enough businesses taking the lead, corporate philanthropy tends to remain stuck in place while the rest of the economy marches on. And that is exactly what has happened over the past decade. Although pretax profits have soared since the mid-eighties, the dollars spent on corporate charitable contributions have crept ahead at a much slower rate of growth.

DOWNSIZING'S SHADOW EFFECT

Also called the it-doesn't-look-right syndrome, the often-unnoticeable effect of downsizing has been especially harmful to corporate philanthropy in recent years. Even when a business scores big with higher earnings and is in a position to expand its social responsibility investments, it balks at doing so. Why? Because even modest increases in so-called nonessential spending don't look right, especially in the face of employee layoffs and other painful cuts in the operating budget.

BAD MANAGEMENT

As one bank executive put it in very unbanking-like terms, "Too many people making corporate philanthropy decisions don't have a clue as to what their jobs are all about." This is a bit harsh, perhaps, and certainly is a generalization that doesn't apply to everyone involved in giving away company funds. However, the statement does raise a critical issue. Exactly what are the managers who handle corporate contributions *supposed* to do? If the answer is don't spend a lot of money and don't make waves, then many of these managers are doing an admirable job. But if a corporation is looking to *leverage its corporate giving to help the business become more successful* (while simultaneously doing good things for society), then this banker may not be far off the mark.

A Critical Issue

All of this may seem monumentally unimportant given other critical issues that businesses have to worry about. Even nonprofit organizations may not view the changes in corporate giving as being all that consequential. After all, businesses have historically played a notoriously small role in American philanthropy. Of the billions of dollars donated annually to religious groups, colleges, human service agencies, and a slew of other nonprofit institutions, businesses have never accounted for much more than 5 percent of the total. (See Figure 3.) If companies turn a little stingier, so what? What difference will it make?

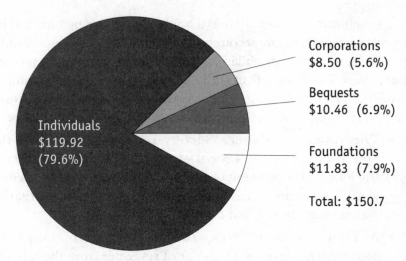

Corporations
$8.50 (5.6%)

Bequests
$10.46 (6.9%)

Individuals
$119.92
(79.6%)

Foundations
$11.83 (7.9%)

Total: $150.7

Fig. 3. Corporate Contributions as a Percent of Total Giving, 1996 (dollars in billions)

Source: *Giving USA 1997;* reprinted with permission by the American Association of Fund-Raising Counsel (AAFRC) Trust for Philanthropy

The difference is greater than you might think.

When focusing only on nonreligious organizations (health, education, civic, cultural groups), corporate charitable donations represent one dollar out of every ten raised by these organizations. For some nonprofit institutions, corporate support is absolutely essential for survival. For others, it provides the seed money needed to raise funds from other sources (private foundations and government, for example). For still other nonsectarian groups, corporate giving comes with a bonus that might prove more important even than the company's tax-deductible gift: time and commitment from corporate executives and employees.

There is a good chance that a nonprofit that gets major financial support from a business also has an executive from that company on its board or one of its advisory committees. This not only means free management consulting for the nonprofit but can also open doors to other services that are quietly donated on the side— for example, printing, accounting, meeting rooms, and so on. These "added value" benefits are likely to fade away along with the company executive serving on the board of the nonprofit organization if a business decides to cut back or eliminate its contributions support.

As mentioned earlier, there is a bright side to this picture that is largely overlooked in any accounting of corporate social responsibility. Although traditional philanthropy has taken a beating in recent years, there has been an upsurge in new kinds of relationships between businesses and nonprofits. Sponsorships, quid pro quo contracts, marketing deals—all are part of a growing trend. Examples:

▸ The American Cancer Society is renting its name to SmithKline Beecham's NicoDerm antismoking patch and to the Florida Department of Citrus. The rentals are reportedly worth a minimum of $2 million a year to the cancer organization, and this sure isn't traditional philanthropy.

▸ A relatively small New York–based retail company, Stonehenge, donates 4 percent of revenues from the sale of its men's ties to Mothers Against Drunk Driving (MADD).

Are these marketing relationships sucking away money that otherwise might have been donated via "usual" contributions channels? Probably not. This is a relatively new kind of revenue stream running into charity's pond that may eventually become a river of change.

The Ten-Step Corporate Social Investment Management Model

Businesses can take the lead in turning this hubbub into a more coherent process. Management is the key. And the ten-step plan outlined in *Corporate Social Investing* is the instruction manual that *any* company—whether a gargantuan multinational or a small service business, whether a laissez-faire Silicon Valley chip maker or a buttoned-down East Coast financial institution—can use to unlock the power that comes from effectively linking up with nonprofit and public sector organizations. Exhibit 1 summarizes the ten-step process.

The following chapters explain in-depth how companies can go about taking these steps to replace philanthropy with corporate social investing.

Step 1. Replace the traditional notions of corporate philanthropy with a broader concept called *corporate social investing*.

Step 2. Identify a significant business reason for every corporate social investment and obtain as much business value from social investments as is allowable and practical.

Step 3. Limit corporate social investments to 501(c)(3) nonprofit organizations and exclusively public institutions (or comparable organizations outside the United States).

Step 4. Make an open statement that endorses corporate social investing or supports a broader concept that allows for social investing to be developed.

Step 5. Send a clear message to employees and other stakeholders that the CEO endorses corporate social investing.

Step 6. Produce a written corporate social involvement report that includes a review of social investments at least once a year.

Step 7. Commit now or by a specified date at least 2.5 percent (3.5 percent for manufacturing corporations that donate product) of an average of a company's last three years of pretax profits for corporate social investing.

Step 7. Amendments for manufacturing companies:

A. Use only salable products that can be provided in a timely manner and in reasonable quantities to any 501(c)(3) non-profit organization or exclusively public institution as corporate social investments.

B. Report all product investments to the public at their retail fair market value (or average manufacturer's price for regulated industries).

C. Regardless of how much product is invested, make cash investments of at least 1.5 percent of a pretax net income (PTNI) three-year rolling average.

Step 8. Postpone some or all social investing if projected business conditions warrant such action.

Step 9. Lock in influential line and staff leaders as co-owners of the corporate social investing program.

Step 10. Assign day-to-day management responsibility for corporate social investing to a position that is no more than one executive away from the CEO or COO.

Exhibit 1. The Ten-Step Corporate Social Investment Management Model

A New Way of Thinking and Acting

Frank Sinatra had nothing on Herbert Stein when it cames to reviving a Golden Oldie. In 1996, Stein, the former chairman of Richard Nixon's Council on Economic Advisers, wrote an op-ed piece for *The Wall Street Journal*. The lyrics may sound familiar: Corporate America—mind your own business!

To rely on "corporate responsibility" to solve major social problems—other than the problem of how to put our people and other resources to work most efficiently—would be a wasteful diversion.

The same song had been belted out by others in previous years. Maybe the most often-heard rendition was Milton Friedman's, which was a hit back in 1970. That's when economist Friedman wrote in a *New York Times Magazine* article that businesses had no business doing anything but generating profits. Friedman complained that corporate social responsibility costs a company money; ergo, a business has to either charge higher prices for its products or lower employee wages—outcomes that are contrary to the best interests of society. And then along comes Herb Stein, putting only a slightly different spin on the same old standard when he tells companies that they "discharge their social responsibilities when they maximize profits."

Those who stand behind Stein and Friedman would contend that hard-core social dilemmas (like homelessness, hunger, domestic abuse, and so on) aren't business problems and shouldn't be taking up space on a company's radar screen. These are distractions that only get in the way of *efficiency*. And efficiency, as people like Herb Stein would tell you, is the nectar of corporate success.

Then there's the other side of the story. There are those who think Stein's music is about as melodic as so-called gangsta rap. They would tell you that William Norris, the founder of Control Data, had it right. Like a lot of business leaders back in the hot summer of 1967, Norris was hit hard by race riots that erupted in different areas around the country. That unrest stirred him to action—partly because one of those riots tore up Minneapolis, which Control Data called home. His company took the lead in hiring more minorities, built a manufacturing plant in (of all places) the inner city, and acted like an overall generous corporate citizen.

Until his company ran into trouble in the mid-eighties, Norris was held up as a corporate Wizard of Oz, the prototype of the benevolent executive. His famous quote, "You can't do business in a society that's burning," is dusted off and used every once in a while, especially when there are rumblings of discontent in America's urban centers.

When Control Data experienced financial troubles in 1985—which ironically turned out to be the watershed year for corporate philanthropy—Norris was retired as part of a corporate restructuring. Unfortunately, some of his social responsibility credibility went out the door with him. There were unfair whispers that he had forced Control Data to be a little too concerned with social issues and that weeds were now growing in the company's core business field. After 1985 things were never quite the same again, either for Control Data or for corporate responsibility.

So, who's right here? Herbert Stein or William Norris? Within the framework of a management approach called corporate social investing—they *both* are.

The Facts About Corporate Efficiency and Social Investing

Corporate efficiency and corporate social investing don't have to be mortal enemies. They aren't mutually exclusive. When structured properly and managed effectively, corporate social investments can actually *enhance* a company's capacity to perform at an optimum level. And here's the kicker: *social investing, which includes tax-deductible charitable contributions, can actually help a business make money!*

Sounds like heresy, doesn't it? Manipulating charitable intent so that it turns into a type of free-enterprise grease that companies can use to fatten their own wallets. Actually, it isn't at all sinister. Rather, it is simply a matter of redefining the way corporate philanthropy has been managed in the past so that it becomes a win-win deal for both business and society.

Before describing how to plan and implement a corporate social investment program, it may be helpful to review a few facts that serve as the foundation for the ten-step process this book describes.

FACT: JUST LIKE CORPORATE CONTRIBUTIONS, CORPORATE SOCIAL INVESTMENTS ARE DEPENDENT ON A COMPANY'S PROFITABILITY

Yes, there are some exceptions. For instance, R. R. Donnelley & Sons took a restructuring charge in 1996 and declared a $157 million net income loss for the year but still made contributions to charity. Occasionally, a business will run into a profit glitch and will continue to support outside causes and organizations. But no business can sustain that practice over a long period of time unless it has a well-endowed company foundation. If contributions are generally dependent on profit, so are social investments. Pure and simple.

Given this fact, it makes sense for those nonprofit institutions that look to businesses for assistance to encourage—even help— corporations to remain successful. That's going to take a different mindset for some nonprofit leaders. Under our new rules, *begging* is out; *partnering* is in.

FACT: BUSINESSES CAN'T SUCCEED IN A VACUUM

Each corporation is dependent on one or more constituencies outside its borders for survival. Keeping those constituencies healthy is important if businesses expect to remain alive and well. Question: Are there ways that corporate social investing can improve the vitality of some of these constituencies? If a corporation is in the business of selling direct to consumers, the answer is yes every time. If a company is a vendor to other corporations or organizations, it may be less obvious as to how social investing can return value to such a business. However, as will be pointed out in later chapters, there are ingenious ways to leverage social investments regardless of what a corporation makes, sells, or services.

FACT: CORPORATIONS CAN WRITE OFF MONEY, PRODUCTS, AND LAND GIVEN TO CERTAIN NONPROFITS AS LEGITIMATE TAX DEDUCTIONS

Businesses can declare up to 10 percent of their pretax profits as tax-deductible charitable contributions each year. Few companies ever get close to this level of giving. If they were to be that generous, it could mean *big* money. Example: if General Motors had decided to contribute a tenth of its 1996 pretax earnings, a whopping $667 million would have been doled out to qualified nonprofit organizations! Instead, GM's reported donations for the year were around $66.7 million—or 1 percent of its before-tax profits—which is closer to what many large companies spend for donations.

For reasons that will be explored later, it is important to note here what the tax collector means by *charitable*. Although subject to interpretation, payments to a nonprofit organization, even if that organization qualifies as an acceptable charitable institution, won't qualify for a charitable tax deduction if there is a quid pro quo involved. Put another way, if a corporation receives or expects to receive a bargained-for benefit, then forget trying to nail down a charitable deduction. This is very gray territory because it is often difficult or impossible to define exactly what a "bargained-for benefit" is. The IRS leaves a lot of room for a business to get significant *indirect* benefits that can be extremely important to a company.

FACT: A TAX DEDUCTION IS A TAX DEDUCTION

When a company takes a deduction for making a charitable gift, it is worth no more and no less than any other allowable business deduction. In other words, the tax advantage to a company is the same if it gives money to the United Way or if it takes out an ad for one of its products in *Newsweek*. It's amazing how many nonprofit fund-raisers miss this point. From a tax perspective, a donation to a charity has no more value than any other expense that is deductible.

Because of this tax fact, corporate social investment's playing field is much wider than corporate philanthropy's notably small backyard. Social investing means that businesses don't have to be constrained to the rules of charitable giving when considering ways to help outside organizations. This point is essential to understand before trying to implement the ten steps for managing corporate social investments.

FACT: CORPORATIONS ARE ENTERING INTO MORE BUSINESS RELATIONSHIPS WITH NONPROFITS THAN EVER BEFORE

Nonprofits are selling their names for endorsement purposes, working out exclusive sponsorship contracts, getting royalties from product sales, and selling services on the open market. Marketing sponsorship payments for entertainment and nonprofit events were estimated to be worth *nearly $2 billion* in 1997, according to IEG Inc., a Chicago research and consulting firm.

FACT: THERE ARE A LARGE NUMBER OF TAX-EXEMPT NONPROFIT ORGANIZATIONS OUT THERE

There are a lot more tax-exempt nonprofit organizations than most people might guess, around 1.1 million or so. (See Exhibit 2.) However, just because an organization is exempt from paying taxes doesn't mean it can give a corporate donor (or any donor, for that matter) a charitable tax deduction. Only organizations that have what's known as a 501(c)(3) tax status—loosely referred to as *charitable organizations*—are generally considered those to which gifts are deductible for income, gift, or estate-tax purposes. Technically, giving money to a 501(c)(3) organization is really not an automatic ticket for a business to declare a tax deduction. The IRS requires that the charity and the business meet other provisions of the tax code. However, this can all get overly complicated. In general, it's safe to assume that if a company makes a donation to a 501(c)(3) organization, the business is probably writing that donation off as a charitable tax deduction.

Category	Description	Number
501(c)(1)	Corporations organized under act of Congress	19
501(c)(2)	Titleholding corporations	7,025
501(c)(3)	Religious, charitable, and so on	626,226
501(c)(4)	Social welfare	139,451
501(c)(5)	Labor, agricultural organizations	66,662
501(c)(6)	Business leagues	75,695
501(c)(7)	Social and recreation clubs	65,501
501(c)(8)	Fraternal beneficiary societies	92,115
501(c)(9)	Voluntary employees' beneficiary associations	14,681
501(c)(10)	Domestic fraternal beneficiary societies	21,046
501(c)(11)	Teachers' retirement funds	11
501(c)(12)	Benevolent life-insurance associations	6,291
501(c)(13)	Cemetery companies	9,433
501(c)(14)	State-chartered credit unions	5,225
501(c)(15)	Mutual-insurance companies	1,185
501(c)(16)	Corporations to finance crop rotations	23
501(c)(17)	Supplemental unemployment benefit trusts	583
501(c)(18)	Employee-funded pension trusts	3
501(c)(19)	War veterans' organizations	30,828
501(c)(20)	Legal service organizations	141
501(c)(21)	Black lung trusts	25
501(c)(22)	Multiemployer pension plans	0
501(c)(23)	Veterans' associations founded prior to 1880	2
501(c)(24)	Trusts described in Section 4049 of ERISA	1
501(c)(25)	Holding companies for pensions, and so on	638
Total		1.1 million

Exhibit 2. Types of Nonprofit Organizations, by Category

Source: Internal Revenue Service, 1995

Because 501(c)(3) organizations will become a focal point for the ten-step corporate social investment management model, it's important to identify which nonprofits fall within this category. In addition to "charities" as they are widely perceived—such as United Way, Girl Scouts, Salvation Army, American Lung Association, and so on—this particular tax class includes (a) religious, (b) scientific, (c) literary, and (d) educational organizations. Nonprofits that do testing for public safety, foster national or international amateur competitive sports, or work to prevent cruelty to children or animals also qualify for this same 501(c)(3) status.

The term *charitable organization* is frequently used to describe any 501(c)(3) nonprofit in this category, whether it's the Lincoln Center for the Performing Arts, the United States Olympic Committee, or the March of Dimes. For ease of making a case on behalf of our corporate social investment plan, we'll ride this same wave and will occasionally use the term *charity* to refer to any 501(c)(3) organization, keeping in mind that the word is a bit misleading because of the wide net that it casts.

With over six hundred thousand IRS-designated charitable organizations in existence, there is no shortage of nonprofit funding opportunities. And the multitude of these organizations is actually even larger than it appears, because many of them have regional, state, and local affiliates, each with the capacity to reach out and touch a business.

In spite of the astounding number of choices available to businesses, most corporations don't spend much time searching for the "right" nonprofit partner. Usually a business is preoccupied with dealing with whatever comes over the transom, which in itself is no easy job. With so many charities competing for funds, businesses are often swamped with unsolicited requests. Some companies log as many as a hundred appeals a day. The process becomes one of hunkering down rather than proactively looking for the kind of relationship that could lead to mutually important advantages for the company as well as the nonprofit institution.

FACT: CORPORATIONS ARE GIVING AWAY LESS OF THEIR PROFITS AS CHARITABLE DONATIONS THAN THEY DID TEN YEARS AGO

Maybe so, a dubious senior executive might argue, but in actual dollars, corporate giving has grown from $5 billion back in

1987 to $8.5 billion in 1996. That's a 70 percent increase! True, but it's not a 120 percent increase, which is how much pretax profits climbed during the same period. Although corporate donations are indeed on a slow growth track compared with profits, this fact brings us to the following critical question.

Does Anyone Care?

For most companies, adopting corporate social investing is going to mean change. Any change, regardless of how seemingly insignificant, can consume an organization's time and tax its fixed resources. So senior management may rightly question whether it is worth the effort to introduce corporate social investing when there doesn't seem to be an overwhelming amount of pressure on the business to make that kind of change. Put another way, management may wonder if enough people really *care* how much the company gives or doesn't give to nonprofit organizations to warrant making a course adjustment.

Truthfully, until now there hasn't been a lot of pressure on companies to revamp their philanthropic activities. However, corporations are beginning to sense interest and concern about this aspect of business, and the rumblings are coming from constituencies both inside and outside the corporation.

▸ MANAGERS OF SOCIALLY RESPONSIBLE INVESTMENT (SRI) FUNDS

There are investment funds that single out socially responsible businesses. One source, the Social Investment Forum, says that one dollar out of every ten now under fund management is part of some type of SRI portfolio. The problem is that the definition of *socially responsible* tends to cover everything from child care services for employees to sprinkler systems in factories. Some of these fund managers do monitor corporate philanthropy, but rarely is it possible to make any meaningful comparisons that show how one company's contributions program stacks up against another.

If fund managers were to have a common yardstick to measure more accurately those transactions a corporation makes with the nonprofit world, they might look more intently at these relationships. Corporate social investing has a good chance of becoming that measuring device.

▶ SHAREHOLDERS

As will be pointed out in Chapter 7, some shareholders are getting restless about—of all things—philanthropy. The noise tends to be from stock owners who think a company is either (a) giving too much money away, or (b) spending the money on the wrong causes or organizations. The unrest usually surfaces around the time a company holds its annual meeting and quite often comes in the form of shareholder resolutions or protestations at the meeting itself.

Right now, shareholders are usually puffs in the private-sector windstorm. Their hit-and-run tactics have had a limited effect on general corporate social responsibility policies. But that may change if enough shareholders learn how to tap more extensively the power of resolutions and annual meetings.

▶ ANALYSTS

There isn't a titan of industry around who doesn't twinge a little when the word *analyst* makes its way into a conversation. With a single word—*downgrade*—an analyst can make the toughest executive shake like Jell-O. The people who forecast a corporation's capacity to create wealth for a stockholder have never been overly concerned about a company's commitment (or lack thereof) to social responsibility.

Suppose analysts had a change of heart? Suppose they suddenly wanted to know how much money, product, or time a company was committing to outside causes and programs? Then, suppose they followed that question with this one: *Tell us the business rationale for why you pared off a portion of your profits for support of certain outside organizations.* Corporate social investing may well prompt these kinds of inquiries on the part of at least a few analysts.

▶ EMPLOYEES

Literally millions of businesspeople volunteer their time to help causes and organizations that are important to them. As astounding as it may seem, very few have any knowledge about their own corporation's grant making. What would happen if employees suddenly became educated about corporate social investing and were able to develop compelling arguments for increasing business assistance to their respective charities? There's a strong probability that companies would boost their support of selected nonprofit organizations.

▶ MEDIA

It is surprising that the popular and business presses haven't investigated the current state of corporate philanthropy. There are some great stories out there, on both sides of this issue. Story line number one: big business gives a cold shoulder to nonprofits struggling to provide for vital human needs. Story line number two: big corporations squander wads of money on irrelevant causes and programs.

▶ BUSINESS ORGANIZATIONS

Federations of businesses such as The Conference Board, the Business Roundtable, the Business Council, the U.S. Chamber of Commerce, and the National Association of Manufacturers think their way through a lot of issues, but frequently come up short on meaty action plans. Still, corporate philanthropy has been a topic of discussion for more than one of these organizations in the past. The emergence of corporate social investing is likely, at the very least, to encourage debate over how corporations should be interacting with the nonprofit world.

▶ ACADEMIA

The Massachusetts Institute of Technology, along with a few other schools, has dipped its toes into the social investment pool. MIT recently joined forces with the Council on Foundations to start a Community Investment Institute, which offers (for a fee) advice and assistance to businesses and other donors interested in "program-related investments." Harvard Business School's Initiative on Social Enterprise is looking at ways in which the private and "independent" (nonprofit) sectors can collaborate.

Prominent business schools that come up with consulting services, programs, and curricula that give more attention to the business advantages of corporate social investing (and related strategic approaches to corporate contributions management) are helping to create the right forum for these issues.

SECURITIES AND EXCHANGE COMMISSION

Back in the 1930s, Congress empowered the SEC to protect investors by requiring corporations to disclose certain financial information. For the past six decades public corporations have had to file periodic reports with the SEC, which to many a senior executive is akin to dancing naked in public. For some reason, however, Congress kept a few fig leaves in the securities acts, one of which has allowed companies to cover their charitable giving. Corporations do not have to tell the public which nonprofit organizations receive company gifts and grants, except for donations made through company foundations, nor do they have to tell how much any of the nonprofits receive.

This cloak of secrecy bothers some people who feel that disclosure is an important requirement to prevent any misuse or abuse of corporate contributions. Pressure is mounting on the SEC to play a more active role in the corporate philanthropy field. Unless businesses become more concerned about controlling their own destiny, regulators may soon be stepping into the ring.

CONGRESS

Two bills recently introduced in the House of Representatives would (if passed) drastically restructure the rules for how businesses deal with nonprofit organizations. Although most congressional observers don't give these bills much chance of getting approved, the proposed legislation may be just the beginning of Washington's interest in the world of corporate contributions.

OTHER CORPORATE CEOS

There are corporate leaders out there who feel strongly that businesses need to do much more to support nonprofit and exclusively public organizations. These tend to be men and women whose own businesses are investing percentages of pretax profits that are five to ten times higher than the average corporate giving level in the United States.

Although it is unusual to find a corporate executive talking openly about why businesses need to increase their support for nonprofit institutions—this topic was far more likely to get discussed fifteen years ago than today—*Corporate Social Investing* may give certain CEOs an opening to speak more freely about their views.

What's the Conclusion?

There appear to be enough people who *do* care—or who are starting to care—about business-nonprofit relationships to justify getting serious about corporate social investing. Even Herb Stein might agree that the ten-step model is worthy of a close look. Corporate social investing may end up infusing billions of additional corporate dollars into society, which is the direction William Norris would have liked businesses to head. But corporate social investing also pushes a company's P&L needle in the right direction. On balance, Mr. Stein might be willing to concede that there are enough potential business benefits tied to corporate social investing to warrant giving it a trial run.

Step 1. Moving from Corporate Giving to Corporate Social Investing

The following is a true story.

Mary X is director of promotions for a large consumer company. She gets paid $100,000 a year plus a bonus to come up with ways to drive sales for a number of popular brands that can be seen in stores throughout the United States. She's very good at what she does.

One summer day, X comes up with an idea. She wants to do a four-week campaign using a popular children's charity to help push fifteen different products her company manufactures. Calling it cause-related marketing, her corporation would promise to send a nickel to the charity for each unit sold during the promotional campaign period. X says it will be a win-win deal—more dollars for the nonprofit organization and more market share for the products involved in the promotion.

X e-mails the corporation's tax department. "Here's my problem," she says. "I don't have the money in my marketing budget to carry the contribution to the charity. I *do* have the money to pick up the costs needed to advertise the campaign and to do in-store promotion."

The tax man wastes no time in responding. He says the proposed payment to the charity is more accurately a marketing or promotion expense and should be considered so for tax purposes.

"But I told you. My marketing budget isn't fat enough to make the payment to the nonprofit organization. However, I know our company contributions fund could absorb the cost of the donation."

"Sorry—it's marketing or nothing."

So, even though the company *could* have absorbed the donation to the charity as part of its corporate philanthropy budget for the year, the idea was scrapped. There was no promotion, no added funding for the children's organization, all because the company couldn't figure out how to maneuver around the accounting and tax issues that cloud the definition of philanthropy.

Here's another true story.

Corporation Z can be found listed in *Fortune* magazine's fifty largest firms in America. It gets a proposal from a prestigious public television station asking the company to underwrite the production of a well-known nationally broadcast series. Sponsorship means on-air credits that will get beamed regularly to upscale viewers known for their "leader level" status in shaping public policy and opinion. The vice president for public relations thinks this is a tremendous opportunity but doesn't have the $1 million sponsorship fee included in his annual budget.

"If we don't do this, one of our biggest competitors is waiting in the wings to take our place," he explains to a group of senior executives in his company. The public relations man proposes that the business pay the sponsorship fee as a charitable donation to the public television station that is asking for the money.

"This isn't philanthropy," some of the executives counter.

"Of course it is—the station is a nonprofit organization that can give us a charitable tax deduction for whatever money we put on the table," the public relations man advises.

"It doesn't matter. This is an advertising or public relations expense and we shouldn't be drawing down close to a million dollars from our philanthropy budget for something like this."

Even though the executives are told that a few large businesses typically carry these kinds of sponsorship expenses as part of their charitable giving programs, Corporation Z can't be sold on using its philanthropy dollars to pay the public television bill. The public relations man isn't able to absorb the cost in his own budget and the program sponsorship shifts to the company's competitor.

These two true examples illustrate the confusion over what corporate philanthropy is—or isn't. The IRS definition of a charitable tax-deductible gift provides ample room for interpretation, which means that one company's gift could easily be considered as anything but philanthropy by another corporation. The tax laws also are written in such a way that they *discourage* corporate cash donations, and here's why.

Tax-deductible charitable donations come with extra baggage compared with most other business expenses. A company has to check to be sure a charitable contribution is going to an IRS-blessed nonprofit organization. For some gifts, the company even has to chase down and then keep on file written receipts or statements from charities in order to satisfy IRS rules. A company also has to worry about staying beneath the cap imposed on businesses for total charitable deductions in any one year (10 percent of pretax profits) although, in truth, few corporations ever get near that ceiling.

Let's go back to the two businesses cited at the beginning of the chapter. Suppose Mary X did have money in her own marketing budget to cover the payment to the children's charity. And suppose Corporation Z put another $1 million into its advertising spending plan to sponsor the public television series. The costs would be considered usual business expenses *and would be taken as regular business deductions that provide the company with the same financial benefits as if they were considered charitable donations.*

For certain kinds of donations (product, land, securities) there *are* tax benefits that can be important to a business. But the cash that corporations write off as charitable contributions is on equal footing with other kinds of deductions a company takes when it files its annual tax return. There are actually very few payments that a company makes that are *not* deductible. Some of them include the following:

▶ Lobbying certain political figures (although firms can deduct costs they incur when dealing with lower-level staffers in some political offices)

▶ Executive compensation in excess of $1 million a year

▶ Fifty percent of business meals

▶ Travel costs for spouses that are paid by a company

▶ Certain club dues and fees

Putting aside whatever moral arguments can be made for corporate philanthropy, it often makes more sense for a company to declare a payment to a nonprofit organization as a marketing, advertising, research, or some other common business expense than as a tax-deductible contribution. By doing so, the company circles around potential accounting and auditing potholes. The process is cleaner and usually less costly to administer. All of this leads to the first of our ten steps for managing corporate giving differently than in the past:

Step 1. Replace the traditional notion of corporate philanthropy with a broader concept called corporate social investing.

Corporate Social Investing: The Basic Components

If corporations are to become stronger allies of nonprofit organizations in the United States, then the rules have to change. The territory has to be expanded so that businesses can go beyond altruism when they look for ways to help nonprofits. Our first step encourages that kind of expansion. Later on, in Chapters 9 and 10, the corporate social investing model will be converted to a more detailed management schematic. But the basic elements are not very complicated. For now, let's review the four main gears in the investment machine. (See Figure 4.)

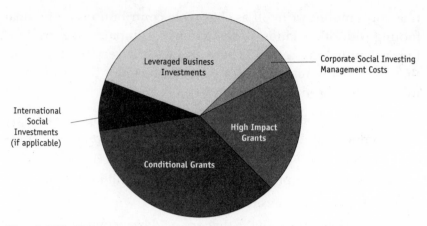

Fig. 4. The Corporate Social Investment Model

HIGH-IMPACT GRANTS

These commitments deliver clearly defined, significant returns to the corporation but still provide the business with charitable tax deductions. (See Chapter 10.)

CONDITIONAL GRANTS

Usually smaller in size than high-impact grants, these payments to nonprofits, which also can be written off as charitable gifts, are made with certain conditions. Donor companies make these grants with the understanding that recipient organizations will use the money to make an impact on specific parts of the business environment that are vital to the corporation's success. (See Chapter 10.)

LEVERAGED BUSINESS INVESTMENTS (LBIS)

Payments made to nonprofits that don't qualify or aren't taken as charitable gifts but still advance the outside organization's main mission are LBIs. Sponsorships, memberships, cause-related marketing, and some types of loans and research awards are examples of this kind of investment. (See Chapter 10.)

ADMINISTRATIVE AND RELATED COSTS

The expenses incurred to plan and manage corporate social investing are included in any public reporting of a company's social investment activities. (See Chapter 10.)

Step 1. Moving from Corporate Giving to Corporate Social Investing

Here's an important observation: charitable gifts are *not* put out to pasture under this new social investment model. Companies can still make donations and write them off as high-impact or conditional grants, which can be deducted as charitable gifts. The big difference is that these contributions will be brought in line with overall business objectives. Using the social investment model, corporate giving as it has been known in the past gets reconfigured into a more strategic, more disciplined business function.

Corporate social investment legitimizes "fringe" philanthropic activities that are already going on. For example, Dime Securities of New York, a brokerage outfit affiliated with Dime Savings Bank, donated 10 percent of the gross commissions paid by its customers to the American Red Cross. Although benevolence may be deep-seated in the business, there was clearly an ulterior motivation for what the company called its Give a Dime program. Dime Securities wanted to distinguish itself from other stock traders by telling the world, *Every time you do business with us, you help the Red Cross!*

Isn't this out-and-out marketing? Of course! Is this a corporate social investment? Of course! Step 1 upgrades this fuzzy transaction with the American Red Cross to a full-blown part of the Dime's social investment total. Furthermore, Step 1 encourages the Dime to think about doing other deals using leveraged business investment funds specifically set aside for these types of market-stimulating, society-benefiting relationships.

If nothing else, our first step takes the blanket off collaborations that would otherwise get overlooked when corporate America's payments to nonprofit organizations are tallied up. If this principle is not in place, we're left looking only at old-time corporate philanthropy when we measure what businesses are doing for society. That's a case of myopia that needs fixing.

Don't misunderstand. Our ten-step plan is mainly about kick-starting *new* corporate social investments, not merely coming up with a different way to count whatever dollars are already on the table. However, it is important to know where we are starting *from*. Industry has done an inadequate job of telling the public what it is spending now on relationships involving nonprofit organizations.

So, just how do corporations collect information about what's going on along the edges of traditional philanthropy? Although it doesn't sound like that big a headache, in medium-sized to larger businesses it can be a migraine. Right now, the elements of corporate social investing are in bits and pieces scattered throughout a company. Pulling that information together means digging into different corners of the corporation. That can take time and cost money, particularly the first year a business converts to social investing. However, the detective work is important and even necessary if a full social investment picture is to be developed.

Delivering a Stronger Punch

Convincing companies to move from philanthropy to corporate social investing becomes easier when businesses are exposed to information that shows what traditional corporate contributions *don't* deliver. There has long been an assumption that philanthropy is an important ingredient in any company's image-building campaign. A recent survey takes the air out of that assumption.

In a study carried out by the international edition of *The Wall Street Journal, Nihon Keizai Shimbun* (Japan's top business newspaper), and a research firm called Bozell Worldwide, Americans were asked to evaluate nine categories of corporate activity to determine how much influence each category had on their opinions of corporations as "good citizens." (See Figure 5.)

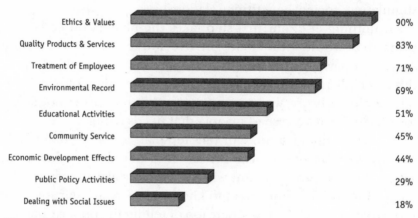

Ethics & Values	90%
Quality Products & Services	83%
Treatment of Employees	71%
Environmental Record	69%
Educational Activities	51%
Community Service	45%
Economic Development Effects	44%
Public Policy Activities	29%
Dealing with Social Issues	18%

Fig. 5. What Makes a Corporate Good Citizen?

Source: Reprinted with permission by *American Advertising*, spring 1996

Step 1. Moving from Corporate Giving to Corporate Social Investing

As the figure shows, a company's ethics and values were important to more of those surveyed—90 percent of them—than any other category of activity. Following that, more than 80 percent thought the quality of a company's products and services were "extremely important" and, following that, more than 70 percent put importance on its treatment of employees.

Two important observations leap out from these results: corporate contributions *do* influence public opinion about what kind of corporate citizen a company is. However, when it comes to building or preserving a company's image, there are a lot of other ways a business can improve its reputation *before* it starts donating funds to outside organizations or causes.

This revelation is contrary to a belief that many corporations have about philanthropic programs. Many—probably most—companies think that if there is any business justification at all for giving money to charity, it's that these donations go a long way in influencing public opinion, especially customer opinion. But this particular research shows that although the public's view of a company is somewhat molded by corporate philanthropy, businesses get a much better gloss on their image when they make it known that they are ethical and work hard to produce quality products and services, which was deemed extremely important by the largest percentage of respondents. Put in different words, the public judges corporate responsibility mostly by the way a company does business and by the quality of products or services it provides.

Now look at Exhibit 3, which reports the results of a second survey carried out by the same group. It ranks some of forty-three specific activities that shape the public's perception of good corporate citizenship. Less than half the consumers surveyed considered any philanthropic activity as being extremely important in influencing their views about a company's corporate citizenship status. For example, a company offering academic scholarships and internships influenced the opinion of only 42 percent of respondents; supporting antidrug or substance-abuse programs influenced only 41 percent; supporting local schools, only 39 percent; and so on down the line. But right up there at the top of the list is "standing behind products and services and honoring warrantees"—91 percent of respondents thought this was extremely important.

31

Leveraging Good Deeds

The study sponsored by *The Wall Street Journal, International Edition, Nihon Keizai Shimbun,* and Bozell Worldwide asked U.S. consumers to evaluate 43 specific activities that influence their opinions of corporations as good citizens. Percentages indicate the number of consumers assessing each activity as "extremely important."

Rank		Percent
1	Standing behind products/services and honoring warrantees	91
2	Producing high quality products and services	86
3	Being concerned about consumer safety	85
4	Providing safe working conditions for employees	85
5	Reporting financial activities accurately	84
6	Not corrupting public officials	84
7	Dealing with ethics breaches quickly and seriously	79
8	Treating suppliers honestly and fairly	75
9	Protecting benefits of retirees	75
11	Participating in recycling programs (raw materials, products, and waste paper)	65
14	Offering environmentally safe packaging	54
18	Offering environmentally friendly products	45
22	Offering academic scholarships and internships	42
23	Supporting antidrug/substance-abuse programs	41
24	Supporting local schools through partnership programs	39
26	Participating in economic development efforts	37
27	Supporting programs to fight major diseases	36
29	Sponsoring research to benefit mankind	31
34	Donating services and products to community	26
35	Supporting youth sports programs	25
37	Sponsoring community events	19
39	Encouraging volunteerism among employees	17
40	Donating money to charitable causes	15
42	Volunteering executives for philanthropic endeavors	13
43	Supporting the arts	8

Exhibit 3. Leveraging Good Deeds

Source: Reprinted with permission by *American Advertising,* spring 1996

A distinction needs to be made here between the public's perception of a company's image and the products it makes and sells. In Chapter 8, the results of a different research study will show that consumers can be moved to make a purchase decision based on an advertised or promoted relationship between a product and an appealing cause. "If you buy what we're selling, we will donate 10 cents to the following charity" is an example of cause-related marketing. Just because a consumer spends money on a product as a result of this strategy does not necessarily lead to a spillover of good feelings about the manufacturer.

It should be remembered that these surveys were carried out in the mid-nineties, a time when very few companies were adhering to the principles of corporate social investing. It is probable that as social investing becomes more prevalent, the public will judge it to be a very important component of corporate citizenship. However, even if that happens, it won't necessarily mitigate public unhappiness with a corporation if its ethics or the quality of the products it makes are perceived to be substandard.

Who Does the Replacing?

A parting shot before we leave Step 1. To move from corporate giving to corporate social investing, there needs to be one or more champions inside a company who will drive the new concept into the heart of the business—a person or persons responsible for replacing the traditional notion of corporate philanthropy and corporate responsibility with a broader concept called corporate social investing. The CEO is a critical player in that transition (see Step 5, Chapter 7), but the CEO probably won't be able to give the changeover the kind of focused attention it needs to be totally successful.

The corporation's chief communications officer, its top public relations executive, the chairman of the company's contributions committee (if there is one), and the staffer who manages the corporate contributions program (whether full-time or part-time) are *all* important in any campaign to shift from philanthropy to social investing. However, rather than leaving the responsibility for transition scattered about the corporation, one senior manager should be assigned to get the job done. (See Chapters 12 and 13 for more on these issues.)

Step 2. Extracting Business Value from Social Investments

October in the Northeast—not the time of year when people are yearning for a double scoop of butter pecan or strawberry swirl. Yet, here's ice cream maven Ben Cohen wandering into, of all places, a Catholic high school to keynote its twentieth anniversary celebration.

What's going on here? It doesn't take the audience long to find out. The cofounder of Ben & Jerry's Homemade didn't accept the invitation from the Sisters of Saint Elizabeth to chat about banana splits.

"Business oppresses people," Cohen tells the group.

There's a rustling in the crowd—maybe from a few people checking to see if they might have wandered into the wrong auditorium. The stirring gets more intense as Cohen begins a history lesson. Religion was the first driving force in society, Cohen preaches. Then came the nation-state. And now (as you might have already guessed) it's business that is running the show. Which brings the ice cream man to a theme that got him summoned to the parochial school in the first place: business is corrupting human spirituality by stepping all over our ethics. Corporations have become obsessed with how many goods can be produced, and corporate workers have become obsessed with the size of their paychecks. The private sector is besmirching our moral fiber.

In case you're not familiar with Ben Cohen and Jerry Greenfield, it bears mentioning that these are not your everyday businessmen. They weren't from the moment they began scooping Rainforest Crunch and they aren't today. Heroes to some and capitalistic bleeding hearts to others, Ben and Jerry are the creators of what might be called—at least by Ben and Jerry—the ultimate caring company. Their corporation gives away 7.5 percent of its profits for the public good, goes out of its way to look for suppliers that employ people who might otherwise not have jobs, and is willing to open its books to any and all.

As admirable as Ben and Jerry's social behavior may be, the company hasn't exactly been a charismatic force that has inspired other businesses to follow suit. Part of the problem may be Cohen's implied criticism of the private sector, which can come across sounding like this: we're right and you're a bunch of greedy, callous, ethically corrupt robber barons. That's not the kind of bugle call that gets the troops rushing to the front line. The inference is that most businesses don't have a moral inner core, and that's not the case. It's just that the core may be a bit skinnier than what Ben Cohen would like to see.

"As we help others, we cannot help but help ourselves." Cohen closes out his appearance before the parochial school audience with an almost biblical authority. His words sound like an amendment to the Beatitudes.

Start with Business

Ben Cohen probably won't like the second principle of our corporate social investment model. It could easily get stuck in his craw like a pit in his Cherry Garcia ice cream, because it rubs against the grain of the message he left with the Sisters of Saint Elizabeth. It mixes the crass side of business with charity—at least at first blush—and to Ben Cohen that may be akin to stirring rancid milk into a batch of fudge ripple.

Step 2. Identify a significant business reason for every corporate social investment and obtain as much business value from social investments as is allowable and practical.

Whatever social investment is made, whether a cause-related marketing contract with the American Dental Association or a donation to the Cub Scouts, it has to start with the business. So says Step 2. Helping society for the sake of helping society isn't in the cards. Just because there is a problem out there, that doesn't mean a company needs to or should invest money and time to solve it. Our model mandates that the problem has to have some relevance to the company's mission if it is to be a candidate for investment consideration.

"This step only proves my point!" Ben Cohen would probably protest if given a chance. "This isn't social responsibility. This is business greed in drag. You're using some warped version of philanthropy to squeeze out a few more almighty dollars for the sake of the bottom line."

Not really. It isn't as pernicious as that. Step 2 doesn't say that each social investment has to pump up a company's profits, just that each investment needs to have some notable link to what the business is all about.

The point has already been made that there are a colossal number of nonprofit organizations out there. A company has literally hundreds of thousands of choices it could make if it decides to "help others." Step 2 gives logic to the social investment process. It is one of the critical defining statements for our model. It is the chalk line on the field that divides fair territory from what's out of bounds.

Businesses that apply the second principle aren't much different than individuals who set about to make a personal contribution. People are not in the practice of writing checks to nonprofit programs or activities that have no meaning to them, *except* if asked by someone they can't (or won't) say no to. Most of the time people give donations because (a) they're self-motivated to support a cause that's genuinely important to them (their own religious organization, a charity researching a cure for a disease that has afflicted someone they know, and so on) or (b) they're arm-twisted or emotionally coerced into dropping a few coins in the can by someone who's too difficult to turn down as long as the cause is not something they dislike or disdain. People will give a quarter to the sweet kid outside the grocery store hustling change for 4-H even though they don't know a capon from a cow. But if that cherub were soliciting for the Saddam Hussein Foundation or something equally as unappealing, hardly a soul would think of parting with a penny.

In the private sector, the process works nearly the same way. As things stand now, companies give most of their contributions to what could be termed very broadly as *business-compatible* causes. Granted, the donations may not be strategic and the recipient organizations may not be the best choices. Nevertheless, companies usually put enough thought into the process to prevent them from giving a contribution to a nonprofit that is openly antagonistic to the private sector.

Of course, being business-friendly isn't a guarantee that an organization is significantly relevant to a corporation. Businesses often make contributions to "safe" nonprofits that have no meaningful relationship to the donor companies. Why? Often it's because of the person doing the asking. Slamming the door on a solicitor is tricky if the person holding out the tin cup happens to be.

▶ the chairman's wife looking for a little something for her garden club

▶ an outside member of the board of directors who thinks the company should help the Muscatine Melon Patchers Quilt Guild (an actual nonprofit located in Muscatine, Iowa), even though nothing links the group with the business

▶ a personal business acquaintance of the CEO who is chairing the dinner committee for a soirée in a city a hundred miles from the company's nearest office

There are ways that Step 2 can help with these types of difficult situations, which are sometimes more of an attempted holdup than a fund-raising exercise. Before demonstrating how the concept can be applied in these circumstances, note that defense is *not* its main intent. The primary purpose of Step 2 is to make social investing more strategic, to bring more discipline to the giving process. It is the North Star for our corporate social investment plan that can keep a company on course.

When the second step does have to be used for defensive reasons, it can be an effective shield against at least some of the unwanted appeals that are constantly fired at the company. Example: whether the business buys into corporate social investing or not, the chairman's wife still has a penchant for gardenias and mums. She's not going to be embarrassed by coming up short for her garden club, so the company will put a few dollars in her watering can no matter what. However, guided by Step 2, the corporation negotiates a deal with the gardening organization. It will give a donation but will channel the funding to beautifying a beat-up park a block from the company's main campus. The city ends up looking a little better, and so does the appraisal value of the corporation's headquarters building.

Step 2 says that if there's not a significant business reason to make a social investment, *don't do it.* Conceding that there are times when a significant business reason is obscure, Step 2 also says, *Create a business rationale if at all possible.*

Seek a Return on Investment

It is the second step in our management model that makes it emphatically clear that corporate social investing needs to be seen as a business resource. It should be recognized as part of a company's overall effort to be successful—that is, to make money. No doubt about it, society is also a beneficiary. However, corporate social *investing,* as the term implies, starts with the premise that the *investor* (in this case the corporation) is looking for a return.

For some, trying to digest this notion will be no easier than swallowing a cantaloupe. People who feel that companies have a moral imperative to be socially responsible without expecting anything back are going to have to think hard about the underlying pillars of the corporate social investing model. Skeptics may have a problem getting beyond what appears to be a clash of two seemingly contrary forces. In this corner wearing white trunks, we have old-time corporate philanthropy, which is pure, unadulterated humanitarianism. In the opposite corner wearing dark trunks is

profit motive, which is a twenty-to-one favorite to eat philanthropy's lunch.

Actually, if the principles of social investing are firmly in place,
this is a battle that should never be allowed to happen. The objective isn't to set up a winner-take-all fight to the finish. Instead, the
goal should be to put together a management design that capital-
izes on the symbiotic relationship that this odd couple has:
Corporate profits make corporate social investing possible. *And in
turn,* social investing uses charity to create conditions that are conducive to making a profit.

"Social investing *uses* charity?" a skeptic might ask with disgust.
"Charity isn't to be used! You're corrupting the whole idea of what
charity's supposed to be all about!"

Not at all. Among other things, social investing *disciplines* a
company's charity (or philanthropy) so that it is focused on the
same general field of interest that the corporation has marked as
its own primary business territory, *strategically applies* funds paid to
external nonprofit organizations (as charitable gifts or other
forms of support) in a way that also helps the corporation, and
leverages whatever gifts or payments are made to nonprofits so that
these allocations end up helping the company continue to be
profitable.

The third statement may again trigger our skeptic's gag reflex.
It still seems *un*charitable to try to take advantage of philanthropy
so that the donor reaps any kind of benefit. But supposing that
donor happened to be a human being and not a corporation.
Would the skeptic have problems if a generous individual's name
were listed on the "patron" page of the symphony orchestra's play-
bill? Would there really be much hand-wringing if a longtime contributor to the local United Way were feted as Person of the Year
at the organization's annual dinner-dance? If individuals can be
given recognition and exposure before their peers, why can't businesses be provided the same kind of acknowledgment to their
important constituencies?

"All right," the skeptic may reluctantly concede. "Maybe there
are times when companies should be given a little publicity for
helping a nonprofit organization. But it sounds like corporate

social investing is looking for a whole lot more in the way of return benefits."

Sometimes, we reply. Where it's appropriate, practical, and legal, corporate social investing digs for more than enhanced name recognition. The benefits that a business might want from these investments aren't much different from those that Homo sapiens look for when they engage in certain kinds of philanthropic activities. Example: like most people, you have probably been subjected to one of public television's telethons, where classy programs are regularly interrupted by high-brow hucksters who try to make you feel guilty for not phoning in a pledge to pay for "your" station. If the televised entreaties eventually get to you, it's time to access that 800 number that continuously rolls across the screen. With credit card in hand, you suddenly find yourself talking to one of the flock of nameless volunteers you've seen manning the banks of telephones to the rear of the telethon's energetic host.

"I want to make a $25 pledge," you say.

"Wonderful! But if you increase the size of your pledge just a little, you get the mug," the volunteer responds, following the how-to-respond-to-a-caller instruction card to the letter.

"What mug?" you ask.

"Make a $40 donation and we send you our designer mug in an attractive box," the volunteer bubbles enthusiastically. "It's a great way to tell people you care about your station." The television station is pushing premiums for larger donations—the mug, the tote bag, the fold-up umbrella, the uncensored CD of Pavarotti's bloopers.

"So what do I get for just $25?" you ask hesitantly, the sensation of miserliness creeping through your body.

"A tax deduction for your donation," the volunteer answers, a slight hint of dejection and irritation in her voice. "You ought to think about the mug. It's really something special."

"Yeah, but it's $40. . . ."

"Which you can put on your credit card," the volunteer responds quickly. It's time to set the hook. "MasterCard, Visa, Discover, or American Express?"

Step 2. Extracting Business Value from Social Investments

As with individuals, part of corporate social investing is about deciding if the premiums are worth it. It's figuring out whether it is in the best interest of the corporation to go for the mug (which, in the world of business, could be a press release sent out by the nonprofit organization praising your company) or the umbrella (a testimonial event sponsored by the nonprofit for your firm that is guaranteed to score points with current and potential customers). Maybe it's the tote bag (right of first refusal to discoveries coming out of basic research that your company is underwriting through a grant to a university). Then again, it could even be the CD (the name of your business chiseled over the archway of the performing arts center, a perpetual corporate reminder to your culturally attuned clients).

Our skeptic protests vehemently. "You're mixing apples and prunes! When people give money to a nonprofit organization and get a premium or a benefit in return, they can't write the value of that premium off as a charitable deduction. It shouldn't be any different for a business."

He won't get an argument here. Remember, corporate social investing isn't handcuffed to charitable giving per se. Unlike individuals who need to worry about what portion of a donation is tax deductible, a business that follows our corporate social investing model will be publicly reporting the *total* payment a company makes to a nonprofit organization, which includes donations plus certain other types of support that don't necessarily qualify as charitable deductions.

Nonprofits aren't known for customizing premiums for different businesses; for the most part, they peddle the same kind of "mugs" to the corporate community. Those premiums tend to be pretty unimaginative. A corporation can be included in the elite "gold sponsor" section of a nonprofit's annual dinner program if it makes a $10,000 donation. For $5,000, the company gets its name on a placard draped over the ball washer at the fourteenth hole of a charity's golf tournament. If a business wants a premium that will give it a stronger return on its social investment, then it is usually up to that corporation to look for a creative opening. A true story serves as a good example:

An American nonprofit organization approaches the U.S. home office of a multinational corporation. The nonprofit asks for

$50,000 as a lead gift to help underwrite an international forum that is to be held eighteen months later. Forum organizers will invite twelve hundred leaders from fifty nations, people the nonprofit knows are of special interest to the business.

The nonprofit offers primary sponsorship credit to the corporation if it puts up the $50,000. That means the company gets a back cover of the program book to be published for attendees and some splashy signs around the meeting venue—pretty standard forget-me-nots that most nonprofits offer potential event sponsors.

The corporation looks apathetic. Then, with a gleam in its private-sector eye, the company wants to know where the forum will be held. The nonprofit says no site has been nailed down, but predictable places like New York and Washington, D.C., have been mentioned. The business, which is located in an out-of-the-way small city, asks if the forum could be brought to its own backyard. It pictures twelve hundred potentially important customers browsing about in the shadow of its main office. The premium has been defined. The equation is this: venue equals $50,000. The nonprofit retreats to see if it can work out the details.

Our skeptic moans. "This is going too far. It's the old story of the corporate bully pushing around some undersized nonprofit. This is absolute manipulation!"

Yes, there is some orchestration going on here. However, the process is much closer to negotiation than manipulation. Keep in mind that (a) the corporation could do a lot of different things with its $50,000, and (b) corporate social investing means that the company should be looking for a significant business reason for each grant it makes. In this example, the firm is working to make the proposed deal more important to the company. If the nonprofit feels it can't live with holding its forum in the corporation's town, then it may have to move on to some other prospect.

This example points out a fact of life that nonprofits need to recognize: when looking for money from a corporation, the competition isn't just with other outside organizations but also with people, departments, and divisions *inside* the company. Let's go back to our real-life forum example to make the point clear. Supposing management has already decided to run a very expensive ad campaign aimed at (among others) those participants who would be attending the meeting. The company is looking for cash to meet the costs of this major ad campaign, which isn't cheap. Using rate-card information, this is what selected publishers and television networks would charge the business for one-time ad placements in 1998 (in fairness, companies often get deep discounts off these published rates):

Reader's Digest (full-page ad, color)	$202,650
TV Guide (full page, color)	$155,185
60 Minutes (thirty-second ad)	$170,000
ER (thirty seconds)	$515,000
20/20 (thirty seconds)	$165,000

That's almost a million dollars for placing just five ads, and the bill for the creative talent to produce the commercials or print advertisements isn't even included! It could be worse. If the corporation were to buy one of the fifty-eight thirty-second spots during the Super Bowl, it would pay over $1 million *per commercial* for the privilege of running an ad during the most-watched televised event.

Let's assume that the manager handling the company's corporate social investment program confronts the ad agency with this argument: "A $50,000 grant may not buy us millions of impressions but it will give us the punch we need to influence a group of people who make major purchasing decisions. We'd be insane to pass this opportunity up."

In this particular example, it is the *business value* that sways the company into thinking seriously about the grant. The money could just as easily have been diverted to help pay for the expensive ad campaign, but a strong hand at the social investing tiller keeps the nonprofit's international forum in the game.

Three Important Points

Identifying and extracting business premiums from grants and other commitments made to nonprofit organizations is not a sometime thing. Social investing requires that we identify a business reason for each investment made, so it makes sense that for virtually every payment to a nonprofit some business value can be extricated. Here are three points to think about when working out a social investment agreement with a nonprofit.

▶ **EFFECTIVELY MANAGING A SOCIAL INVESTMENT PORTFOLIO MEANS KNOWING THE RULES**

In other words, companies must know what's *allowable* in the way of a premium or benefit and what's not. As noted earlier, this has to be a special concern if a social investment is to be written off as a charitable deduction because there are constraints on how much quid pro quo value can be extracted from that kind of an investment. Remember our earlier advice: if in doubt, *don't* declare a payment to a nonprofit as a charitable gift. Remember too that noncharitable support for a nonprofit or an exclusively public organization has the same social investment value as a tax-deductible contribution.

▶ **IN SOME SITUATIONS, EVEN IF A BENEFIT IS ALLOWABLE, AN INVESTMENT SIMPLY ISN'T STRATEGICALLY APPROPRIATE**

Example: Anderson Consulting (the worldwide management and technology consulting company) made a major commitment to the National Gallery of Art in Washington, D.C., to sponsor a large exhibition of Van Gogh masterpieces. The exhibit with all its advertising and publicity tie-ins got the Anderson name in front of the country's top business decision makers and potential clients. So far, so good. Now supposing Anderson were approached by exhibit organizers to take the seventy pieces of art on the road to out-of-the way rural locations in America. Although this would be a wonderful way to expose people who might not otherwise ever get to see original works of great artists, it would require funding for an activity that has little if any meaningful strategic value to Anderson.

▶ **THE WHOLE PROCESS OF EXCAVATING BUSINESS VALUE FROM A SOCIAL INVESTMENT ALSO HAS TO BE PRACTICAL**

It may not be worth the time and effort to capitalize on a premium even though it's there for the asking. Small donations generally yield small returns. It just doesn't warrant a lot of time and energy trying to pluck out meager benefits when there are bigger fish to fry.

....

The Deft Hand of a Competent Manager

Managing Step 2 of the social investing process requires a strong knowledge of the business mixed with equal parts of common sense and good intuition. As already stated, it also means knowing just how far a company can go without violating any rules, regulations, or ethical boundaries that surround a social investment. Getting "allowable, strategically appropriate, and practical" business value from a social investment requires talent—the more extraordinary the management, the more extraordinary the premiums to the business.

Trying to implement a really effective social investment plan without strong management is like Ben and Jerry trying to make a banana split with a cucumber. The end product won't turn out the way it should. So unless a business is willing to start with a decent banana, it might as well not even bother mixing together the rest of the social investing ingredients.

Ben Cohen says that there is a spiritual aspect to business and would like every company to begin the search for nirvana. Although Step 2 is not a map that will lead a business to the holy grail, it is a navigation system that can guide companies toward a different way of thinking about their external social responsibilities. Maybe our principle doesn't come with exactly the kind of cherry on top that Ben and Jerry would like to see. Still, if it helps to get more corporate money into the nonprofit world, Ben Cohen might have to concede that it's a sweet treat all the same.

Step 3. Which Nonprofits Qualify—and Which Don't

They come in all different sizes and shapes. Some operate on a shoestring and a prayer. Then there are others like the YMCA of the USA, which rakes in $2 billion a year to conduct its activities. There are quite literally hundreds of thousands of them and they are known as the citizens of the nonprofit world, an aggregation of all kinds of organizations that are becoming more and more of an economic powerhouse in America. Gross revenues of service groups, education institutions, community hospitals and certain other nonprofit operations exceed more than *a trillion dollars a year* according to some estimates, and that doesn't include what many churches, synagogues, and other religious agencies are collecting.

Finding the most appropriate business-relevant organizations as candidates for support is what Step 2 of the corporate social investing process tells us that we need to do. This is quite a feat given the mammoth size of the options. So where does a corporation begin the sorting process? Believe it or not, the best place to start is by calling upon our friends at the Internal Revenue Service.

There's a section in the IRS tax code that has become famous in the nonprofit world. As we saw earlier, Section 501(c)(3), as it is called, designates which tax-exempt organizations can provide a charitable tax deduction to donors. The qualifying nonprofits must be "organized and operated exclusively for religious, charitable, scientific, testing for public safety, literary, or educational purposes, or to foster national or international amateur sports competition (but only if no part of its activities involve the provision of athletic facilities or equipment) or for prevention of cruelty to children or animals."

In order to get 501(c)(3) classification—which most nonprofits consider more valuable than platinum—an organization has to tell the IRS that it will not direct any personal benefits, including dividends or anything else that might be disguised as profits, to members or officers. The organization also has to pledge that it won't participate in or attempt to influence political campaigns, although it can engage in voter education activities such as conducting public forums, giving testimony on party platforms, and providing issue briefings for candidates.

What we have here is the IRS serving as a kind of free quality-control agent for our social investing process. Without costing companies anything, the government helps weed out organizations that potentially could be a problem to corporate donors. Consider it life insurance, compliments of the IRS, that reduces the odds that corporations will get entangled with nonprofits that could blemish a company's good name. This is not foolproof insurance, mind you. There are plenty of pitfalls even among those organizations blessed with what the IRS calls a 501(c)(3) "determination letter." Nevertheless, it's not a bad first screen for our sorting-out process.

Indeed, this tax provision is such a useful culling mechanism that it's inserted into the heart of the next step in our corporate social investment model. Along with another provision drawn from Section 170(c)(1) of the tax code, it leads us to the next step in the corporate social investment model:

Step 3. Limit corporate social investments to 501(c)(3) nonprofit organizations and exclusively public institutions (or comparable organizations outside the United States).

· ·

Excluded Groups

In the United States this step narrows the corporate social investment field to just 501(c)(3) organizations and public sector entities such as the federal government, states, U.S. possessions, and the District of Columbia. By making this declaration, a lot of other tax-exempt nonprofits are left on the outside. Some of the excluded groups include these:

SOCIAL WELFARE ORGANIZATIONS

Most of these nonprofits are awarded a 501(c)(4) tax status and include local employee associations and certain civic leagues. Some are kissing cousins to 501(c)(3) organizations. A notable difference between a status of (3) and (4) is that the latter organizations have more latitude to influence those who hold government positions.

BUSINESS LEAGUES

Local chambers of commerce and other like organizations may be exempt from paying certain taxes, but they aren't covered by Step 3 because they can't get 501(c)(3) approval.

FRATERNAL SOCIETIES, ORDERS, OR LODGES

Although these groups often carry out important projects in the community, they're usually not 501(c)(3)s and therefore don't qualify when it comes to corporate social investing.

Even though these non-501(c)(3)s may be excluded from a company's social investment program, that doesn't mean that they should be denied corporate funding. However, whatever payments are made to these organizations should be counted over and above commitments made for corporate social investing purposes. Why limit social investing to 501(c)(3)s and exclusively public organizations? As a rule, these are the nonprofits that (a) are the "safest" social investment partners, and (b) offer the greatest potential for addressing critical social needs.

The 501(c)(3) Pool

Remember that there are a *lot* of fish in the 501(c)(3) pool—over six hundred thousand organizations, representing an astounding number of choices for a business. (See again Exhibit 2 in Chapter 2.) Categories include the following:

CHARITIES

The IRS has been fairly liberal in its definition of what it considers to be a charity. A nonprofit organization has a good chance of getting a 501(c)(3) passport if it has as its main mission

- working to provide relief to the poor, distressed, or the underprivileged
- erecting or maintaining public buildings, monuments, or works
- lessening of the burdens of government and the promotion of social welfare—a gigantic gateway for organizations to climb into the 501(c)(3) nest

SCIENTIFIC INSTITUTIONS AND AGENCIES (INCLUDING GOVERNMENT ORGANIZATIONS)

If these organizations conduct research that is in the public interest, then they can apply for 501(c)(3) classification.

EDUCATIONAL ORGANIZATIONS

Colleges, universities, professional schools with faculties, course offerings, and students are the kind of organizations you would expect to find in this category. But surprisingly, the government also considers the following to be educational institutions: museums, zoos, planetariums, and "public discussion groups." What *won't* qualify under this particular category are organizations that have as their principal purpose the presentation of "unsupported propaganda" or groups that practice discrimination in either their hiring or admissions practices.

RELIGIOUS ORGANIZATIONS

About half the 501(c)(3) exemptions awarded by the IRS go to religious groups. That means there are approximately three hundred thousand religious institutions that qualify as candidates for corporate social investments. However, even though Step 3 leaves the door open for businesses to assist such religious organizations, most corporations rule out support to these groups *unless* they provide nonsectarian services. Examples: nonprofits such as Catholic Charities USA, Salvation Army, Jewish Board of Family and Children's Services, and many other religious agencies lend a hand to abused women and children, the homeless, and so on, usually without regard to the religious persuasion of those in need.

OTHER 501(C)(3) ORGANIZATIONS

Over the years, Congress has tacked on a few other smaller categories to those included in the original 501(c)(3) legislation. Right now, these "addendum" organizations include groups that work to prevent cruelty to children or animals and those nonprofits set up to foster national and international amateur athletics.

Most 501(c)(3) organizations can be found with other nonprofits listed in an IRS directory called *Publication 78* (also often referred to as the Blue Book or the Cumulative List). Thumbing through this two-volume tome (plus appendix), you get an appreciation of the extraordinary diversity of nonprofit organizations in America. As noted, not all organizations in the book are 501(c)(3)s but every one of them is exempt from federal income tax. As the following randomly selected list of nonprofits makes it clear, there's something in *Publication 78* for everyone:

▶ American Heartworm Society (Batavia, Illinois)

▶ Elvis Presley Memorial Foundation (Memphis, Tennessee)

▶ Herb Society of America, Inc. (Kirtland, Ohio)

▶ Shoplifters Anonymous (Jericho, New York)

▶ World Darts Federation (Bellflower, California)

COMPATIBLE PARTNERS

Some businesspeople may have a knee-jerk reaction to 501(c)(3) organizations as being "do-good" agencies that companies should avoid. Actually, most nonprofits can prove to be very effective business partners if corporate social investing principles are applied. The following is one of many examples.

Not that long ago, the yogurt maker Dannon discovered that *environment* was a magic word among a respectable number of young yogurt eaters and their families. The product manager for Dannon's Kids Businesses division worked a deal with the National Wildlife Federation (NWF): the company agreed to commit 1.5 percent of its Danimals brand sales to NWF for the life of the product.

The company's cause-related marketing strategy included packaging that was educational and environmentally friendly and brilliantly targeted to both children and their parents. It proved to be a "green" idea in more ways than one:

▶ First year sales of Danimals yogurt shot past projections

▶ NWF ended up with a $450,000 donation after year one of the project

There's a long list of other successful business–501(c)(3) partnerships and we'll be citing examples in the course of the next several chapters.

Exclusively Public Institutions

In addition to allowing investments in 501(c)(3)s, Step 3 also keeps the door open for "exclusively public institutions"—those designated under 170(c)(1) of the IRS tax code—which gives companies the go-ahead to extend social investments to local, state, or national government agencies. This also leads to the following questions:

"You mean a company can get a tax deduction for giving a donation to the government if the contribution is to be used for public purposes? " *Answer:* Yes.

"But the company has to pay taxes to the government. Why would it also want to make a contribution?" *Answer:* Grants to government agencies can sometimes provide a company with certain strategic advantages that just aren't attainable any other way. Besides, the grant is deducted from the company's taxable income, which means the company is going to pay less taxes.

"But even if it gets a little tax relief, a company still ends up spending more if it makes a donation to the government—doesn't it?" *Answer:* Yes. However, the company can earmark its grant to those government programs or projects that are in line with a corporation's own interests. The company gets a much bigger bang for its buck than it does from its tax dollar.

"How commonplace is it for a business to make a grant to a government agency?" *Answer:* It's unusual except in cases where corporations support public universities and colleges. Otherwise, donations tend to be few and far between. But the grants that are made can be very advantageous to the donor company.

It boils down to this: there may be times when a company would be well-served by committing cash, products, or even land to local school systems, state parks, or U.S.–run cultural agencies. Step 3 permits that to happen.

6

. . . .

Step 4.
Making a Declaration
for Corporate Social
Investing

There are those who think Robert Haas is Moses with a profit motive. The chairman of the world's largest apparel maker has a reputation for leaving his San Francisco office and ascending into the Sierras to conjure up big ideas for Levi Strauss & Company. One never knows what Haas will bring down from the mountain. Maybe a new business development strategy. Or possibly something still dripping of transcendental meditation, like a notion to improve the "psychic ownership" of his company.

Haas isn't just another California oddity who by some quirk of fate has been plopped onto the throne of one of America's big businesses. The man has had remarkable success turning Levi Strauss into the archetypal values-driven company. The firm's Aspirations Statement, written in 1987, is a model for employee empowerment and effective organizational leadership. The statement covers a lot of territory as it highlights everything from diversity to the need for striking a balance between personal and professional obligations. It is the company's manifesto for enriching the business and the people who work for it.

Almost as well known as the firm's aspirations is its vision statement. It plots a course for the company and does so by committing the organization to certain business practices. Part of the vision reads: "Our success will be measured not only by growth in shareholder value but also by our reputation, the quality of our constituency relationships, and our commitment to social responsibility."

Levi Strauss is one of those companies that tries to do things right when it comes to external affairs. Robert Haas isn't the kind of CEO who tiptoes through his professional career hoping to sneak past questions about what his company is doing to help the world outside his business. He gets people believing that the words in his company's vision statement actually mean something. That leads folks to conclude that Levi Strauss is dead serious about social responsibility. And they're right.

Of course, the company's vision statement isn't exactly overflowing with specifics. What *is* social responsibility anyway? At Levi Strauss, Haas can retort with a pretty impressive definition and can even make a convincing case about how social responsibility helped resurrect his business back in the mid-1980s when the company had a bad case of the financial blues. However, many other corporations that openly babble about how committed they are to doing their fair share for society can't hold a candle to Levi Strauss. Of course, most businesses don't take a public stand on social responsibility at all, and of those that do, many go heavy on the fluff and light on substance.

Why Make a Statement?

This brings us to the question that is at the heart of this chapter: Why *should* a company make an open statement about social responsibility?

On the surface, it may seem that making a proclamation about confounding concepts like corporate philanthropy, corporate citizenship, and social responsibility generates more downsides than upsides. After all, these are not issues that will ever get full consensus among all of a company's stakeholders. Remember the conflicting views of Herbert Stein and William Norris described in Chapter 2? Well, the world is full of people who don't see eye-to-eye when social responsibility is put on the table as a topic of discussion. So why should a company wave that kind of red flag when instead it could just stay silent?

There's no arguing that it is easier for a corporation to say nothing about its social responsibility beliefs. However, keeping quiet isn't golden if a company is serious about corporate social investing. Open statements about social responsibility (even if not very explicit) give the word to those inside the company that it's okay to spend some time and attention thinking about external relations. Corporations need to *sanction* social investing and that starts by hanging out a sign that says (in so many words): "We take a reasonable approach to social responsibility."

Going public with the right comments about social responsibility gets close to what is called in psychobabble *validation*. Anyone who has watched a daytime talk show or has read an advice column is well aware of the concept:

It's okay to hate the Spice Girls.

It's okay to despise the ring in your kid's navel.

It's okay to have fantasies about llamas (as long as you don't act them out).

In adapting validation for our purposes, here's the message that needs to be delivered to the workforce and others outside the business who have an interest in the company:

It's okay to make social investments.

A corporation can send out the word in different ways. It can include the statement as part of a widely circulated vision or mission statement. Or it can add a paragraph or two to its annual report. Maybe a company's internal house organ is the right vehicle. Some corporations produce general-purpose brochures that can get the job done effectively. A few firms take a bolder approach and use wall plaques and posters to get their point across.

These statements don't have to be splashy, multicolor, banner-headline declarations. It's the message that's important here and not the medium. A simple but clear statement of commitment is fine. It needs to be written with the following audiences in mind:

STOCKHOLDERS

Somewhere, somehow, the word needs to get out to people who "own" a corporation that the business has its head on right when it comes to philanthropy, community relations, and public affairs. It has already been noted that institutional fund managers who buy and sell a company's stock are not overly concerned about a corporation's social responsibility policies. However, there are more and more shareholder "guerrilla groups" that *are* concerned. As these proactive shareholders push corporations to demonstrate social responsibility, businesses will find some comfort in being able to point to a policy statement that says, in effect, "We subscribe to the principles of social investing and have a well-managed, business-relevant program in place."

NONMANAGEMENT EMPLOYEES

Even though there is a little rust on the trust that once was perceived to exist between worker and employer, most employees feel a sense of pride about their company when the business does something that shows it has a heart. Social investing does encourage employees to feel good about their company.

However, there is another dimension to a corporation's investment program. When a business says it is committed to a carefully developed social investment strategy, that corporation is making it clear to employees that those investments are included in the cost of doing business. That expense, which is driven largely by the pretax profitability of the company, *has no bearing on whether the employee will get a raise or a bonus, or be downsized out of a job.* It's important that employees understand this point.

A well-communicated mission statement (or some reasonable alternative) that makes reference to social investing takes the steam out of the oft-heard argument that says when a company is cutting staff, the timing isn't right to shell out more money for nonprofit organizations or other external relations. Under the rules of a well-planned social investment strategy, that argument is spurious. It's simple—as long as a business is earning a profit, social investing continues. Making this kind of investment commitment has nothing to do with a corporate decision to shrink the workforce or to seek other efficiencies. It has everything to do with maximizing the benefits both to the company and society from whatever investments a business decides to make.

MANAGEMENT

It is especially important that those leading the corporation know that (a) it is perfectly all right to deal with the outside world, as long as (b) those dealings take place within the framework of certain guidelines. In most companies, management is totally confused about where the line is drawn (that's assuming there *is* a line) when it comes to external affairs. For this audience, a general proclamation about social investing is too thin.

Managers want answers to questions like these: "How much am I supposed to put in my budget for social investing?" "What specifically do you want me to do, and by when?" "Will my own performance evaluation be affected by how enthusiastic or lackadaisical I am about social investing?" The trick is to get managers to think of social investing not as a duty but rather as an opportunity. A fully implemented social investment plan gives managers a chance to compete for money that can be used to drive the business beyond the limits of a manager's own budget. A more detailed description of the social investing process can get that point across—and also stir up enthusiasm for the concept.

NONPROFIT ORGANIZATIONS

Put yourself in a pair of nonprofit loafers. What do you want to know about a corporation? The cold hard truth is you want to figure out if you can extract a few dollars (or free product, services, or employee time) from the company. Effective nonprofits know that fund-raising is 90 percent research and 10 percent asking. So before approaching the business, you study the corporation and discover that the firm's vision statement says (in part): "XYZ Company subscribes to corporate social investing management principles." That information tells you this is a socially responsible corporation that gives priority to *business-relevant* investments with outside organizations. Now you make a choice. Either you forget about asking XYZ Company for financial support because its business is too far removed from the main mission of your organization—*or* you put together a proposal that blends your nonprofit interests with XYZ's business objectives.

A company's open commitment to social investing puts the onus on nonprofit organizations to develop fund-raising appeals that mesh with the corporation's business concerns. Truthfully, nonprofits often fall short when it comes to creativity. However, once in a while there's a pearl in the oyster and a broadly communicated statement about social investing is a good way to bring it out of its shell.

OTHER STAKEHOLDERS

A corporation has a *lot* of stakeholders (see Figure 6). Not all of them will have the same level of interest in a company's views about corporate responsibility. However, at some point in time, any one of these stakeholders may raise questions about what kind of strategy stands behind a company's decision to fund (or not to fund) certain nonprofit organizations.

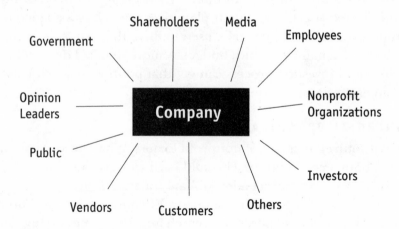

Fig. 6. Corporate Stakeholders

Conclusion: there are more advantages than disadvantages in signaling the world that a company has thought enough about its corporate responsibility to voice a position. This all leads to our next principle:

Step 4. Make an open statement that endorses corporate social investing or supports a broader concept that allows for social investing to be developed.

For companies that aren't ready to implement a full-scale social investing program, this step provides some breathing room. It allows for a wide-net approach whereby a company can make a much more general comment about social responsibility, à la Levi Strauss. However, be cautious about broad statements or proclamations. "Our commitment to social responsibility" works for Robert Haas because the words are the wrapping paper for a very well-developed program. People inside and outside Levi Strauss either know the specifics about the firm's social responsibility practices or can easily find out. For a business where there is no clear-cut social responsibility program, sweeping generalizations may sound nice but they could come creeping back to bite the company on its haunches.

In spite of the warning about sending out empty missives, it is still better to say *something* that will keep the door open for developing a more clear-cut plan in the future.

"This company recognizes the importance of social responsibility" or some other nonspecific wording plows a field that should be fertile enough for social investments to take root. It may take a little time, maybe even a lot of time, for businesses to develop a full-blown social investment strategy, but letting management and employees know that they have a ticket to make the effort is the least a company can do.

Examples of Strong Validation Policies

When it comes to validating social responsibility and social investing, a few businesses are at the front of the pack. Here are a couple of examples—one, an industry giant and the other, a comparatively small company.

JOHNSON & JOHNSON

The world's largest health care corporation is powered by a deceptively simple philosophy that Johnson & Johnson calls its Credo (see Exhibit 4). The four-paragraph statement of purpose has been scrutinized by business schools and contemplated by private and public sector leaders for years. With only a few small changes since it was written in 1943, the Credo continues to be the nucleus of a company that has ballooned into a $23 billion megabusiness with ninety-one thousand employees and sales in 175 nations.

WE BELIEVE OUR FIRST RESPONSIBILITY IS TO THE DOCTORS, NURSES, AND PATIENTS, TO MOTHERS AND FATHERS AND ALL OTHERS WHO USE OUR PRODUCTS AND SERVICES. IN MEETING THEIR NEEDS EVERYTHING WE DO MUST BE OF HIGH QUALITY. WE MUST CONSTANTLY STRIVE TO REDUCE OUR COSTS IN ORDER TO MAINTAIN REASONABLE PRICES. CUSTOMERS' ORDERS MUST BE SERVICED PROMPTLY AND ACCURATELY. OUR SUPPLIERS AND DISTRIBUTORS MUST HAVE AN OPPORTUNITY TO MAKE A FAIR PROFIT.

WE ARE RESPONSIBLE TO OUR EMPLOYEES, THE MEN AND WOMEN WHO WORK WITH US THROUGHOUT THE WORLD. EVERYONE MUST BE CONSIDERED AS AN INDIVIDUAL. WE MUST RESPECT THEIR DIGNITY AND RECOGNIZE THEIR MERIT. THEY MUST HAVE A SENSE OF SECURITY IN THEIR JOBS. COMPENSATION MUST BE FAIR AND ADEQUATE, AND WORKING CONDITIONS CLEAN, ORDERLY, AND SAFE. WE MUST BE MINDFUL OF WAYS TO HELP OUR EMPLOYEES FULFILL THEIR FAMILY RESPONSIBILITIES. EMPLOYEES MUST FEEL FREE TO MAKE SUGGESTIONS AND COMPLAINTS. THERE MUST BE EQUAL OPPORTUNITY FOR EMPLOYMENT, DEVELOPMENT, AND ADVANCEMENT FOR THOSE QUALIFIED. WE MUST PROVIDE COMPETENT MANAGEMENT, AND THEIR ACTIONS MUST BE JUST AND ETHICAL.

WE ARE RESPONSIBLE TO THE COMMUNITIES IN WHICH WE LIVE AND WORK AND TO THE WORLD COMMUNITY AS WELL. WE MUST BE GOOD CITIZENS—SUPPORT GOOD WORKS AND CHARITIES AND BEAR OUR FAIR SHARE OF TAXES. WE MUST ENCOURAGE CIVIC IMPROVEMENTS AND BETTER HEALTH AND EDUCATION. WE MUST MAINTAIN IN GOOD ORDER THE PROPERTY WE ARE PRIVILEGED TO USE, PROTECTING THE ENVIRONMENT AND NATURAL RESOURCES.

OUR FINAL RESPONSIBILITY IS TO OUR STOCKHOLDERS. BUSINESS MUST MAKE A SOUND PROFIT. WE MUST EXPERIMENT WITH NEW IDEAS. RESEARCH MUST BE CARRIED ON, INNOVATIVE PROGRAMS DEVELOPED, AND MISTAKES PAID FOR. NEW EQUIPMENT MUST BE PURCHASED, NEW FACILITIES PROVIDED, AND NEW PRODUCTS LAUNCHED. RESERVES MUST BE CREATED TO PROVIDE FOR ADVERSE TIMES. WHEN WE OPERATE ACCORDING TO THESE PRINCIPLES, THE STOCKHOLDERS SHOULD REALIZE A FAIR RETURN.

Exhibit 4. Johnson & Johnson's Credo

If anyone has any doubts about how seriously Johnson & Johnson approaches the business of dealing with the outside world, pay particular attention to the following excerpt from the Credo:

> We are responsible to the communities in which we live and work and to the world community as well. We must be good citizens—support good works and charities and bear our fair share of taxes. We must encourage civic improvements and better health and education. We must maintain in good order the property we are privileged to use, protecting the environment and natural resources.

Johnson & Johnson has consistently been among the most generous corporate philanthropists in the world. One reason is that— it uses cash and product contributions to fuel the "good citizen" segment of its high-powered Credo. This is a company that openly tells the world that it intends to "support good works and charity." It would be tough for Johnson & Johnson *not* to have a top-notch philanthropy program.

Johnson & Johnson is also a company that doesn't do much grandstanding. It resists buttering up its citizenship or good works with a lot of hype. However, the corporation is never shy about pointing to its Credo. It appears on everything: it is printed on company publications, hangs on office walls, and is carved into a huge block of limestone in the front foyer of its headquarters building. The corporation regularly probes employees with what it calls Credo surveys to find out if the mission statement is still alive and well.

The Credo isn't an antidote to every problem Johnson & Johnson bumps into, and it doesn't prevent the company from occasionally stumbling. From time to time, a dismissed employee or some disenfranchised outsider will accuse Johnson & Johnson of hypocrisy for flag-waving a philosophy that isn't always translated into action. Given the colossal size of the corporation, it would be impossible for the company to make a blanket claim that the Credo doesn't get nicked every so often. However, the violations are few and far between, and when they do occur, Johnson & Johnson is quick to apply an organizational bandage to whatever scratch it finds. If there is a serious Credo breach, company managers are rounded up to figure out why it happened and what can be done to prevent the problem from recurring.

Interestingly, shareholders are relegated to the very end of the company's Credo. This isn't an accident or an oversight. The company unabashedly says that if the company properly tends to all the other individuals and groups mentioned in earlier paragraphs of the Credo (consumers, employees, and community) then the shareholder will come out just fine. So far, the theory seems to be on track, since the company has seen its net earnings jump nearly fivefold over the past decade and has managed to increase its dividend every year since 1963. You can understand why there aren't a lot of Credo critics around.

Few corporations have so loudly proclaimed that it is okay to deal with forces outside the business per se. In fact, it's more than okay. At Johnson & Johnson, it's mandatory.

TOM'S OF MAINE

When NBC stitched a five-part series on American philanthropy into its evening news broadcast a while back, the network reserved one installment for a thumbnail look at corporate giving. The producers of the segment could have used the airtime to showcase the contributions programs of big-hitting businesses like IBM, Exxon, or Philip Morris. Instead, they turned their camcorders on a relatively tiny company—around $20 million in sales at the time—tucked away in Kennebunk, Maine.

Tom's of Maine says it is the country's leading producer of natural personal care products (toothpaste, soap, deodorant, antiperspirant, and so on). The business has only been around since 1970 but its fennel toothpaste, honeysuckle shampoo, and other products are on sale in more than thirty thousand stores in the United States and are exported to Canada, Israel, Japan, and the United Kingdom.

Tom's is the brainchild of Thomas and Katherine Chappell. Besides putting their entrepreneurial arms around an interesting marketing concept, the two anchored their business on a social responsibility platform. Today, the company seems to get more media mileage (at no cost) for being a corporate citizen standout than it does from its paid product advertising.

Tom's is one of those businesses that matches whatever it says about social responsibility with plenty of money. The company donates 10 percent of its annual pretax earnings (the most a company can deduct in any one year) to nonprofit organizations *and* urges it employees to donate 5 percent of their *paid* time at work to volunteering. This isn't an occasional gesture—Tom's makes this commitment every single year. It's no wonder Tom Chappell makes network news.

This company largesse stems from a Statement of Belief that the Chappells take very seriously (see Exhibit 5). In a separate declaration, the corporation turns its beliefs into action by pledging:

> To address community concerns, in Maine and around the globe, by devoting a portion of our time, talents, and resources to the environment, human needs, the arts, and education.

> To be a profitable and successful company while acting in a socially and environmentally responsible manner.

We believe that both human beings and nature have inherent worth and deserve our respect.

We believe in products that are safe, effective, and made of natural ingredients.

We believe that our company and our products are unique and worthwhile, and that we can sustain these genuine qualities with an ongoing commitment to innovation and creativity.

We believe that we have a responsibility to cultivate the best relationships possible with our co-workers, customers, owners, agents, suppliers, and our community.

We believe that different people bring different gifts and perspectives to the team and that a strong team is founded on a variety of gifts.

We believe in providing employees with a safe and fulfilling work environment, and an opportunity to grow and learn.

We believe that competence is an essential means of sustaining our values in a competitive marketplace.

We believe our company can be financially successful while behaving in a socially responsible and environmentally sensitive manner.

Exhibit 5. What We Believe

Tom's of Maine may be a lot smaller than Johnson & Johnson but its vision statement certainly is no less grand. Tom Chappell preaches "common-good capitalism," which a lot of businesspeople might find a tad radical. However, that doesn't stop Chappell—

the Harvard Divinity School graduate who has become the Billy Graham of the private sector—from beaming his beliefs to anyone who will listen. If you don't get enough of him on television or in *The New York Times Magazine,* then pick up his book, *The Soul of a Business: Managing for Profit and the Common Good.* You can't miss his vision, his company's vision, because it's flying high on the Tom's of Maine flagpole for all to see.

Is there one employee working for Tom's of Maine who hasn't gotten the word? Is there one supplier who doesn't know that this is a business committed to coupling capitalism and morality? It's doubtful that anyone could possibly be confused about the company's strong commitment to society. Not everyone may buy Tom and Kate Chappell's business beliefs, but no one can fault the couple for making it clear what their company stands for.

The Bottom Line

Powerful tools like the Johnson & Johnson Credo or the Tom's of Maine Statement of Belief aren't required components of a corporate social investment program. Not every business is going to have a Robert Haas who's willing to stand tall in his Dockers and wave a we're-for-social-responsibility banner. Most corporations are going to be more subtle when addressing external affairs. And that's perfectly all right, as long as corporations put something in writing that creates the right climate for social investing to germinate and blossom.

Step 4 is the decree that legitimizes social investing. It is the notice tacked on the company's front door that says "This business supports an intelligently managed approach to social responsibility."

Step 5.
The CEO Endorsement

Social investing doesn't have a chance unless a company's chief executive gives it the nod. Hence, this chapter is dedicated to every CEO—especially those whose companies are going to be in the black this year. If you're a chief executive, please read the next few pages. If you're an employee who doesn't happen to be the company's CEO or if you're a stakeholder who has a special interest in a corporation, please mark this chapter and send the book to the individual sitting in the front office. Although it would be gratifying to have a CEO read Corporate Social Investing *from cover to cover, enough information can be gleaned from this one chapter to do the trick.*

David Rockefeller's speech at the New York Economic Club in September 1996 bubbled through the senior executive ranks like a freshly popped bottle of Dom Perignon. The then eighty-one-year-old Rockefeller told corporate leaders that they should think seriously about "reassuming the role of what we used to call *business statesmen.*" With his usual polish, Rockefeller made this point: "In recent years, business leaders appear to have devoted themselves to making more and more money and find themselves with less and less time to devote to civic and social responsibilities and to sinking roots in their communities and showing their loyalty."

Rockefeller recollected the days when prominent CEOs like Tom Watson, Reg Jones, Irving Shapiro, and Walter Wriston were vocal and visible when dealing with external affairs. He observed that things have changed, and although he didn't use these words, no one missed the main point of his message: things haven't necessarily changed for the better.

Rockefeller went on to criticize the "self-serving behavior" of modern-day CEOs. He warned that such conduct could make the views of business more irrelevant to the important issues of the day. He said, "We must accept the fact that we have responsibilities that are broader than simply running our businesses in an efficient, profitable, and ethical manner."

David Rockefeller—the eminent banker and bearer of one of the greatest business names in America—had taken the CEOs of today behind the woodshed. And, quite remarkably, many of those chief executives understood why they were there and absorbed the sharp smacks on their egos without resentment.

David Rockefeller isn't the only one to put CEOs on the carpet for their decreasing attention to social responsibility. Another critic is Stanley Karson, who once directed the Center for Corporate Public Involvement, a Washington, D.C.–based group that works with over six hundred health insurance companies on community responsibility issues. Karson has complained that the hundred-plus businesses that endorsed a 1992 Declaration of Interdependence have backed away from that statement of beliefs, which included the following promise: "Our industry cannot prosper if society fails—thus, we pledge that, to the best of our ability, our companies, of whatever size and location, will use available resources—including financial, time, talent, and leadership—to improve the social and economic conditions that bear on the quality of life in our communities."

Karson contends that changes in leadership in the insurance industry and a shift in priorities have led many of the companies that signed the Declaration to "diminish their commitment." Karson maintains that the troubling changes in the insurance field aren't confined to that industry alone. He wrote, "Many chief executives in dozens of other industries probably believe in concepts of social responsibility. . . . But many business executives who have those views feel philosophically marooned and that paralyzes them. They fear that if they seem too preachy or take a totally different view from their peers, then they will be isolated because of their dissent."

Pertinent Questions

Karson is perceptive. Most CEOs *do* genuinely care about the problems of society and believe that businesses have a role to play in addressing those problems. Karson's also right about CEO paralysis, but he may be wrong about the cause of the problem. Most chief executives don't freeze because of a deep-seated fear that some out-of-the-box comment will get them ostracized by their colleagues. What brings CEOs to a dead stop when dealing with external affairs is total confusion over what exactly their companies should be doing to meet their social responsibility obligations. CEOs want specifics—not vague generalities—that can become the building blocks for a *manageable* and *defensible* social responsibility strategy. They want straight answers to pertinent questions.

HOW MUCH?

"How much should my company be budgeting for social investing?"

Someday, science will reveal a remarkable similarity in the genetic makeup of all CEOs. One common gene zips through the bodies and brains of those people who percolate to the top of their respective corporations, and that gene forces chief executives to avoid—whenever possible—making an up-front commitment of money for anything. Why? Because business leaders know that spending always expands to a budget. Never give subordinates a clue as to how much money is available for a project; let the project be presented first and assign the dollars later. That's pure, unadulterated CEO thinking.

With corporate social investing, CEOs have to grit their teeth and do something they normally don't do. They have to pledge a certain amount of money at the start of the fiscal year. They have to trust that there will be a lengthy menu of business-relevant funding opportunities that will more than justify whatever money is reserved for social investing.

CEOs need to accept the premise that the level of social investing is largely a by-product of a company's historic profitability. In a nutshell, here's how it works. Corporations invest a percentage of an average of the pretax earnings of their previous three years. There is an emergency brake that can be pulled if needed—the CEO retains the power to stop social investing in its tracks if the current year's profits are in jeopardy. The formula is spelled out in much greater detail later in this book, but this general explanation should be sufficient for most CEOs.

What percentage are we talking about? For companies that don't manufacture products, it's a minimum of 2.5 percent of this three-year rolling average. For businesses that do manufacture products, it's 3.5 percent. The reason for the difference is the favorable tax treatment given to products that manufacturing companies can include as part of the social investment program. The rationale for the 2.5 percent and 3.5 percent targets is presented in Chapter 9, but to assuage any CEO anxiety, it should be stated here that these investment levels are quite realistic. They equate to about what the average corporate contribution levels were in the early 1990s.

Regardless of what size corporation a CEO happens to be running, the formula remains the same. It is inexorably fair. For a non-manufacturing company that records an average of $2 billion in pretax earnings over three years, the $50 million in annual social investments has no more or less of an impact on the business than the $125,000 paid out in investments by the nonmanufacturing firm that made an average of $5 million in pretax dollars over the same three-year period.

THE RED-FLAG PROBLEM

"I'm against waving a red flag in front of stockholders. No matter what the pretax percentage level of our contributions might be, if too much money gets handed over to nonprofit organizations in any one year, that's a red flag, isn't it?"

Many CEOs don't relish being put in a position where they have to defend what could be considered a company's overly large commitment to charity. The reasons for this uneasiness are understandable since there are such mixed stakeholder views about corporate social responsibility in general. To date, chief executives have had no solid rationale to fall back on when facing challenges about spending too much or too little for philanthropy, community relations, or other external activities. The more money a corporation doles out for "social responsibility" purposes, the bigger the target for unhappy shareholders and others.

With corporate social investing, everything changes. By adopting the ten management steps that the social investment plan offers, a CEO of any size business can state, "Our company invests the recommended percentage of pretax earnings as called for in the social investment model adopted by well-managed corporations. The financial commitments we make under this plan not only address social needs, problems, and opportunities but also return value to our company."

Few CEOs have had this kind of platform under their feet. Corporate social investing provides chief executives with a logic for making funding decisions that extend outside the company—and for explaining those decisions.

COMPETITIVE ISSUES

"Supposing my competitors don't make social investments at the level suggested in the management plan—their profits go up and my company starts looking a lot less interesting to investors. Isn't that right?"

No. A business that doesn't subscribe to a prudent social responsibility strategy has a weak spot. Increasingly, it will be competitively unwise *not* to implement a corporate social investment program—a company will be putting itself at risk for being criticized in a way that could harm its ability to do business. The cost is too small and the benefits are too important not to implement such a program.

Still, reality says there will always be those corporations that will stay outside the circle. Will they have a financial advantage over a company that is spending a percentage of its pretax earnings on social investments? No—for two reasons.

First, these are investments that are returning value to the companies that spend the money. If social investing is working properly, the funds paid to nonprofit organizations are creating conditions or stimulating markets that are advantageous to the business.

Second, even if the return on social investments happens to be less than dramatic, CEOs should keep in mind that these funds are drawn from earnings that are subject to federal and state taxes. In other words, if the investments aren't made, the tax collector will be subtracting a healthy portion of the funds that could otherwise have been invested. For this reason, companies that elect not to implement the ten management steps might get a small uptick in their after-tax profits but lose the chance to use social investments to grow both their top and bottom lines.

MANAGEMENT TIME

"What impact does social investing have on head count and overall management time?"

Until a corporation starts paying out more than $5 million a year in social investments, it probably won't require full-time investment management. Companies with larger programs should commit full-time manpower to ensure that investments are achieving their full potential. (A general formula for determining staffing levels is presented in Chapter 12 of this book.)

What's important to remember here is that full-time or part-time manpower costs associated with corporate social investing are factored into the 2.5 percent or 3.5 percent of pretax earnings (based on a three-year rolling average) that a company annually commits to corporate social investing. These are not added or "hidden" expenses.

THE CEO'S TIME

"What about *my* time? How many hours and days does a CEO have to carve out for social investing or related social responsibility commitments?"

A chief executive doesn't need to give much time at all to the mechanics of a corporate social investment program. A CEO *does* need to stay on top of a company's social investments and usually can do that at two critical points: (a) during the budget approval process, a few months before the start of an upcoming fiscal year; and (b) prior to the corporation's annual meeting (assuming the business is a publicly held company).

Quite aside from social investing per se, David Rockefeller would probably contend that CEOs have an obligation to commit a respectable portion of their time to general external affairs. The partnerships forged with nonprofits as a result of social investing will open a lot of opportunities for CEOs to strike up those kinds of outside relationships.

What's the "right" amount of time? There's no hard and fast rule. We know that twenty years ago when The Conference Board, a business research group based in New York, surveyed 185 chief executives, researchers found that a majority of the CEOs (103 of the 185) were spending 25 percent or less of their time on "external affairs," which was defined as government, investor, special interest, media, and community relations. When splitting out just community and civic affairs along with government meetings or discussions that were held to discuss nonbusiness social issues like education, crime prevention, health care, and so on, it appeared that CEOs were spending 5 percent or less of their time on these functions.

That benchmark data, even though two decades old, might not be a bad reference point for CEOs. Using that information along with observations of more proactive CEOs who participate in nonprofit (nonbusiness) activities today, here's a guideline for chief executives to think about:

Companies with one top executive. CEOs of corporations that do not have a separate office of the chairman should target 5 percent of their time, at a minimum, for participation in nonprofit activities that are relevant to their businesses—board meetings, special events, fund-raising calls, and so on. That's about one day a month. This doesn't include time spent with business associations (business roundtables, chambers of commerce, and so on) unless such organizations are dealing with wider social issues.

Companies with two top executives. When a corporation has two top-end executives—e.g., a CEO and a chairman—the chief executive is usually considered the "inside" manager, and the "outside" responsibilities are left to the chairman. Quite often, the inside executive is excused from virtually any external involvement. Actually, this dual leadership setup should give the CEO more latitude to engage in social responsibility functions than executives who have to shoulder both the chief executive and chairman roles. In situations like these, a day and a half a month might be a reasonable time allotment for a CEO to devote to outside activities. The chairman should be spending at least 15 percent of his or her time on external affairs, that is, three days a month.

Getting the Message Out

Corporate social investing has to be blessed from the top. It absolutely has to have a CEO's approval if employees are going to treat the concept seriously and if stakeholders are going to get the right message. Even though the CEO's role in the social investing process is minimal, there is no more important player in the game than the chief executive. That is why one of the ten steps deals exclusively with the role of the CEO:

Step 5. Send a clear message to employees and other stakeholders that the CEO endorses corporate social investing.

In addition to occasionally casting an eye on the company's social investment portfolio, a CEO needs to take just two simple but essential steps to launch a full-scale social investment program:

SAY THE WORDS

Without mumbling, a CEO must tell employees and others (via whatever company communication channel is most appropriate— internal house organ, annual report, special brochure, and so on) that "our company is committed to the ten-step corporate social investing management plan" and follow that with a brief explanation of what the plan is.

If that is too much of a mouthful for a CEO, then an alternative statement should be sent out that says, "Our company is committed to moving toward the ten-step management plan for corporate social investing that has been adopted by other well-managed businesses."

This fallback position (see Step 4, Chapter 6) gives a company the time and space needed to take all ten steps included in the management model. Although the statement may be a little soft, it is enough to signal those inside and outside the corporation that social investing is something the CEO thinks is important.

PICK THE RIGHT MANAGER

Just as critical as communicating the proper message is the need for a CEO to choose an effective manager to make social investing happen. If the job is dumped on a lower-level staffer, that belies the CEO's endorsement of the concept. "I really believe in social investing so I am assigning an inexperienced, unknown, completely unempowered junior manager to lead this initiative." This kind of hypocrisy is sure to take the life out of a corporation's social investment initiative.

It takes a high-level executive to run a social investment program. That executive should be a solid *business*person who is wired into the marketing, sales, finance, and public relations corners of a company. The job should be given to someone who can put together a strategy that will yield a respectable investment return for the business as well as make an impact on society.

Benefits

Corporate social investing not only is likely to be right for a CEO's company but also is not a bad deal for the CEO's personal image. This is an era when corporate leaders are being attacked for (a) cutting too many jobs, (b) being too focused on short-term profits, (c) making too much money in wages and options, and (d) destroying any semblance of loyalty among employees deep in the organization.

IMAGE ENHANCEMENT

To counter charges that some CEOs are "corporate killers" while others are uncaring dolts driven by selfishness and insensitivity, top executives are being urged to expose their soft sides. A few companies have stepped harder on the public relations pedal and have rolled out worker-friendly policies and anecdotes about environmental improvements as examples of CEOs who care. Corporate responsibility is often used as sandpaper to smooth the rough edges of the top company executive.

Now along comes corporate social investing. It gives a CEO the ability to send out a signal that everyone can interpret the same way—sort of a social responsibility Morse code, if you will. Chief executives who subscribe to the corporate investment management plan, or who at least state openly that their companies will work toward adopting such a plan, are making a powerful statement. There's no need for a lot of extra public relations ballyhooing. If you're a CEO of a company that is committed to social investing, you're not just talking a good game, you're converting intentions into actions that will have a positive influence on both society *and* your business.

Corporate social investing should not be much of a stretch for most CEOs. One reason why is that these people really do want to do what's right—their moral compass is pointing in the proper direction. At a time when executive-bashing is so prevalent, that may be hard for some to accept. However, anybody who has come to know a cross section of CEOs will testify that corporate leaders are not insensitive to social needs. Many of these people make their own personal donations to nonprofit causes and organizations, and it's curious that gifts made by some of these CEOs vastly outpace what their own companies spend in grants, sponsorships, and the like. Exhibit 6, which lists the top ten philanthropists in the United States as ranked by *Fortune* magazine and the origins of each donor's wealth, illustrates this point clearly.

It's true that many corporate executives, like most wealthy people in general, tend to delay their biggest spurts of generosity until they are older even if they have money in hand now. Bill Gates, for instance, has told the media that he intends to give most of his money to charitable causes "later in life" (which Gates defines as age fifty or sixty). Warren Buffett will leave the bulk of his fortune (estimated at around $21 billion) to the Buffett Foundation when he dies, according to Roger Lowenstein, who wrote *According to Buffett: The Making of an American Capitalist.* This wait-until-I'm-old-or-dead mentality may fuel the fires of distrust among those who don't have much use for CEOs no matter what they say or do. As Exhibit 6 shows, however, these individuals aren't exactly skinflints. (Gates already places fourth on the top ten list.) Chief executives have a fairly good view of the world from their exalted positions and the scenery is not always pretty. Allowing for a few exceptions, CEOs are not disinclined to want to make things better for those outside as well as inside the companies they run.

Philanthropist	Total Donations in 1997	Origin of Funds
Ted Turner	$1 billion	Turner Broadcasting
Kathryn Albertson	$660 million	Albertson's (supermarkets, founded by her husband)
George Soros	$540 million	Soros Fund Management
Bill Gates	$210 million	Microsoft Corporation
Leonard Abramson	$100 million	U.S. Healthcare
Michael and Jane Eisner	$89 million	Eisner Foundation and the Walt Disney Company
Mitchell Wolfson, Jr.	$75 million	Wometco Enterprises
Phyllis Wattis	$70 million	Utah Mining & Construction Co. (merged with General Electric)
Raymond Nasher	$50 million	Nasher Foundation, real estate
Dwight Opperman	$50 million	West Publishing
Leslie Gonda	$50 million	International Lease Finance

Exhibit 6. America's Most Generous Donors, 1997

Source: *Fortune* magazine, February 2, 1998

THE SHAREHOLDER FACTOR

Those CEOs who run publicly held businesses should have an extra-special interest in corporate social investing's ten-step plan. It gives these chief executives an effective means of responding to unhappy shareholders.

Increasingly, stock owners are getting wise to certain privileges afforded them by the Securities and Exchange Commission. The

SEC gives any person who has owned at least $1,000 in a company's stock for over a year the right to submit a shareholder resolution. Corporations do have ways of deflecting some resolutions, but those that survive have to be sent to all stock owners for a yea or nay vote.

As most CEOs have come to learn, shareholder resolutions can be powerful weapons. They have been used to get retail companies to adopt new standards for selecting vendors and suppliers. Resolutions calling for a change in environmental practices have been lobbed at a number of corporations over the years. Maybe the most publicized use of such resolutions came in the early 1970s when the Episcopal Church put pressure on U.S. corporations to pull out of South Africa because of that country's apartheid practices.

A stockholder who has learned how to leverage these kinds of resolutions has a finger on the *Detonate* button of an explosive device. With a light touch, the shareholder can create a lot of noise, and corporations know it. Why has the SEC extended such power to the common man? The reasoning is as follows:

1. As a stockholder, you are an owner of the corporation.

2. Management is accountable to you (and everyone else who owns the company's stock).

3. Therefore, you can exercise your SEC-given right to influence company policies and practices by filing shareholder resolutions.

What's interesting about shareholder resolutions (especially those that deal with social responsibility issues) is that *almost no one expects them to get enough votes to pass if they are opposed by management.* In fact, those that get more than a 10 percent favorable vote are considered astoundingly successful. So what's the secret ingredient that gives a shareholder resolution its real power? *Answer:* V-E-X-A-T-I-O-N.

Resolutions can make a CEO squirm, particularly if they are likely to find their way into the media. Many corporations end up agreeing to meet with protesting shareholders to find out what it would take to keep the proposed resolution from going to a full stockholder vote. Sometimes businesses make concessions and the resolution is withdrawn. In other instances, the company holds firm and takes its chances.

A few organizations have developed shareholder activism into an art form. The Interfaith Center on Corporate Responsibility and the Investor Responsibility Research Center are a couple of examples. These groups have been known to make companies quiver, especially when dealing with environmental issues. Another 501(c)(3) nonprofit called Co-Op America ("dedicated to creating a just and sustainable society by harnessing economic power for positive change") published a column in the 1997 edition of its publication *Co-op America's National Green Pages* that opened as follows: "David beat Goliath and you can too. Shareholder resolutions are a powerful tool for individuals to make their voices heard in corporate policy."

The same publication reports an Investor Responsibility Research Center accounting of "the most active" shareholder resolutions that were filed in 1996 (see Exhibit 7), a list that should dispel any notion that resolutions are a quirk.

Issue	Number of Resolutions
Tobacco	47
Environment and energy	44
Board diversity	29
Equal employment	27
Workplace issues	27
Human rights	13

Exhibit 7. Most Active Shareholder Resolutions, 1996

Source: *Co-op America's National Green Pages*, 1997 edition

Co-Op America also highlights "resolution successes" for 1995 and 1996 that include these:

▶ *Kimberly-Clark:* agreed to spin off its tobacco operations.
▶ *3M:* said it would no longer accept tobacco ads in its outdoor media business.

▶ *RJR Reynolds:* split off its Nabisco foods division from its tobacco business.

▶ *PepsiCo:* decided to sell its Burmese operations because of that country's alleged human rights violations.

▶ *Mobil:* agreed to issue a report on its Nigerian operations regarding human rights matters.

Environmental issues, human rights, diversity—these have been the more traditional targets for shareholder resolutions. It has been unusual for shareholders to get exercised about a corporation's philanthropy or its general social responsibility policies—so far. However, the corporate weather map shows a disturbance heading toward publicly held businesses, and that impending storm is being fanned by charges that senior management may be mishandling contribution resources. As New York Law School professor Faith Stevelman Kahn puts it, "Corporate executives have control over billions of dollars of corporate (and corporate foundation) resources, which they may allocate to charitable entities independent of commercial considerations and according to their own pleasure."

This shareholder uneasiness over the possible misuse of contribution resources accounts for an emerging interest in what's called the Berkshire Hathaway model. Developed by Warren Buffett, the financial genius who heads Berkshire Hathaway, the company invites people and institutions holding Class A stock to designate one to three charities or private foundations to receive company contributions. Berkshire Hathaway then sends checks (or stock) to these nonprofits with the amount that is contributed determined by the number of shares a stockholder owns (in 1997, the "contribution value" of each share equaled $16). The concept works for Berkshire Hathaway mainly because there are only nine thousand shareholders or so, but the plan could turn into a managerial nightmare for larger businesses.

The dream of giving shareholders a loud voice in determining which nonprofits a corporation should support led to the introduction of House Resolution 945 by Congressman Paul Gillmor (R-Ohio) in March 1997. If passed and signed, the bill would "afford to shareholders the opportunity, on the basis proportional to the number of shares owned or controlled by such shareholders, to participate through a proxy, consent, or authorization in the designation of recipients (of charitable contributions)." In other words, the Berkshire Hathaway model would become the law of the land.

Companies with large numbers of shareholders reacted sharply to the proposed bill, as did many nonprofits. Critics predicted that such a law would create such managerial headaches that businesses would be discouraged from giving anything at all to nonprofit organizations.

Even if companies *could* design ways of cutting their social investment pies into thousands of tiny slices so as to appease every shareholder, it would mean sacrificing an important business asset. *That's* the message CEOs need to deliver to concerned shareholders. Corporate social investing is an assurance to anyone who owns a company's stock that the business is trying to get a two-for-one return from its external affairs investments—supporting nonprofits that have some relevance to the business and paving the way for the company to be even more successful in the future. Without it, or some similar kind of strategic plan, shareholders can easily be left with the impression that philanthropy and social responsibility dollars are up for grabs. And that can lead to shareholder questions about whether these funds are being used to glorify the deep-pocket reputations of CEOs as well as other high-end executives and company directors.

Blazing a New Trail

David Rockefeller's appearance at the New York Economic Club got unusually good reviews. His message filtered out of Manhattan as copies of his speech circulated through the upper levels of the private sector. CEOs talked and wrote about the wisdom of Rockefeller's remarks.

"We in business need to move beyond simply supporting the traditional social welfare, educational, and cultural institutions of our contemporary society," Rockefeller said. "We need to blaze new trails and build new partnerships—alliances, joint ventures, collaborative efforts—across the sectors and within our communities."

Corporate Social Investing

This call for an inventive way to hook business to society is the springboard for corporate social investing. The esteemed Mr. Rockefeller has given us the vision; social investing provides the right engine. All it takes now is for CEOs to push the *Start* button.

••

Step 6.
The Annual Social
Involvement Report

Ⅰf you've put on a few too many pounds or if you think you look
anorexic, the thought of slipping into a bathing suit and heading for the beach might not thrill you.

Such is the state of mind of most businesses in America after
giving their corporate responsibility profiles a once-over. Do you
really want to expose yourself when you presume that anyone who
glances your way is going to be turned off?

There are a lot of good reasons why businesses aren't pulling
back the covers on their corporate philanthropy, community relations, and social responsibility activities. The primary concern is
that showing off too much may be absolutely abhorrent to anyone
who thinks money spent on external affairs is pure unadulterated
business fat. Now along comes the next step in the social investing
management model:

Step 6. Produce a written corporate social involvement report that includes a review of social investments at least once a year.

A nervous ripple works it way through the private sector. "Don't take me there!" corporate captains implore. Business leaders usually learn (often the hard way) that the written word can turn on you like a mad dog. Particularly in light of the mixed views people have about corporate social responsibility, reducing a company's corporate responsibility activities to print seems to be a ticket to the dark side. That kind of report might win a few kudos for the company, but it also could be a hand grenade for some angry, don't-give-away-my-dividend shareholder.

In spite of the possible negatives (yes, Step 6 does bring with it an element of risk), social investing has to have a provision for disclosure. It's the price for credibility. Without an annual (or more frequent) report on a company's social investments, skepticism rules—particularly if companies are prone to bragging about their deep concern for communities and society in general.

Actually, the arguments for going public with specifics on a company's social responsibility initiatives are a lot stronger than those that are based on hanging a veil of secrecy over such activities—*if*, that is, a business has adopted the ten-step management plan. Circling back to the beach analogy, think of it this way: corporate social investing is a kind of organizational weight management and exercise program that can make a business look decent *before* it strips to its Speedo.

For companies that are somewhat anemic, corporate social investing can serve as a high-protein supplement that bulks up the organization. For the few businesses that may have the opposite problem—companies that have let their philanthropy, community relations, and social responsibility functions get a little too heavy—corporate social investing can tone up those sagging folds.

Another important point: our latest step doesn't mean that a company can't keep a few of its parts covered. You might think this smacks of selective truth telling (only go public with what's absolutely safe to talk about). That's not the intent. The idea is to produce a report that communicates the big picture and doesn't get into every agonizing detail of a company's social investing program.

Of course, even minuscule tidbits are important to some people. For these individuals, the company may want to provide additional information. A printout of all investments a corporation made last year (which, by the way, doesn't have to include a dollar amount for every small commitment a business makes) can be slipped into the main report for those who want that information.

Why Bother?

There are two good reasons why Step 6 is important to a corporation: (a) impending pressure and (b) opportunity.

IMPENDING PRESSURE

With or without corporate social investing, businesses may be moving toward a day when public reporting of a corporation's charitable donations (and perhaps other social responsibility activities as well) will be expected if not required. At least that's what Professor Kahn—the New York Law School professor mentioned in Chapter 7—would like to see happen.

Professor Kahn is not happy about the cloak of secrecy that hides a corporation's philanthropy, and she contends that in the absence of any accountability there is too great a risk that charitable dollars can be misused. She says that throughout the country, state laws and regulations that affect corporate contributions are all the same in one respect: "They authorize seemingly unlimited philanthropic contributions from corporate capital without regard to whether the firm will be benefited thereby."

Professor Kahn shouldn't be taken lightly. She's one of the plates pushing into a major fault line. She's causing tremors that could well be the harbinger of a much more powerful quake down the road. Kahn is not alone in her contention that "the potential for abuse arising from managerial control over corporate charitable giving . . . necessitates that some system of accountability be established—optimally, one based on obligatory disclosure of corporate contributions information."

This is the kind of talk that gets people thinking—people like Congressman Gillmor, the lawmaker who wants shareholders in publicly held companies to decide which nonprofits should get corporate contributions (again, see Chapter 7 for more on Gillmor's proposal). The congressman also introduced a bill in 1997 that called for an amendment to the Securities and Exchange Act of 1934. If passed, the change would require corporations and any investment funds regulated by the SEC to disclose in their annual reports to shareholders "the identity of and the amount provided to each recipient" of a charitable contribution. This bill (H.R. 944) ended up in the Commerce Committee's Subcommittee on Finance and Hazardous Materials, which then sent it to the SEC for a thorough feasibility study. Not many people thought H.R. 944 would ever find its way to a White House signing ceremony, but a lot of nervous businesses did wonder if the bill might push the SEC to require companies to produce more information about their charitable activities.

To prevent getting legislated or regulated into making disclosures, companies would be far better off if they volunteered to implement their own manageable and logical reporting procedures. That will happen if they adopt corporate social investing including Step 6.

OPPORTUNITY

A good disclosure report should be a convincing case statement for the company's social investing program, not just an accounting of payments made to nonprofit organizations. It should have energy and excitement. The report demonstrates how creatively and effectively the company is using investments to move the business ahead *and* address social needs.

Not many companies would consider using this report as part of a direct-to-consumer marketing device. Yet making it known that the report is available to consumers on request could prove beneficial to certain companies. Here's why.

On and off over the years, researchers have been hearing consumers say that their buying decisions are influenced by how good a corporate citizen the manufacturer or marketer is perceived to be. Cone Communications (a Boston consulting company) found that 76 percent of consumers would buy products to help charity as long as they didn't have to sacrifice price or quality (which is an upward change from 1993 when 62 percent of consumers surveyed said a charity tie-in would make a difference in their buying behavior). Okay, sounds reasonable. There's a problem, however. The Council on Foundations (a Washington, D.C.–based nonprofit organization that is just what its name implies) and an Indianapolis marketing company called Walker Information recently conducted a poll among six hundred heads of households. Forty percent of those included in the survey said that if they knew a product purchase would help a charity, that would be a "tie breaker" for them if price and quality were comparable. Then those 40 percent were asked to identify companies that donated proceeds from sales to charity—90 percent couldn't do it. Stated differently, an overwhelming majority of consumers who say they want to support socially responsible businesses don't seem to have a firm grip on which companies are "good, socially responsible corporations."

When asked for a reaction to this piece of research, a Whirlpool Foundation spokesperson told *The Wall Street Journal* that she was "real disappointed," because that company (one of sixteen firms involved in the study) had been an active supporter of women's and other social issues. Presumably, all the other businesses included in the survey that had a history of pumping money into social causes couldn't have felt much better about the results.

The research makes it apparent that many companies that are doing the kind of socially responsible things that might turn on consumers just aren't getting the word out. Somewhere between the corporation and its potential customer, the messenger either got lost or the information the messenger was carrying didn't have the force needed to punch through the hype-ridden atmosphere that enshrouds every consumer in America.

An Effective Report

This is an argument for developing a corporate social investing statement into something more than just a list of those organizations a company supports. The main ingredients of an effective report might include these:

A STATEMENT ABOUT CORPORATE SOCIAL INVESTING

"We use a ten-step management plan widely accepted by the business community to plan and carry out our social investment program" is not a bad opener.

A LOOK AT THE COMPANY'S BIGGEST SOCIAL INVESTING COMMITMENTS

Anyone curious about a company's external affairs practices wants the lowdown on those organizations or programs that are getting the most attention by the business. However, a long discourse on even the most important investment a company makes is not necessary and could turn out to be a detriment. The majority of readers will get satisfaction from an informative headline and a few well-chosen words about the major social investments the company is making.

Does that mean the report should overlook the small change the corporation is putting out for second-tier investments? No and yes. No, the corporation's report doesn't have to expound on every minuscule commitment, but yes, the report should say something about the lump-sum value of these smaller investments. A way to do this is to bundle these minor investments into subcategories (for example, investments under $500, matching grants to schools, and so on) and show how much money is being spent on these clusters.

AN EXPLANATION OF THE PERCENTAGES

A respectable disclosure report should openly acknowledge that a company sets an annual investment goal based on a percentage of the pretax net income figures averaged out over the past three years. Think of this percentage information as the logic chip in your disclosure statement. It says, "This company hasn't flipped a coin to figure out how much it's spending on its social investments; our business works within well-defined and generally accepted parameters to decide the investment level." This will be reassuring to a good many readers who, more than anything else, want to know that there is a clearly understood rationale for this kind of spending.

INFORMATION ABOUT DOLLARS AND SENSE

An explanation of percentages invariably leads to a disclosure of the cash value of a company's social investing program. That kind of financial information is often absent from social responsibility brochures that some businesses produce. Such vanity publications generally include self-painted and self-glorified portraits of the company's "community and social commitments," but they're skimpy on what those commitments cost. Step 6 calls for a report that requires numbers, not just adjectives.

The statement should also show, by referencing specific funding commitments, that the company is making *sensible* investments that have a positive impact on the business, as well as on the "community and society."

DESCRIPTION OF THE COMPANY KEYHOLE

One audience for a corporation's disclosure report will be those nonprofit organizations that are prone to probe for cracks in the company walls—small openings that might be entryways into the business.

Nonprofit executives and board members (remember that some of these board people might also be company employees or stockholders) may be inclined to use the report like a steel-toe shoe that can be jammed in the corporation's front door. That's why it is important to make the gateway as narrow as possible, so that only extremely relevant proposals can filter into the business. In the philanthropy field, "guidelines for giving" have long been used as a similar screening device. This same type of keyhole is even more important when a company implements a social investment strategy.

THE WHOLE STORY

There's usually more to a corporation's social involvement than just its social investing. Employee volunteerism (which only a few companies are likely to track as social investments—see Chapter 10) is a big part of the story, as is the purchase of goods and services from nonprofits. These "extras" don't get factored into the formula used to calculate a firm's social investment spending target, yet they are chapters that should be included in the overall story of a corporation's "social involvement" activities. Hence, *a company's disclosure report should be as inclusive as possible and show the full range of commitments a company has made to the non-*

profit field. Exhibit 8 outlines the elements of a social involvement report.

Statement of Commitment
Brief comment about the corporation's adherence to the ten-step management plan for social investing. Optional: list ten steps as a part of the report or as an addendum.

Level of Commitment
Describe the formula used to calculate amount of money/resources directed toward social investments. Acknowledge that other information in the report may be based on estimates if data are not available.

Report on Corporate Social Investments
  • High-impact grants

  • Conditional grants

  • Leveraged business investments (sponsorships, memberships, cause-related marketing expenses, risk investments)

International Social Investments
Provide dollar amount or estimate of company support of non-U.S. organizations comparable to 501(c)(3) or exclusively public organizations.

Commercial Support
State dollar total of fee-for-service, clinical/applied research, direct product purchases that involved 501(c)(3) organizations that were not counted in any other categories of the report.

Employee Volunteerism
Estimate the number of hours employees volunteered as a result of corporate-initiated projects or programs.

Corporate Social Involvement Summary Statement
Reemphasize the business logic that runs through all the corporation's social involvement activities.

Exhibit 8. Annual Report on Corporate Social Involvement

"It's impossible to get the data for certain sections of the report," some companies will protest. Well, maybe not impossible, but perhaps impractical. Counting every hour that employees work as volunteers outside the company or trying to figure out to the ruble or peso how much social investing is going on in foreign locations isn't a prudent use of time. So for certain parts of the report, extrapolations are permissible as long as there is an explanation included as to why estimates are being used.

Distribution

Once a corporation accepts Step 6 and produces an annual disclosure report, who gets it? Answer: It depends on the company.

Virtually every business will use the report to respond to inquiries from the outside. Some larger corporations get dozens of requests each day from nonprofit organizations looking for information about a company's philanthropic policies and guidelines. Public relations offices regularly get calls asking for details about the firm's community involvement or social responsibility activities. And, of course, there are those stockholders who want to know more details about "their" company's stand on certain social issues.

Aside from the defensive value of a social investing report, the information can be used proactively in certain circumstances. Some companies will find the report helpful in reaching out to the following audiences.

EMPLOYEES

It's not uncommon to hear people inside a corporation say that they know little or nothing about what the business is doing in the social responsibility field. If there is an effort made to get this news to employees, it's usually delivered in fragments—a story here or there in the company house organ about one noble undertaking or another. In most businesses, workers aren't given a composite picture of a company's corporate responsibility commitments because the organization isn't transmitting that kind of wideband signal.

By sending employees a report that details a corporation's total social investing program, a company can really get the workforce juices flowing. In most cases, if this information is delivered once a year it will be like a shot of vitamin B-12 to those companies looking for ways to improve productivity and attract new recruits.

SOCIAL INVESTMENT FUND MANAGERS

The financial wizards who oversee social investment portfolios have their work cut out for them. If they want a reasonable profile of a company's social responsibility agenda, they'd better have a sturdy shovel because they'll need to do some digging.

A publication called *Business Ethics* recently noted that 67 percent of Fortune 100 companies claim they produce something in writing about their charitable giving. That's probably a higher percentage than most people might think because few individuals have ever laid eyes on a corporate charitable-giving report. Even if they did get their hands on such a statement, they probably wouldn't find an overload of pertinent information. It only takes a quick review of some of these reports to realize that if the devil is in the details, he isn't living between the covers of those particular documents.

Business Ethics also surveyed a group of smaller publicly held businesses in the Boston region and found that only 16 percent of these firms issued a report on corporate giving. That's probably more typical of the overall universe of medium and larger businesses. Generally speaking, the smaller the firm the less likely anything is said publicly about its corporate responsibility activities.

Those businesses interested in scoring points with social investment managers should seriously consider sending them an annual disclosure report (this assumes, of course, that the company has a viable social investing program under way and therefore has something worthwhile to say).

SELECTED MEDIA

If you haven't noticed, America's corporate image has been scratched up pretty badly lately. Not so long ago, Max de Pree, former chairman and CEO of Herman Miller Inc., lamented that he couldn't remember any time in recent history when antibusiness rhetoric had been so strong. Then there's Benjamin Barber, who directs Rutgers University's Walt Whitman Center for Culture and Politics of Democracy. He blasted corporate America for not having an interest "in the public good."

There's more. G. J. Meyer, author of a book called *Executive Blues: Down and Out in Corporate America,* claims "corporations are alienating large numbers of Americans with their behavior. . . . The only way to change anti–big business feelings is to change that behavior."

Patching up corporate America's reputation will take more than a report or two from businesses with exemplary social investing programs. However, this kind of information placed in appropriate media certainly won't hurt. Occasionally, the popular press can be convinced to do a story about the shiny side of corporate responsibility. Keeping business editors informed about a company's overall social investing activities is a good way to spark more of that kind of media interest.

An annual report of a company's social involvement (with heavy emphasis on social investing) doesn't have to be fancy, long, or expensive. Small businesses might cover the territory with a couple of sheets of paper; larger corporations will need more space but don't have to produce multicolored masterpieces. The goal is to tell the social investing story the way Warren Buffett suggests businesses should communicate in general: simply. The true test of the report will not be how it looks but what kind of impression it makes on employees, shareholders, and anyone else who reads it.

Note to Small Businesses

Disclosure is not just for publicly held companies or megacorporations. Small companies often have amazing social involvement stories that rarely get told. These businesses can deliver their messages plain and simple, often on a single 8½ by 11 inch sheet of paper. Although such a deceptively elementary handout can serve a multitude of important purposes, it isn't often used by smaller companies. That will change if social investing's ten steps work their way into the ranks of the nation's vast conglomeration of medium and small businesses.

Step 7. Committing to the Corporate Social Investment Model: Part I, Percentages

S tep 7 is big enough and important enough that it merits coverage in two chapters: this one and the next. Both chapters are essential reading for whoever is going to be given responsibility for corporate social investing within a business. They are also important for those nonprofit managers and volunteers who solicit support from the private sector. Others who have a general interest in corporate social investing but don't need a deep understanding of the inner workings of the ten-step plan, can skim through these two chapters.

Presented in the pages that follow is the schematic for the corporate social investing model—a detailed explanation of how the social investment "motor" works and how much "fuel" is needed each year to keep the motor running. To make it easier to understand the model, the chapters dissect the plan so that each element can be studied separately. However, it is important to keep in mind that this is a management process that needs all of its parts. So, for those charged with planning and implementing such a program, remember to reassemble all of the pieces before activating the corporate social investment engine.

A One-Size-Fits-All Plan?

If Steffi Graf wants to add a little more zip to her serve, she should give Ed Kleiner, Jr., a call. Even though the owner of a Reno, Nevada, company called Comstock Seed never played at Wimbledon, Kleiner has a terrific forehand. The young businessman makes his living wandering around the western part of the United States using a secondhand tennis racket to smack seeds off plants and shrubs into canvas collection bags.

Comstock Seed has only six full-time employees (that includes Kleiner and his wife) and hires teams of part-time pickers to help with the harvest. Still, the business managed to literally bushwhack tons of specialty seeds in 1996—enough to ace $586,000 in sales.

Another, slightly larger U.S. corporation also did well in 1996. The accountants at General Electric Company's headquarters in Connecticut put in late nights counting the beans because there were a lot of them that year. GE got within a whisker of raking in $80 billion in sales during 1996—$79.2 billion to be exact.

Can a single corporate social investing model really be applied to a company as large as GE and as small as Comstock Seed? Is it truly a one-size-fits-all plan? The fact is, as with most off-the-rack products, social investing does require a little tailoring. With a nip here and a tuck there, the strategy can work for the half million or so corporations that are in the same size category as Comstock Seed or the more than seventeen thousand that (like GE) have sales of $50 million or more. (See Exhibit 9.)

Although alterations are permitted on some parts of the social investing strategy, there should be little compromising on Step 7 in our management plan. It stands as a giant signpost at the center of the proverbial fork in the road, and it gives a company no choice but to go in one direction or the other. Which way a business decides to turn will determine whether corporate social investing is seen as a sham or gets implanted into the company's DNA.

Under $25,000	967,652
$25,000 to under $50,000	256,394
$50,000 to under $100,000	396,700
$100,000 to under $250,000	874,758
$250,000 to under $500,000	542,757
$500,000 to under $1 million	439,279
$1 million to under $2.5 million	360,956
$2.5 million to under $5 million	151,036
$5 million to under $10 million	83,846
$10 million to under $50 million	74,132
$50 million or more	17,080

Exhibit 9. Number of U.S. Corporations, by Annual Sales

Source: Statistics of Income, Department of the Treasury, Internal Revenue Service, 1993

So here it is. If a corporation goes along with this step, then everything else that follows is merely a matter of tactics.

Step 7. Commit now or by a specified date at least 2.5 percent (3.5 percent for manufacturing corporations that donate product) of an average of a company's last three years of pretax profits for corporate social investing.

This is an inherently equitable requirement. It doesn't matter whether a corporation makes billions in pretax profits or a thousand times less money, the formula still holds. Businesses that subscribe to corporate social investing agree to ante up (as a minimum) the same percentage of profits in order to get into the game—and ante up again every year in order to stay in play. Some businesses may decide that they want to pitch more than 2.5 percent or 3.5 percent of their averaged pretax earnings into the pot, which is fine as long as the other management steps are used to guide the added spending. Step 7 isn't meant to discourage higher investments; it's the ground floor for those businesses practicing corporate social investing.

Why does the plan call for 2.5 percent or 3.5 percent of pretax profits (based on a three-year rolling average) in annual social investment commitments? Why not 1.5 percent or even 5 percent? Answer: The percentages included in the model bring corporate support for nonprofits back to a level of spending close to what corporations were allocating as charitable contributions in the early 1990s. This was a period when businesses (on average) were committing around 1.5 percent of current-year pretax earnings for donations, and we estimate that they may have been spending some 30 percent more for support of nonprofits not reported as part of the gifts and grants total—which would bring the annual payout in those years to close to 2 percent of current-year pretax profits. Because the corporate social investing percentages are calculated using a three-year rolling average and because the model is more liberal in the way it accounts for product donations and some other payments to nonprofits, the 2.5 percent and 3.5 percent targets are in the same range as the 1.5 percent to 2 percent range of business support for nonprofits recorded only a few years ago. In other words, Step 7 is not some radical departure from what businesses have done in the past.

Throughout the 1980s, corporate support to nonprofits never dipped below 1.5 percent of current-year pretax earnings. Many who follow the corporate philanthropy field felt that the eighties made 1.5 percent an impenetrable floor for corporate giving.

The corporate social investment model does more than stabilize company support for nonprofits at a reasonable level; it provides a much clearer framework for deciding what gets counted and what doesn't. And, again, remember the words "at least" in Step 7. The percentages are minimums. Companies may wish to go beyond the 2.5 percent and 3.5 percent targets if they can obtain a return benefit from such investments.

Large Corporations

As a general rule, the larger the corporation, the tougher it is going to be to comply with Step 7. Why? Because big companies have tended to pull back their overall social responsibility spending for all the reasons mentioned earlier in this book.

The Conference Board annually reports the giving activities of between 250 and 300 companies. The median level of giving for those companies in 1995 and 1996 was just 0.7 percent of their

Corporate Social Investing

Industrial Classification	Number of Companies	Total Consolidated Pretax Income ($ Thousands)	Total U.S. Contributions ($ Thousands)	Median Consolidated Pretax Income ($ Thousands)	Median U.S. Contribution ($ Thousands)	Median U.S. Contribution as a Percent of Consolidated Pretax Income
Aerospace and defense	5	$4,545,100	$37,937	$1,223,000	$10,627	.08%
Chemicals and allied products	16	18,850,059	104,534	488,000	2,235	.06
Computers and office equipment	7	18,677,779	223,261	1,944,000	16,000	.08
Electrical machinery (noncomputer)	8	14,936,052	74,374	521,500	4,018	.06
Food, beverage, and tobacco	11	24,124,352	213,156	917,000	13,999	1.3
Industrial and commercial machinery	9	4,671,707	29,209	162,781	1,418	0.7
Paper and allied products	8	2,432,254	29,101	291,885	2,261	1.3
Petroleum, gas, and mining	19	35,445,589	175,482	265,000	1,919	0.5
Pharmaceuticals	9	15,945,563	441,188	2,031,000	28,820	1.7
Scientific, photographic, and control equipment	6	4,867,620	52,840	389,501	6,258	1.2
Soaps and cosmetics	5	6,674,358	64,722	647,200	5,888	1.0
Transportation equipment[1]	7	20,270,918	138,251	302,000	7,366	0.6
Other manufacturing[2]	18	3,038,865	47,289	48,487	657	1.0
Total manufacturing	**128**	**$174,480,216**	**$1,631,344**	**$344,572**	**$3,031**	**.08%**
Banking	21	$23,249,367	$169,693	$338,363	$2,138	0.7%
Finance	6	6,356,324	41,050	893,150	2,596	0.5
Insurance	34	13,163,398	90,834	218,722	1,059	0.6
Retail and wholesale trade	9	4,823,146	91,338	330,000	6,802	2.2
Telecommunications	7	23,063,212	156,376	3,267,000	24,500	0.6
Utilities	29	14,868,989	79,676	383,948	1,966	0.6
Other service[3]	8	3,174,607	30,572	102,167	1,760	1.3
Total service	**114**	**$88,699,043**	**$659,539**	**$348,512**	**$2,122**	**0.7%**
Total all companies	**242**	**$263,179,259**	**$2,290,883**	**$348,512**	**$2,319**	**0.7%**

Note: Loss companies excluded.

1. Includes tire manufacturers.

2. Includes agricultural products; building materials; fabricated metal products; primary metals; printing, publishing, and media; and textiles and apparel.

3. Includes accounting; advertising; engineering and construction; health care; management services; and transportation.

Exhibit 10. U.S. Contributions as a Percent of Consolidated Pretax Income of 242 companies, by Industry, 1996 Reprinted with permission by The Conference Board. Sources: *Corporate Contributions in 1996,* The Conference Board

consolidated pretax earnings. (See Exhibit 10.) Remember, these statistics only reflect what corporations declare as the value of their charitable contributions. Sponsorships, memberships, cause-related marketing expenses, and some other payments that should be folded into the social investment model were not included in that figure. For the sake of making a case, assume that these other social investment activities added up to 50 percent of the philanthropic payments of these corporations (20 to 30 percent would be more in line with what may actually be the norm for businesses). That would hike the total median social investing to around 1.1 percent. That's still a far cry from 2 percent of current year pre-tax profits, which equates to investing 2.5 to 3.5 percent of the average of a company's pre-tax profits over the previous three years.

The sledgehammer effect of Step 7 on a megacorporation becomes apparent when we look at its impact on a specific company. Let's return to Connecticut for a moment. Remember the $79 billion in sales that General Electric collected in 1996? After GE sorted out all its expenses, it dropped $10.8 billion to the bottom line before taxes.

Now let's jump a year forward to 1997. We don't know exactly how much GE spent on what we define as social investing. Even GE probably doesn't have a handle on that figure because like most large businesses, the corporation had no reason to tally up the commitments it made to nonprofit organizations beyond what was spent on charitable donations. However, we can take a stab at sizing up the company's social investment total for the year. We know that GE distributes some of its contributions through a company foundation called the GE Fund. Based on that foundation's level of giving in 1996 ($28.4 million), the company probably paid out between $30 and $35 million in gifts and grants from that fund in 1997. The company also makes contributions outside the GE Fund, with those payments coming from other parts of the business. We will use a very liberal estimate and say that this nonfund amount was equal in size to what was paid out through the company foundation. So for purposes of this illustration, we estimate GE's charitable giving in 1997 at $70 million—$35 million from the GE Fund and a like amount directly donated by the company.

In addition, on top of its purely philanthropic dollars, GE might possibly find another $35 million (50 percent of its giving total) that it paid to nonprofits for basic research, sponsorships, memberships, and so on, which also qualify as social investments. This is money that would not normally be reported as part of the corporation's philanthropy figures. So by adding everything together, our best guess is that GE had a social investing total of around $105 million for 1997 (although, to repeat, this estimate is probably on the high side).

Now let's place Step 7 on GE's broad corporate shoulders and see what it would have done to that company had it been implemented in 1997. GE is a manufacturing company, so our formula says the firm needs to be at 3.5 percent of an average of its last three years of pretax profits. Doing the math, we find that GE should have spent $340 million for social investing purposes in 1997 if it had been complying with Step 7. That's *$235 million* more than what we think GE spent on corporate investments in 1997!

At this point, GE's John Welch, Jr.—one of the most celebrated CEOs in the history of American business—is using various colorful terms that all express pretty much the same meaning. Like many corporate leaders, Welch may have been swept along by the intellectual underpinnings of social investing until he bumped into Step 7. To lay out $235 million more than what GE already put on the table for nonprofit support seems to be a proposal too extreme to be taken seriously.

This example shows how difficult it will be for some corporations to leap from their current levels of corporate philanthropy to the social investment targets prescribed in our model. That's why Step 7 gives businesses some "wiggle room" to get to the designated investment levels by including a provision that says a business can either move to the spending target immediately or "by a specified date." For corporations that need time to get to Step 7, an important caveat goes along with this privilege. They should be willing to state how soon they plan to reach the 2.5 percent or 3.5 percent investment levels. Our model doesn't impose any fixed time limits on a company, and it's possible that without any hard-and-fast requirements, a few businesses may crawl toward minimum investment goals when they could walk or run. That could be a risky tactic because some stakeholders are bound to be impatient, particularly if competitive businesses have already met or exceeded the provisions stated in Step 7. Few corporations will be able to make a defensible case for taking any more than three years to reach the minimum percentages.

Exhibit 11 shows what a randomly selected list of corporations would have had to invest in 1997 in order to have been at either the 2.5 percent or 3.5 percent levels that year that year. (For gen-

Company	Pretax Earnings (MM)			3-Yr. Avg.	2.5% of Avg.	3.5% of Avg.
	1994	1995	1996			
3M	$2,011	$2,168	$2,479	$2,219	$55.5	$77.7
Alcoa	823	1,470	1,082	1,125	28.1	39.4
Allied Signal	1,111	1,261	1,553	1,308	32.7	45.8
AT&T	7,240	5,255	8,866	7,120	178.0	249.2
Bristol-Myers Squibb	2,555	2,402	4,013	2,990	74.8	104.7
Chevron	2,803	1,789	4,740	3,111	77.8	108.9
Cigna	805	251	1,601	886	22.1	31.0
Deere & Co.	921	1,093	1,287	1,100	27.5	38.5
Eaton	488	592	485	522	13.0	18.3
Exxon	7,804	10,442	11,916	10,054	251.4	351.9
General Electric	8,661	9,737	10,806	9,735	243.4	340.7
General Motors	7,098	8,349	6,676	7,374	184.4	258.1
Gillette	1,458	1,670	1,525	1,551	38.8	54.3
GTE	3,973	4,004	4,412	4,130	103.2	144.5
Honeywell	370	506	610	495	12.4	17.3
JC Penney	1,699	1,341	909	1,316	32.9	46.1
Johnson & Johnson	2,681	3,317	4,033	3,344	83.6	117.0
Merck & Co.	4,415	4,797	5,541	4,918	122.9	172.1
Merrill Lynch	1,730	1,811	2,566	2,036	50.9	71.2
MetLife	413	744	1,406	854	21.4	29.9
Monsanto	895	1,087	540	841	21.0	29.4
Olin	119	204	446	256	6.4	9.0
Pfizer	1,830	2,299	2,804	2,311	57.8	80.9
SBC	2,434	2,792	3,267	2,831	70.8	99.1
Schering-Plough	1,227	1,395	1,606	1,409	35.2	49.3
TRW	436	625	302	454	11.4	15.9
Xerox	1,514	1,849	1,944	1,769	44.2	61.9

Exhibit 11. Dollar Amounts Represented by Minimum Social Investment Percentages, Selected Large U.S. Corporations (Dollars in Millions)

eral comparison purposes, both numbers are shown for all companies, whether they happen to be manufacturing or nonmanufacturing businesses.) The cold, hard truth is that a large percentage of big businesses is going to have to come up with more cash (and, in some instances, more products) in order to meet the requirements of Step 7. Based on an extrapolation of charitable donation information collected by The Conference Board (see Figure 7), only a few of the top forty-eight corporate donors in the country may already be at or over the 2 percent level. Most of these very large corporations have contributions programs that equal about 1 percent of their annual pretax profits. But nine are actually paying 0.5 percent (a half of 1 percent) or less for their philanthropy activities (which means their total social investments are probably well under 1 percent of their before-tax profits). The majority of these corporations have a good distance to travel before reaching the minimum support levels specified in Step 7.

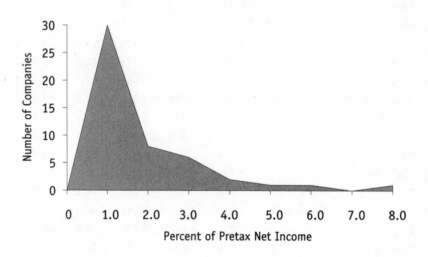

Fig. 7. The Forty-Eight Largest Corporate Donors, 1995

Source: Based on data compiled by The Conference Board

Small Fry

So much for huge businesses. Let's circle back to Ed Kleiner. Question: Why worry about how Step 7 affects small companies when their revenues and earnings (and, therefore, their social investments) tend to be so meager?

Here's one reason: there are a whole lot of Ed Kleiners. Of the 3.9 million corporate tax returns filed in 1993, over 30 percent came from companies like Comstock Seed that grossed between $100,000 and $499,000. There are more than a million companies in this country big enough to have stock. America is awash with pint-sized companies and the collective impact they have on social investing is significant.

There's another point worth mentioning here. The Wirthlin Worldwide consulting group recently collected information from 419 businesses with annual sales between $1 million and $3 million. The firm's research leaves no doubt that these smaller businesses are more generous than their larger counterparts. Small service businesses, for example, reported that they give 4.8 percent of their revenues to community charitable activities each year! Compare that with the 0.7 percent of pretax profits that many large businesses pay out to charity on an annual basis!

The Wirthlin Worldwide research also shows that smaller businesses may understand and appreciate the importance of strategic relationships with nonprofits better than do larger corporations. Most of the small companies questioned said they don't think giving to local programs or charities leads to a drop in profits.

Although small businesses might concur that there is a definite payback when supporting the right local nonprofit cause or program, it doesn't mean corporate social investing is easy for a small company. That is because small business owners are confronted with a barrage of in-your-face solicitations that constantly force them to apply social investing principles. It's the mom-and-pop operation that gets constantly hustled by its customers and other off-the-street solicitors. Retail and service operations are most vulnerable to this hassle factor. You run a bakery, sell flowers, or own a gift shop? You're on the "Compliments of . . . ." hit list for some organization's silent auction. You manage a restaurant, travel agency, or Swedish massage parlor? You'll be solicited by a local nonprofit to take a quarter-page ad in its dinner-dance journal.

THREE IMPORTANT TIPS

Here are three important tips for small businesses.

WRITE IT DOWN

Keep a pad next to the cash register and make a note of the retail cost of that layer cake or fruit basket you just donated to the high school glee club or local hospital. Keep records. Add up the totals at year-end. When appropriate, use that information to let the public know how responsive your business already is to community needs.

There is a vast underrecording of cash and goods donated by small businesses to nonprofit organizations. If these companies were to keep more accurate records, their generosity when calculated as a percent of their profits would probably make most multinational corporate giants blanch.

GET STRATEGIC

A small company will be whipsawed from one end of town to the other if it doesn't limit most of its social investing to clearly defined causes or areas of interest. Whatever that focus happens to be, it should line up with the company's main raison d'être. A small business doesn't have the capacity to be Santa Claus to every community organization that drops in looking for loose change. It needs a way to say, "Sorry, we can't help," without offending customers or potential customers.

Pick an organization, cause, or more general interest area (for example, senior citizen housing, children's health, clean streets, and so on) that has an impact on your business. Not every social investment needs to be pointed in this direction, but the company's high-profile commitments should.

DEPERSONALIZE THE "NO"

Getting shot down after asking for a contribution isn't going to leave a solicitor with a warm feeling. Although rejection will never be appreciated it can at least be better understood, and that can happen if a company uses a brief written statement to help the business say "so sorry." Exhibit 12 is an example of a one-page handout that will make rejection easier to take. The implied message is "We may think the world of your organization but we have this predetermined policy that prevents us from making a commitment." This simple explanation of a company's investment policy is many things: (a) a disclosure statement (see again Step 6); (b) a definition of the "keyhole" the company uses to decide which appeals will get funding consideration and which won't; and (c) a resource that makes it easier to turn down requests in the least offensive way possible.

ACME DINER AND DELI

In addition to working hard to give our customers good food and service, Acme is committed to being a good neighbor and citizen. Like many responsible businesses, we have adopted the ten steps of corporate social investing (see back page). Each year, Acme actually *exceeds* the recommended level of funding for nonprofit organizations as called for in the social investing statement.

While we want to help as many community programs and projects as possible, our funding can only stretch so far. That's why we have decided to focus our investments on needs that coincide closely with our business expertise. Acme limits its support to nonprofit [501(c)(3)] and publicly funded organizations that

- provide food to the needy and elderly
- offer vocational training to those interested in restaurant and food service careers
- educate children on nutrition and good eating habits

Acme also supports the United Way as a means of preserving and improving the quality of life in our community.

Last year, Acme made available over $5,000 in cash and products to Meals on Wheels, the Vo-Tech High School foodservice program, Cub Scout and Brownie nutrition projects, and Second Harvest.

So many of our customers and friends ask Acme if it would be possible to donate cash or food to help other worthy causes in our town. It is difficult for us to decline these invitations. However, after careful thought, we think Acme can make the greatest contribution to our community by holding fast to the priorities in our investment guidelines. We hope you agree.

Exhibit 12. A "Gentler" Rejection Letter from Acme Diner and Deli

UNINTENDED RESULT?

There is the possibility that a more disciplined approach to social investing will actually reduce the level of support small businesses now provide to their respective communities. Simply by doing an inventory of what they're already giving away, a few small companies might be convinced to scale back their support to non-profits—especially after learning that bigger corporations are much tighter with their dollars. There also may be small businesses looking for an excuse to shrink the size of their commitment, and with Step 7 their search may be over. So, yes, there may be some reduction in small-company support for community nonprofits. Overall, however, things should balance out. More small companies will use Step 7 to increase their investments because for the first time they will have an inkling of what they should be spending. That will more than offset the constriction effect that causes other businesses to pull back their community funding. Finally, to repeat a point already made, Step 7 establishes minimum investment levels for businesses—moving to a higher level of social investing may be appropriate for many corporations.

In Aggregate

Step 7 has significant economic importance if it were to be implemented by all corporations, large and small, in the United States. Nonprofits would receive an extraordinary increase in resources, and corporations would be creatively using added dollars (and/or products) to address their commercial concerns as well as helping society. Assume that all U.S. corporations that filed a tax return in 1996 had paid out 3 percent of their three-year rolling average pretax profits (splitting the difference between 2.5 percent and 3.5 percent) for social investment purposes. Here's what would have happened:

U.S. Corporate Pretax Profits
(In billions of dollars)

1993	1994	1995	Avg/3-yrs	3 Percent
$464	$528	$601	$531	$15.9

How close did companies actually get to paying out $15.9 billion in social investments in 1996? No one knows. The only figure we can point to is the $8.5 billion that companies took as charitable deductions for the year (see Chapter 1, Figure 3). Add to that number a 50 percent uptick for other kinds of social investing that may have gone on during the year and that's an additional $4.3 billion (remember that this is a *very* liberal estimate). Our best guess is that total corporate social investing for 1996 could have been somewhere around $12.8 billion.

Even using the high end of our estimate, it brings us to this conclusion: If Step 7 were adopted by all profitable businesses in the United States, nonprofits would receive at least another $3 billion a year in corporate social investments.

This boost in corporate spending for nonprofit programs and activities isn't going to occur unless corporations can be convinced that Step 7 makes sense. Arguing that businesses should hike their budgets for the good of mankind won't do the trick in most cases. The majority of companies will not move to these higher percentages unless they truly understand and accept the business relevance of corporate social investing.

Manufacturing Companies

A dollar is a dollar. But a product, that's a different story altogether. When a business manufactures a product (and a "product" in this instance can be anything from an automobile to a cracker), it creates something with a multiple personality.

VALUING A PRODUCT

When a product is provided to a nonprofit organization, it can be valued in at least five ways.

COST

The cost is the "book" expense for manufacturing an item. The figure covers what the company paid for component parts, ingredients, labor, marketing, warehousing, and general/administrative overhead. It's the true cost of the product to the manufacturer.

DONATION TAX VALUE

The IRS gives companies (with some exceptions) an incentive to donate products to certain nonprofit organizations: (a) those that use the product solely for the care of the ill, the needy, and infants, and (b) schools and charities that promise to use computers and other technology equipment donations to educate children in kindergarten to grade twelve. In these circumstances, corporations can take 50 percent of the difference between cost and retail fair-market value as a "stepped-up" charitable tax deduction that can be added to the cost of the product as long as the total write-off does not exceed twice the cost. Here are two illustrations of how the rule is applied:

Widget A

Book cost of widget	$1.00
Retail fair-market value (FMV)	$2.00
Difference between book and retail FMV	$1.00
Step up (50 percent difference)	$0.50
Possible deduction (step up plus book)	$1.50
Maximum deduction allowed (twice cost)	$2.00

In this case, because the possible deduction is well below the allowable ceiling, the company gets to write off $1.50 for every widget it donates to a qualified nonprofit organization. But look what happens when the retail value represents a huge markup over cost (which is the case for some products):

Widget B

Book cost of widget	$1.00
Retail FMV	$8.00
Difference between book and retail FMV	$7.00
Step up (50 percent difference)	$3.50
Possible deduction (step up plus book)	$4.50
Maximum deduction allowed (twice cost)	$2.00

Even though the possible deduction is $4.50 in this example, the ceiling limits the actual tax write-off for Widget B to just $2.

WHOLESALE VALUE

Whatever a manufacturer charges to the retailer or middleman (if there is one) represents another dollar amount that can be picked out as the worth of product given to a nonprofit.

AVERAGE MANUFACTURER'S PRICE (AMP)

In certain industries (for example, pharmaceuticals), manufacturers may be required to calculate an average selling price for their products, a price that takes into account discounting and other adjustments. For such products, the AMP is usually considered the fair market value even though the products might have a higher advertised or promoted retail price.

RETAIL FAIR-MARKET VALUE

Whatever a willing buyer pays a willing seller for an item determines its retail value. It's the price a nonprofit organization would normally have to pay for the product if it were not donated, and it's the fifth way a manufacturer can look at the value of a donation or investment.

Until now, most companies have treated products that are given to nonprofits as donations, not as social investments. It is not clear whether corporations are consistent in the way they report product donations to the IRS—some may take the "step up" and some may not. But what we do know is that when communicating to the general public, companies have been notoriously inconsistent in what they say about these gifts. Some have considered it a moral breach to take credit for anything more than the cost of the product they are giving away. A few regulated businesses report AMP as the worth of their product donations, while others go whole hog and claim the full retail value. Many think that the cost plus step-up deduction is the right figure to use with the public. This total lack of uniformity has made a mess out of attempts to develop an apples-to-apples comparison of overall corporate philanthropy programs.

Example: The media played up Microsoft as the top (that is, most generous) corporate donor in America in 1996. This is a business that wasn't even in the running as the number-one corporate contributor the year before. So what accounted for this meteoric rise to stardom? Product. The retail value of a load of software was added to a very modest amount of cash that Microsoft doled out as gifts during the year. The company reported the combined cash-product total to an outside organization that monitors corporate philanthropy and presto! Bill Gates's business leapfrogged to the front of the line.

Although Microsoft's decision to take the highest possible value for its product irked some businesses (especially companies that don't have product to give away), the corporation wasn't acting inappropriately. Lots of businesses use retail value when publicly reporting their product contributions; of course, many others do not. And therein lies the problem. There simply is no way to put Microsoft's total giving program in perspective because there is no uniform reporting system for products. If such a standard existed and if all corporations communicated the same way to the public about their product contributions, Microsoft would end up as an afterthought on the list of top corporate donors.

AMENDMENTS FOR MANUFACTURING COMPANIES

What is badly needed is an agreed-upon, common approach to how businesses should publicly state the value of products given to nonprofit organizations. Three amendments to Step 7 establish an important framework for reporting this information to the public:

> *Step 7, Amendment A. Use only salable products that can be provided in a timely manner and in reasonable quantities to any 501(c)(3) nonprofit organization or exclusively public institution as corporate social investments.*

> *Step 7, Amendment B. Report all product investments to the public at their retail fair market value (or average manufacturer's price for regulated industries).*

> *Step 7, Amendment C. Regardless of how much product is invested, make cash investments of at least 1.5 percent of a pretax net income (PTNI) three-year rolling average.*

These are significant points for any company that produces original product—from apple sauce to airplanes, from baskets to batteries.

AMENDMENT A

Amendment A says that product giving is just as legitimate a corporate social investment as cash if certain conditions are met. A key word in the amendment is salable, meaning that the product which is being donated is still on the market at the time the contribution is made. It isn't out of date and it isn't junk. Product investments are very visible corporate commitments, and they need to reflect the same quality standards that are applied to those goods that are being sold in the marketplace. If a company tries to pull a fast one and unloads questionable products on some charity that has a reputation for being a dumping ground, it may contract a serious case of bad press. The media doesn't take kindly to corporations that are suspected of shipping their mistakes to nonprofits and then taking a sweetened tax deduction for pulling off the slippery deal. An article in *New Scientist* magazine headlined "Dud Drugs Dumped in Crisis Zones" is a good example of how sharp the media's knife can be. The following is an excerpt:

> Donations of useless drugs are blighting international aid and disaster relief efforts, says a new report from some of the world's leading aid charities.
>
> The report, from a group that includes Médecins Sans Frontières and the World Council of Churches, says that "drug donations may be more trouble than they are worth." Most of these donations, often made by the manufacturers, are not requested. In many cases, the drugs are obsolete or of no use in the recipient country, which is then saddled with the cost of disposing of them. For instance, appetite stimulants have turned up in famine-hit Sudan, and indigestion tablets have been shipped to Rwanda.

Not exactly a glowing endorsement of the pharmaceutical industry. However, in fairness to the drug manufacturers, charges like these may not convey the whole story. Most corporations play by the rules that the IRS established for product giving. Often, however, these companies see their good intentions get sidetracked by Father Time. When companies send dated product (drugs, certain foods, and so on) to a nonprofit, they usually do so well in advance of the expiration month and year that's stamped on the items being shipped. (If they don't, the companies forfeit the privilege of taking the important stepped-up tax deduction). The problem is that the charities accepting the donations often have to jump a number of time-consuming hurdles to get the product to the end user—volunteers are sometimes recruited to pack the materials, heavily discounted space on a cargo ship has to be located, then comes the hassle of getting products cleared by bureaucrats overseas. The sea freight transportation and handling process can take six to nine months, sometimes even longer.

Amendment A should get companies thinking about a rather commonsense practice. When providing a nonprofit with dated product, the corporation should do so with this stipulation: "Don't hand out our product if it has expired."

Manufacturing companies need to consider carefully a couple of other words in Amendment A: reasonable quantities. Shipping a boatload of donated space heaters to Nigeria is probably not the smartest move a business can make. Even though corporations often want their contributed products sent to locations where they aren't being marketed, oversaturating one destination with these kinds of goods is not only a waste of material but also a red flag to the media, which always has its antennae out for this kind of abusive practice. There are plenty of places that can use space heaters. It may mean spreading the donated product around so that two or three nonprofits are brought into the act. Sure, that's more of a hassle for the company—different shipping consignments, more paperwork, and so on. But seeing to it that the right amount of product (1) ends up in places that won't embarrass the company, and (2) legitimately helps people is good social investing and therefore good business.

AMENDMENT B

Amendment B is going to make some corporations uncomfortable. Companies that manufacture products that customarily get marked up five or eight times over cost (sometimes even higher) will be concerned that their giving totals will go too high if they report the retail market value of their noncash donations. Nevertheless, this standard is the best industrywide option for these two reasons:

1. *Common valuation.* The retail FMV or, in the case of regulated industries, AMP is what many nonprofits use when recording the value of products they receive. Amendment B brings corporate reporting in line with what nonprofits are already reporting to the public. The goal is to have the business and the nonprofit recipient assign the same value to the product investment.

2. *Most practical alternative.* Many businesses won't disclose any number except the retail FMV or AMP because they fear that stating product values any other way will give competitors or stake-

holders information about the book cost of their manufactured goods (information that is usually closely guarded by most companies). Given this immovable position on the part of some companies, getting every corporation to use either the retail FMV or AMP is the only practical option there is.

Important announcement: If this one amendment is adopted by all manufacturers, it will bring order to an incredibly confusing reporting system. A recent informal poll of thirty of the largest corporations disclosed that a third use retail FMV (or AMP) when telling the world what their product donations are worth, another third use book value, and the rest of the companies use tax value. The current situation is chaotic. Amendment B will straighten it out and will paint a much more accurate picture of the true value of corporate social investing in this country.

AMENDMENT C

Amendment C is a "fairness" provision that many nonmanufacturing companies feel product-producing corporations need to adopt. It is clear that manufacturers get a big perk by being able to use retail FMV or AMP to hit their social investment targets. Nothing irks banks, insurance companies, and other service companies more than seeing manufacturing businesses make a donation of slow-moving inventory that might ultimately be heading to the scrap heap—and then get a stepped-up tax deduction for contributing the product. To create a more level playing field, nonmanufacturing businesses argue that manufacturers should put a reasonable amount of cash into the corporate social investment pool in addition to whatever product they are turning over to nonprofit organizations. Based on a review of manufacturing company cash and product giving over the past few years, 1.5 percent (of a three-year rolling pretax profit average) looks like the right number for manufacturers to use in budgeting the cash component of their social investment programs.

There will be some manufacturing companies that will definitely balk at Amendment C. A few companies use product in a big way to "make the numbers." For these businesses, this amendment means they will need to spend a lot more cash—something that may rub against the grain. There are those who are convinced that product and cash are of equal value and no distinction should be made between the two.

"What's the difference if we give our 3.5 percent in product or cash?" asks a piqued manufacturing company.

An equally piqued nonprofit organization might answer this way: "We can't pay salaries, rent, or the telephone bill with product. Bartering hasn't been popular since the nineteenth century. Even if we could trade your product for chickens and butter, the IRS wouldn't let us get away with it—the law says no exchanging donated product for money, other property, or services. Give us a break—organizations like ours need some amount of cash to keep us going!"

Given the benefits manufacturing companies get from investing their products, these businesses should agree to add a dollop of cash to their donated goods. The 1.5 percent cash–2 percent product formula seems fair and strikes a balance that should ease the frustrations of those companies that aren't in the manufacturing field.

Let's pay a return visit to General Electric to see how Amendment C would impact a real business. Remember that based on 3.5 percent of a three-year rolling average, GE would have needed to shell out a whopping $235 million more than what we think their corporate social investments were worth in 1997 in order to have been faithful to Step 7. Closing that gap is a lot easier to do thanks to Amendment C.

Using 1.5 percent of the PTNI rolling average to calculate the minimum cash requirement for GE, the company would have needed to invest a minimum of $146 million during the year—that's about $41 million more than the $105 million in cash we think the company may have paid out for social investing in 1996. The company could have then relied on product (at retail FMV or AMP) to make up the remaining $194 million needed to get to 3.5 percent.

Beefing up GE's cash investment total by $41 million a year won't be a cakewalk. But when product investing can be used to carry $194 million of the company's total investment burden, Step 7 suddenly looks a lot more viable for General Electric.

Here's a last word on product. About-to-be-obsolete or slow-moving products are not the only items corporations end up donating to selected nonprofit organizations. A growing number of companies are actually producing products for the sole purpose of handing them over to private voluntary organizations. If a corporation has a couple of open hours on its manufacturing schedule (when labor and overhead costs are going to be paid no matter what), it can keep its production line busy and produce product for charity. In spite of what accountants may list as the book cost for these goods, the company is really spending little more than what it paid for ingredients and packaging to manufacture this product investment. Keeping in mind that the company gets an extra tax deduction for these contributed items, this is a good deal for manufacturing businesses.

ANY 501(C)(3) ORGANIZATION

Yes, manufacturing companies are being asked to put more cash on the table than some might otherwise be inclined to spend. However, they get something back in return. Tucked away in amendment A is the innocuous word: "Any." It gives businesses the ability to invest product with any nonprofit organization—if it has a 501(c)(3) status—or exclusively public institution and then publicly claim full retail value. Companies don't have to be concerned if organizations are using the products for the ill, needy, or infants, or if they are using computers to help educate kids, which are the current guidelines for getting a stepped-up tax deduction. Any qualified nonprofit will do.

There will forever be debate over whether product investments have parity with cash. Some manufacturers will insist that their product is their most valuable currency, more precious than cash. Other businesses will complain that product giving is a boondoggle with manufacturers using nonprofits to help them get tax breaks for disposing of slow-moving or excess inventory or for carrying out a disguised product-sampling campaign. Those that hold these two points of view are unlikely ever to come to a middle ground that is mutually acceptable. The amendments to Step 7 bring businesses to a DMZ that seems to be the right place to draw the line.

Straightening out how manufacturers deal with product commitments to nonprofits is essential if there is to be order in the social investing field. It's time for manufacturing businesses (big and small) to agree to Step 7—as amended.

One last word on this subject is this. Manufacturing companies that choose not to give product as part of their social investing activities should target 2.5 percent of their three-year rolling average base as their annual cash investment total. This statement should eliminate any confusion about how much cash a manufacturer should set aside for social investing if product is not included in the equation.

Step 7. Committing to the Corporate Social Investment Model: Part II, Strategic Plans

lizabeth and Robert Noyce split in 1976. With a divorce settle-
ment worth $40 million, Betty left her home in California's
Silicon Valley and put a whole continent between herself and
Intel Corporation, the company her ex-husband had founded. She
relocated to Maine and drove her roots into a state not known for
embracing outsiders, even if they happen to be rich.

Twenty years later, sixty-five-year-old Betty Noyce died, and an
extraordinary thing happened. A couple of thousand dyed-in-the-
wool down-easters showed up at the memorial to pay tribute to the
remarkable woman they had made one of their own. They were
there to honor a lady who had turned her wealth into a salve that

had been skillfully applied to the bruised economic exterior of the southern part of the state.

Betty Noyce could have taken her fortune and lived the fabled life of a well-heeled divorcée. Instead, she inoculated her adopted state with an estimated $50 million as part of a personal crusade aimed at preventing a massive job exodus from Maine. At first, it was standard-fare charitable giving. But then she converted it into something else that would eventually be called *economic philanthropy*. Betty Noyce used her treasure chest to create and keep jobs in the region. As *Boston Globe* columnist Ellen Goodman put it, "She went into business without a profit motive. . . . She went into the charity of employment."

Betty Noyce saved banks, revitalized business zones, and even salvaged a foundering bakery. She turned her money into financial flypaper that kept small companies stuck to the region. The woman didn't turn her back on the cultural, educational, and health-organization needs of her community. She continued to help certain nonprofits that she judged to be making an impact on Maine's quality of life. However, she refused to lose sight of her primary mission: reviving the local economy.

RODES Scholar

Betty Noyce did something that many corporations don't do when it comes to corporate philanthropy, community affairs, and other corporate responsibility matters: she learned how to plan before opening her checkbook. Sure, businesses are quick to tell you that they never spend money on external affairs without first concocting some type of plan. However, in far too many cases, the "plan" is light on the well-thought-out business logic that a company would insist upon if it were about to launch a product or make an acquisition decision.

It's important that companies get the message that designing a social investing program without planning is like trying to make crêpe suzettes without a recipe. To get the maximum return benefit from a social investment, a corporation has to think like Betty Noyce. It needs to put a defensible, workable programming strategy ahead of the first dime it shells out as a social investment.

To produce a sound programming plan, a business should *R*esearch, *O*rganize, *D*esign, *E*ngage, and *S*pend, in that order. With the key points reduced to the acronym RODES, the planning process begins in a way that would have made the late Betty Noyce proud.

RESEARCH

There's nothing glamorous or enticing about the usually tedious business of collecting information. Yet without adequate facts and data, a corporation can easily find itself sailing in the wrong direction. Here's a way to set the right course for a company:

BUSINESS CHECKUP

Start with a thorough examination of your company—customers, products, opportunities, problems. Where is the corporation heading in the short term and what are some of the roadblocks that are lurking around the corner? Keep coming back to the premise that corporate social investing is a tool to help the business do better.

OPPORTUNITY APPRAISAL

What programs, organizations, sponsorship options, and events intersect with the interests and requirements of your corporation? Do a thorough job of scouting.

QUALITY-OF-LIFE ANALYSIS

What forces and pressures (crime, education, health care, homelessness, culture.)are making (or could make) an impact on the communities in which your business has a presence? Get a reading on how many of these problems (or opportunities) are being met through umbrella funding organizations like the United Way. Find out which employees serve on the boards of any nonprofits in these communities.

PRIVATE SECTOR ENVIRONMENTAL SCAN

Determine what other businesses are doing in (a) priority interest areas that have been identified for your company, and (b) communities where your corporation is active.

This is pretty basic stuff—gathering information that can make the difference between a real plan and something that looks like one. However, in larger companies, those who manage corporate philanthropy, community relations, or other external affairs programs have frequently skimped on this aspect of the job. As for small companies, they usually don't give a second thought to this kind of research because they are consumed with so many other day-to-day pressures on the business.

Research is so crucial to making good social investment decisions that it is worth finding a way to scoop up pertinent information no matter what size the business happens to be. Suggestions:

LARGER COMPANIES

Outsource the assignment. A decent consultant or management consulting firm should be able to do this work without charging the company a fortune. Later on, we will make the point that these consulting costs (if within reason) can be charged to the company's social investment program. They count as part of the 2.5 percent or 3.5 percent of the multiyear pretax net income (PTNI) average that is budgeted for investment purposes.

SMALLER COMPANIES

Ask commonsense questions when attending chamber of commerce, trade association, Rotary, United Way, or other business or civic meetings. Intelligence gathering is generally not that complicated.

Another option for any size business: make your company a living laboratory for a local college. This is a tremendous opportunity for business or social science students to do the legwork in picking up information a company needs—and to do a case study of the business itself. A small grant to the school should cover the costs related to the project.

Regardless of how a company chooses to get the job done, the true test for the *R* in our RODES program development plan is to locate more investment opportunities than a corporation can afford. The goal is to present the business with a true dilemma: how to sort out the best of a lot of good funding choices.

ORGANIZE AND DESIGN

Once a company finishes its research, the business needs to separate the information it collected into different piles. The idea is to *organize* (the *O* in the RODES acronym) the facts and data in a way that suits the *design* process (the *D* component).

A handful of chambers constitute the main engine of the corporate social investment model, as Figure 8 illustrates.

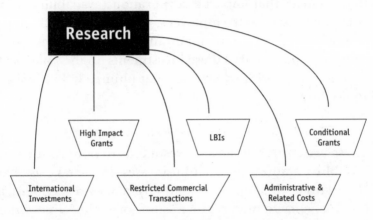

Fig. 8. Organization and Design Chambers of the Corporate Social Investment Model

The challenge for the company's investment program manager is to pick out the most pertinent bits of research and *organize* those facts by putting the data into the right chamber. Once that's been done, the manager or social investment "designer" can start being creative and develop a menu of programming alternatives. This part of the design process works best when the designer has a good grasp of each of the following chambers (described in more detail beginning on page 123):

HIGH-IMPACT GRANTS

These are dollar or noncash social investments that qualify as charitable deductions and that have a clear, major influence on a business (as well as on the nonprofit that receives the grant). High-impact grants generate very concrete—but not always precisely measurable—returns to the corporation. Example: a medical supply company makes a large social investment that can be taken as a tax-deductible donation to a nonprofit hospital and gets its name prominently displayed on the institution's surgical suite.

CONDITIONAL GRANTS

Corporate social investments that have a less direct influence on a business and that are also written off as charitable donations are found in this chamber. They are called conditional investments for two reasons. First, they have an effect on the *conditions* or circumstances that impact a corporation (availability of qualified new hires, safety of employees, general quality-of-life standards that can attract and maintain employees, and so on). Second, a company makes these investments on the *condition* that they actually be used for purposes that ultimately will be beneficial to the business.

LEVERAGED BUSINESS INVESTMENTS (LBIs)

These are corporate social investments to nonprofit or exclusively public organizations that businesses do *not* take as charitable deductions. Example: a company makes a payment to a 501(c)(3) agency to underwrite a "sponsor night," an event used to recognize attendees and also to give top corporate marketing people a chance to interact with prospective or existing customers. The corporation carries the charge as a business expense (not a charitable donation). There are many kinds of LBIs: sponsorships, memberships, cause-related marketing expenses, and risk investments.

INTERNATIONAL SOCIAL INVESTMENTS

The payments a company makes to organizations outside the United States that equate to 501(c)(3) or exclusively public institutions in this country fall in this chamber. North American–based international corporations quite often vastly underestimate the monetary value of their social involvement activities in overseas locations. To the extent that much of the business community has become globalized, social investing needs to reflect the international characteristics of the private sector.

RESTRICTED COMMERCIAL TRANSACTIONS

Not every check that's made out to a nonprofit counts as a social investment. On occasion, a business buys products from 501(c)(3) organizations. Or a company may contract with a nonprofit to perform specific work on a fee-for-service basis. These commercial transactions should be tracked and dropped into this particular chamber. As part of its annual disclosure report, the corporation should consider including a statement that reminds the public that there are many kinds of economic ties between nonprofit organizations and corporations, some of which fall outside the dollar amounts reported as social investments.

ADMINISTRATIVE AND RELATED COSTS

Regardless of how big or small a corporate social investment program might be, it's going to cost money to develop and administer. Even the smallest company that spends only a few hours thinking about how to design a simplified version of the ten-step plan outlined in this book is devoting management time to the process—and time is money. It's okay to fold reasonable administrative expenses into the social investing pot. (See Chapter 12 for more information on administration costs.)

As might be expected, not all companies will organize and design their investments the same way. Some will make high-impact grants their prominent design element, while other corporations are going to put more resources into different types of leveraged business investments. Almost all corporations will make some types of conditional grants, but the number and size of those commitments will vary greatly among businesses.

Figure 9 is a replay of Figure 4, which was introduced back in Chapter 3. The pie chart shows how a "typical" medium to large international business might organize and design its corporate social investments. This is not a prototype that will work for every company. The size of the chambers will vary from business to business depending on each corporation's needs, interests, and investment opportunities.

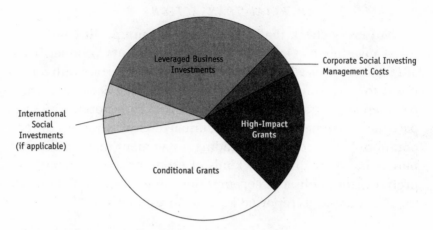

Fig. 9. The Corporate Social Investment Model

Note: Restricted commercial transactions not included in the model.

O and *D* are the essence of corporate social investment strategic planning. This is where management competence is most needed.

ENGAGE

Good research, effectively organized information, a well-designed social investing plan—all systems are go, right? Not exactly. The greatest investment strategy on earth won't fly if the corporation's senior managers won't let it on the runway. A company's top brass might make a statement in favor of social investing, but the words won't mean much unless a specific investment plan is presented and endorsed.

Engaging management early in the planning process helps grease the approval skids. If the top decision makers are converted into co-owners of the social investing plan, two things happen. First, they have a vested interest in seeing that the program gets a green light (they become advocates rather than potential critics). Second, more likely than not, they are going to bring their own ideas and concepts to the planning table that will enrich the program.

The *E* in the RODES acronym can work beautifully if the company has a high-level investment committee in place. That committee should include a cross section of highly placed executives who are widely regarded within the corporation. Of course, such a committee isn't always relevant to a very small business; however,

122

even a small company can benefit from a process that engages a few employees in social investment planning.

Although the main goal of engagement is to sell the proposed investment plan, roping in the right people during the planning phase can give the program added zip long after it is launched. The big E can populate the corporation with a cadre of cheerleaders and doers who can make marketing future social investment plans a lot less challenging.

SPEND

Congratulations. The investment plan has been researched, organized, designed, and sold to the key people inside the business. Now (and only now) it is time to release the dollars and other resources needed to execute what's been approved.

RODES is a system that puts the right kind of planning ahead of paying out 2.5 percent or 3.5 percent of a company's averaged multiyear PTNI. To stretch this concept to its limits, the ideal social investment manager for any company would be an individual who understands how to apply RODES—a RODES scholar, if you will. That role should be filled by someone who understands that simply slapping together a budget for doling out social investments won't do. The person should be a skillful manager who learns how to take full advantage of different types of social investing strategies. The remainder of this chapter presents a more in-depth review of the strategies that were briefly introduced earlier.

High-Impact Grants

Lobby: To solicit or try to influence the votes of members of a legislative body.

On any given day in the nation's capitol, a buttoned-down army of "special interest representatives" (otherwise known as lobbyists) can be found working in the District of Columbia. There are approximately sixty-eight thousand of them buzzing around the Hill, trying to pollinate legislators and their staffers with their vested points of view. You see them everywhere—a legislative breakfast at the J. W. Marriott, lunchtime powwows at the Old Ebbitt Grill, a cocktail reception at the Watergate. It's a frenetic, nonstop, expensive whirlwind that in many cases is—*nonproductive.*

Put yourself in the position of a state or federal lawmaker who consistently gets besieged by people paid to persuade. There are four times as many "issues salespersons" in Washington today as there were thirty years ago, and they can be as pesky as flies at a political party barbecue.

Still, getting legislators (or, perhaps even more important, their legislative aides) to understand an organization's perspective can make the difference between an Aye and a Nay in a floor vote. So if a corporation or any other special interest group doesn't lobby, how can it expect to communicate its point of view?

Coming on too strong is usually a good way *not* to succeed, and coming on strong is a trait that has never been bred out of the private sector. Businesses want to get right down to business. They spend a lot of money and energy on information dispensing but forget about the preliminaries that frequently make public servants more inclined to really listen to what a company is saying. Sometimes it's the prenuptial activities that decide whether a lawmaker will end up happily married to whatever position an organization happens to be peddling. And this is where high-impact grants make their entrance. They can put public officials in the right mood.

High-impact grants are not lobbying expenses. They are not payoffs. They are not "soft money" or "walking around" expenditures that could get a business (and government officials) in hot water. They are 100 percent legitimate social investments that are used to do good things that are of mutual interest to a corporation and the public sector.

High-impact grants also don't guarantee that a company will have its way with a lawmaker. They can, however, create a positive mindset among the right people in public office, which ultimately will help a lobbyist get a fair and attentive hearing. In the turbulent world of government affairs, that's worth something.

JOHNSON & JOHNSON'S CRYSTAL AWARD PROGRAM

For over ten years, the health care giant Johnson & Johnson has been using high-impact grants to create conducive atmospheric conditions in Washington and elsewhere around the nation. The Johnson & Johnson Community Health Care Crystal

Award Program is currently funded through the company's philanthropy budget. One American Medical Association official familiar with the initiative said it's the most powerful example he's ever seen of how an organization can score points in Washington.

For over a decade, Johnson & Johnson has poured millions into its Crystal Award program. Here's how it works:

1. Each year, the corporation targets regions of the United States that are important to the business (areas where the company has operations or other interests).

2. Nonprofits that provide or could provide health care services to the medically underserved in those regions are invited to compete for the piece of Tiffany-designed glass that's become the most coveted symbol of excellence in the field of community health. Incidentally, a $100,000 donation from Johnson & Johnson (paid over two years) just happens to accompany the crystal trophy—that's the cash value of this particular high-impact grant.

3. An independent selection panel chooses winners from the nominations received. The panel, which includes representatives from a few of the country's most prestigious health care organizations, is above reproach. That's important, because the company doesn't want the credibility of the award to be tarnished. It also wants to be able to say to those organizations that didn't get selected that it was the panel and not the company that made the win-or-lose decisions.

4. Victorious nonprofits are given the option of accepting an additional $2,500 grant that can be used to organize and conduct a local event where the Crystal Award can be presented. Nearly every organization that has won the award in recent years has exercised this option and most of the events they have held have been showstoppers.

5. Using a how-to-do-it booklet produced by Johnson & Johnson, the nonprofits are encouraged to include legislative representatives in their local Crystal Award ceremonies. Does it work? Senators, congressmen, state legislators, mayors, and even a politician named Bill Clinton have

attended these events, which have been held in many parts of the United States and Puerto Rico since 1986. The award ceremonies usually draw ample media coverage in regions that are very important to Johnson & Johnson.

Yes, the program works.

Crystal Award events are not setups for Johnson & Johnson executives to arm-twist politicos. Instead, they become forums where the Johnson & Johnson name is held high, not by the company but by those who are the recipients of the firm's grant making. If you're an elected official, it's hard not to feel good about a business when two hundred or more of your constituents sing the praises of a corporation—and with some justification, because no other business in America infuses so much money into programs aimed at providing medical services to people living at or below the poverty line.

The corporation knows that a Crystal Award ceremony won't brainwash a legislator. But it has discovered that these local award ceremonies lessen the chances that the corporation is going to feel like Rodney Dangerfield when it visits a lawmaker. Johnson & Johnson gets respect from legislators for its high-impact grants. That respect has a way of opening the doors of the men and women who set public policy or are paid to administer it. And in a nation where there are so many lobbyists competing for any public official's undivided attention, that counts.

High-impact grants are jumbo-sized corporate social investments (jumbo, that is, in relationship to most of the rest of the company's commitments to nonprofit organizations) that a company writes off as charitable donations. To some, this still may seem incomprehensible. How can a company make a charitable contribution and still get something back in return?

If an investment paid to a nonprofit or exclusively public organization (a) advances the general purposes of the recipient agency or institution and is not extraneous to the organization's mission, and (b) doesn't result in an excessive quid pro quo for the company, then it can legitimately be declared a high-impact grant that is written off as a charitable tax deduction.

Hold on a minute. Excessive or not, isn't just about any kind of return benefit a quid pro quo? If so, then every time a company makes a high-impact grant, is it out of bounds as far as the rules for charitable giving are concerned? In the land of quid pro quos, fuzziness prevails. The IRS permits companies to get some recognition and exposure for the charitable contributions they make. Of course, too much recognition and a payment to a nonprofit starts looking more and more like a leveraged business investment. (See the following section.) Sometimes it's a judgment call as to where the investment should be placed on the continuum shown in Figure 10. A competent manager of a social investment program will eventually get the feel for this rather mushy process.

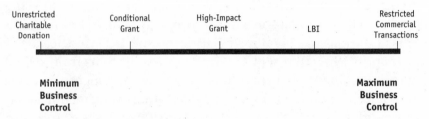

Fig. 10. The Business Benefit Continuum

OTHER CORPORATIONS' PROGRAMS

Nowhere are examples of high-impact grants as plentiful as in the telecommunications industry. Corporations like AT&T are using these types of strategically placed grants (often a combination of a little cash and a lot of product) to get a foothold in the nation's education system. The AT&T Learning Network is a heavily hyped drive that includes $50 million in high-impact grants paid out of the corporation's foundation and several more millions of dollars in LBIs. The money and materials are being used to help wire the nation's 110,000 public and private schools to the information superhighway. The advantages to the company (as well as to a lot of students and teachers) are fairly obvious.

AT&T is only one of many telecommunications companies courting the country's education establishment. U S West is another corporation that is trying to get closer to educators and kids by moving to the front edge of the "technology convergence" era. So in 1995, when U S West said it was redesigning its philanthropy program and would fund projects that addressed the role of new media in kindergarten through grade twelve, the announcement didn't come as much of a shock. The company initiated a campaign called Connecting Teachers with Technology that does exactly what the title implies—it provides teams of instructors with laptops, printers, modems, and a little cash ($12,000 per team), which are used to hitch educators to new technology-based teaching techniques.

Then there's Oracle Corporation (the second-largest software producer), which has trumpeted a program aptly titled Promise. The firm has committed $100 million to provide network computer capabilities to schools around the nation.

If there were a technology-industry Academy Award for using products as high-impact grants, IBM would certainly be a top contender. The corporation runs a program called Reinventing Education that has certain similarities to the U S West teachers' project. In 1994, IBM sent out a call for applications from school systems looking for help to fund innovative technologies. Ten sites were selected and the company donated equipment, technical services, and assistance to the winners (small cash awards were also given, which amounted to about 10 percent to 15 percent of the selling price of the corporation's donated products). The $25 million project got IBM good exposure and created a handful of excellent demonstration sites.

Social investing would treat any of these examples like high-impact grants if the product and cash given to nonprofits qualified as charitable contributions and were recorded as tax-deductible donations. Some of these companies may already be including these commitments as part of their corporate philanthropy programs. In these cases, a bit of relabeling is all that's needed to convert these superstrategic charitable gifts into high-impact grants.

These high-tech examples may leave one with the impression that the private sector is teeming with powerful examples of strategic philanthropy. That's not the case. Most companies don't have a grab bag of contributions that could be transformed into high-impact grants. For these businesses, moving ahead with this type of social investment means starting from scratch.

BENEFITS OF HIGH-IMPACT GRANTS

It's possible—in fact, probable—that some computer companies will never consider product or cash given to schools or certain other nonprofits as philanthropy, even if the equipment or money might legitimately qualify as a charitable deduction. Fine. Corporations can still claim these commitments as corporate social investments by declaring them as LBIs. There are, however, a couple of good reasons for companies to make high-impact grants even if they do subject corporations to a few added constraints. A high-impact grant

Taps the primary power of the recipient organization. The strength of a nonprofit or exclusively public institution is in its core mission. If a company is going to enter into a relationship with a nonprofit, then it's a no-brainer that the business will probably get the most out of the arrangement if it stays in the organization's main channel and doesn't push the nonprofit into some secondary stream.

Helps the nonprofit organization the most. If it just takes a little design creativity to ensure that a social investment is delivered as a high-impact grant, then a company should put in some extra effort to make that happen. Here's the reason why. If a corporation's support to a nonprofit is something too distant from the nonprofit's stated objectives in its charter and bylaws, it can create financial havoc. It's possible the organization might even have to pay taxes on the company's investment should it be ruled as "unrelated business income."

HIGH-IMPACT GRANT PROPOSALS

Deciding to make a high-impact grant (instead of a leveraged business investment) to a nonprofit is one thing; getting a proposal from a 501(c)(3) or exclusively public organization that warrants doing so is quite another. Businesses may have to take the initiative and help nonprofits understand what should go into a high-impact grant proposal. Here are some points that a company might want to encourage organizations to include in that kind of request:

HYPHENATED NAME RECOGNITION

In cases where the nonprofit name is perceived to be as valuable or even more valuable than the company name, then a "hyphenated" relationship between the two might be something a corporation would present as an option. Example: if your company sells children's vitamins, a visible connection with a highly regarded children's nonprofit can give your business a point of difference in the marketplace. Not every nonprofit will be at ease in entering into a hyphenated relationship with a business. But a surprisingly large number of nonprofits will agree to this arrangement if the high-impact grant is sufficiently large, and if they feel the company name will also bring added value to the organization.

From a corporation's perspective, hyphenated relationships have only limited importance unless they are advertised or promoted. So, in addition to a high-impact grant, it's often in the company's best interest to work out a way to leverage the nonprofit partnership as part of its overall public relations and advertising plan. Remember that any wraparound advertising dollars should *not* be counted in the corporate social investment totals.

MARKET IMPACT

Often, a high-impact grant can drill a company's name into a market niche better than any other type of advertising or promotional campaign. Nonprofit organizations often overlook the market power they have. They should emphasize that their members, clients, or beneficiaries are also potential consumers for certain businesses.

If a nonprofit has an especially strong connection to Hispanic Americans, for example, that organization can become a marketing avenue for a company that wants to crack this rapidly growing segment of the U.S. population. Hispanics are known to have strong product loyalty, and it may take more than a continuing onslaught of television, radio, or print ads to get people to think about switching to a product alternative. Connecting to the right Hispanic American organization or cause could prove fruitful for certain businesses.

THE CREDIBILITY FACTOR

A company that thumps its own chest isn't going to draw much of a crowd. However, a nonprofit that trumpets the virtues of a corporation is going to draw attention to the business. There's no substitute for someone else singing your praises.

High-impact grants give nonprofits plenty of opportunity to say nice things about their corporate partners in front of the right people. On the flip side, corporations can publicly pat their nonprofit partners on the shoulder in front of important audiences. A good high-impact grant proposal spells out how these public displays of mutual affection will be orchestrated.

CONTROVERSIAL HIGH-IMPACT GRANTS

There are occasions where high-impact grants run into controversy. One example: Freeport-McMoRan (the large New Orleans–based mining and development company) has been a longtime supporter of the well-known Audubon Institute. The corporation has been under fire from a few environmental organizations for its gold, silver, and copper mining operations in Indonesia. When it donated $5 million for something called the Freeport-McMoRan Audubon Species Survival Center, critics went into an uproar. Audubon countered saying that the company was, in its estimation, "a good corporate citizen." It offered no apologies for accepting the company's high-impact grant and reminded the world that Audubon's role was to work with businesses (not against them) to come up with answers to environmental concerns. This is a classic example of a prominent nonprofit speaking up for a corporate supporter.

Obviously, these kinds of high-profile relationships can easily backfire if nonprofits go too far in accepting large social investments, especially if they have inappropriate strings attached. In other words, organizations need to think carefully about the businesses they are soliciting for high-impact grants. A nonprofit might get a short-term windfall only to find that its principles have been so compromised that it ends up going out of existence. Just as important, businesses have to weigh whether there are possible negative consequences in making a high-impact grant commitment. There are times where it is far better for a corporation to lay low than to put itself on public display.

All in all, high-impact grants can deliver results for both a company and a nonprofit organization recipient as long as both parties are clear about the potential ups and downs of this very visible kind of relationship. For a business, the most effective high-impact grant is one where the corporation gets the greatest return possible and still manages to declare the payment as a charitable donation. It's not always easy to pull off but usually worth the effort.

Conditional Grants

There are businesses that treat corporate philanthropy as a watering hole for the company's top brass. This is the oasis that makes shareholders mad as hell. The mere thought of executives who earn six- or seven-figure salaries sucking up company donations to quench the thirst of their personal nonprofit interests is enough to make some stockholders see scarlet.

It shouldn't be a revelation that under the old way of handling corporate philanthropy, contributions have had a tendency to ooze into places they shouldn't go. And even when that didn't actually happen, there has been an aura of suspicion (at least among some outsiders) that philanthropy is just another word for executive *perk*.

The antidote to this kind of real or perceived misuse of corporate contributions is the ten-step plan for social investing. If a company has adopted this management model, there's a significant business reason behind *every* commitment a company makes to a nonprofit. There are no exceptions to this rule—not even for the highest-level corporate officer who may be looking for the smallest company donation.

A corporate social investing program is no assurance that heavyweight executives won't continue to put pressure on the business to make picayune payments to nonprofit organizations that have no special connection to the company. Their argument has been and always will be, "Why get exercised over only a few hundred dollars?" The answer is that it only takes a few dollars going to the wrong place to create major problems. This kind of executive favoritism can easily go awry and has the potential to become a huge burr under a disgruntled shareholder's saddle.

There has to be ample room for companies to make the right kind of relatively small commitments to nonprofit organizations. The social investing model calls for up to 40 percent of these types of cash investments to be set aside for *conditional grants*.

As we saw earlier in the chapter, conditional grants influence or alter those conditions that affect a corporation's ability to do business. Even investments that don't involve a lot of money or product commitments that have a low cash value can have an impact on the atmosphere or environment in which a company lives. Conditional grants can help a corporation become more successful in many ways:

▶ recruiting employees
▶ retaining employees
▶ reinforcing customer ties
▶ creating new customer relationships
▶ stimulating market awareness
▶ building legislative linkages
▶ improving company asset values

Putting conditional grants to work so they deliver returns that are important to a business isn't something that comes easy to many corporations. There is a tendency for companies to shotgun these small investments, firing a little money at a lot of nonprofits regardless of whether they are part of a general investment strategy or not. This spread-the-money-around mentality is a carryover from the old philanthropy days when companies used token gifts to appease nonprofit organizations. A charity might ask for $10,000 and end up being shown the door with $500 in "go away" money.

Social investing necessitates putting down the shotgun and picking up the rifle. A company should only aim and fire at conditional grant opportunities that have some demonstrable value to the business. It bears repeating that just because a conditional grant happens to be on the small side doesn't mean that it is exempt from Step 2 of the ten-step management plan. That is, all investments—no matter what the size—need to have a connection to the business. If a proposed conditional grant doesn't have significant relevance to the corporation, then it shouldn't get funded.

This all may sound cut-and-dried. Unfortunately, the significant-business-reason litmus test is much more difficult to apply to conditional grants than to high-impact grants or (as we will see in the next section) to LBIs. The business significance of many conditional grants often falls in a hazy, gray zone—so much so that what might be considered relevant by one company could be viewed as totally extraneous by another.

The next few pages include guidelines that will help a company determine what should or shouldn't be considered a conditional grant. However, even these guidelines won't eliminate all the vagueness from this segment of the social investing model. Although a company may think a conditional grant has a clear and apparent business connection, outsiders may need a lot of coaxing before they see it that way. Because of this potential quandary, a company risks having its whole corporate social investing program turn murky if it leans too heavily on these particular kinds of social investments.

Conditional grants need to be a part of the model but they should not consume all or even most of a corporation's social investing resources. If that happens, a company may find itself spending too much time defending what appear to be an overload of "soft" investments. A significant part of the social investing plan should be so obviously tied to the corporate interests that it needs little or no explanation.

To keep conditional grants in check, the social responsibility model includes funding guidelines for four different categories of conditional grants: (1) *employee-focused investments,* (2) *quality-of-life investments,* (3) *customer-centered investments,* and (4) *government relations investments.* There's plenty of flexibility built into these funding guidelines. One company might choose to invest heavily in employee-focused investments whereas another might put most of its conditional grants into government-relations investments. As a rule of thumb, the composite of *all* conditional grants, regardless of how the categories are apportioned, shouldn't be more than 40 percent of a company's total social investing budget. (See Figure 11.)

Here's a closer look at each of the main conditional grant categories:

EMPLOYEE-FOCUSED INVESTMENTS

There are a couple of ways conditional grants can be used by corporations to get and keep top-notch employees. First, they can be integrated into a company's recruitment strategy. Second, once employees are hired, they can be used to build or sustain worker allegiance to a company. Both types are employee-focused investments.

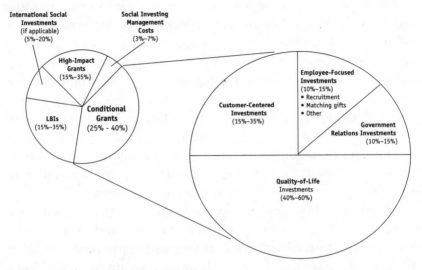

Fig. 11. Types of Conditional Grants

There is probably no more important goal for any company than to capture the best and brightest people as employees. For corporations that have college recruitment staffs, it pays to earmark a few conditional grants that can be used to establish solid connections to top priority colleges or universities. For smaller businesses that regularly look for manpower at local institutions (four-year colleges, two-year community colleges, vo-tech high schools, and so on), small conditional grants can let educators know that companies are very serious about meeting their recruitment objectives.

Businesses that make these types of conditional grants usually are given a good window on promising graduates. Some might see this as no different than greasing the right palm, tipping the headwaiter at a good restaurant, or something far more perverse. However, because the money goes to the educational institution and is usually earmarked for student placement services, the grant is actually a legitimate tax-deductible contribution. In fact, recognizing that businesses as well as students benefit from student placement programs, a case could be made that corporations should be paying a lot more than they usually do to educational institutions for the services these schools provide to the private sector.

Once the right people have been recruited into a company the next challenge is getting them to stay put. The supermagnet for holding people in place will always be, of course, a decent salary and benefits package. However, other perks can make an employee feel good about a company. Take matching gifts, for instance.

A matching-gift program is the ultimate employee-focused investment. A worker makes a personal gift and the company matches the donation, sometimes by a multiple of two or three. You give a dollar to your alma mater and your corporation puts an extra one, two, or three dollars on top of your donation.

At least six thousand companies sponsor matching-gift programs. According to a survey of over one thousand of these businesses by the Council for Advancement and Support of Education (CASE), 99 percent of these programs are set up to match donations to colleges and universities. Only 41 percent match anything other than educational institutions. Conclusion: matching gifts are used mainly to satisfy the educational (usually college and university) interests of employees.

Matching gifts can make workers feel good about a business, but just how much money should a corporation spend to create that rosy glow among its workforce? How a company answers that question will determine whether it has a well-managed social investment program or is conceding its investment potential to old-fashioned philanthropy.

Corporations need to put a cap on their employee-focused investments—especially matching gifts. What's more, they also need to steer these investments in a direction that is consistent with company interests. Businesses that overspend in this area or allow their employee-focused dollars to go to nonprofits that have no relevance to the company are not getting the most out of their corporate social investing resources. In addition, they're waving a red flag in front of critics who can revert back to the argument that companies are excessive in their use of pretax profits to support the personal charitable interests of employees.

Step 7. The Social Investment Model: Part II, Strategic Plans

Exhibit 13 shows how dominant matching gifts have become among some large corporations. Earlier, we stated that there's no fixed rule that mandates what a business should be spending on employee-focused investments. There may be valid business-related reasons why some of the companies listed in the exhibit are putting so many eggs into the matching-gifts basket. However, as a general guideline, corporations should keep all employee-focused investments (including matching gifts) to 10 percent to 15 percent of their cash social investing payments. Anything more than this amount usually yields diminished returns.

	Employee-Matching Gifts	Percentage of Cash Giving
Georgia-Pacific	$2,236,000	50.79 %
Wal-Mart	21,200,000	42.40
Hewlett-Packard.	5,546,000	37.23
Enron Corporation	1,780,000	33.40
Salomon	1,342,022	31.79
Atlantic Richfield	5,765,879	26.61
IBM	10,500,000	25.80
J. P. Morgan	3,661,233	25.20
Exxon	13,500,000	24.37
Textron	1,313,996	24.11
Motorola	1,103,457	23.11
Citicorp	5,796,521	22.88
General Electric	10,100,000	21.91
Phillips Petroleum	1,891,301	21.78
Apple Computer	300,000	20.00

Exhibit 13. Companies That Used 20 Percent or More of Their Cash Gifts to Match Employee Donations, 1995

Source: *Chronicle of Philanthropy,* July 1996

Companies should carefully consider pulling in the reins on matching-gift programs that provide support to nonprofits that don't have some connection to the business. A few corporations match employee donations to *any* 501(c)(3) organization. That's asking for trouble, because the company could find itself supporting nonprofits that are actually antibusiness.

There are other employee-focused commitments a company can consider making. One of the more popular investments is underwriting nonprofit-run scholarship or student exchange programs for children of employees. This edges so close to the self-interest borderline that it could be viewed as a fee-for-service expense that should be excluded from corporate social investing totals. Our management model allows these payments to be added to the pot as long as generally accepted eligibility rules are followed when making decisions about who gets the benefits from these programs—and if underwriting is kept to a reasonable level.

Conclusion: in moderation, employee-focused investments can be a productive type of conditional grant. Taken to an extreme, however, such investments can drain a company of its ability to use its resources for more strategic purposes.

QUALITY-OF-LIFE INVESTMENTS

Just about any social investment a corporation makes has an impact on the quality of life, so in some respects the name given to this conditional grant category is misleading. The investments included here are those that are aimed at sustaining or improving the quality of life in those communities where the company has a presence. There are a number of advantages to a business when it focuses a portion of its cash investment pool on the needs of a neighborhood, town, or city where the corporation has a plant or major office location:

▸ upholding the property value of a company's real estate (assuming the corporation owns land and buildings)

▸ providing a safe and attractive working environment that can help lure and hold workers

▸ protecting the company's buildings and equipment from vandalism and theft through support of anticrime programs

▸ sustaining good relations with community officials empowered to tax and regulate business

Conditional grants paid out as quality-of-life investments can be made directly to nonprofits and exclusively public institutions, or through umbrella organizations such as United Way, America's Charities, or other federated campaign agencies.

Step 7. The Social Investment Model: Part II, Strategic Plans

Keep in mind that we're presenting broad funding guidelines for all four categories of conditional grants. Businesses can expand or contract the spending within each category to suit their particular circumstances. That having been said, companies still may want to consider this *general* recommendation: large and mid-sized businesses should allocate 50 percent of all conditional grants to quality-of-life investments; small businesses should consider committing a higher percentage.

Remember our opening recommendation: put up to 40 percent of all cash investments into conditional grants. Now we're suggesting that larger companies take half of that 40 percent and use it for quality-of-life purposes. For some businesses, this will prove to be a lot of money. To illustrate that point, return to General Electric for a moment. Remember that when our social investment formula was applied to the company in Chapter 9, we found that GE would have needed to spend a total of $146 million in cash during 1997 to meet the provisions specified in Step 7. Here is how a portion of those dollars would be distributed if the company were to have followed the guidelines outlined in this section:

Total cash investments	*$146 million*
of which 40 percent would be . . .	
conditional grants	*$58 million*
of which 50 percent would be . . .	
quality-of-life conditional grants	*$29.2 million*

Distilling business relevance from nearly $30 million in quality-of-life grants is not an easy undertaking. For large corporations like GE, this component of the social investment model might prove to be the most challenging to manage.

For smaller businesses, spending half of whatever conditional grant dollars are available shouldn't be a problem and in fact, the smaller the firm the more likely it is that quality-of-life investing will consume a larger share of the company's conditional grants. And for good reason. Many of these corporations are easy prey for community solicitors looking for contributions that fall in this investment category. Local United Way chapters or comparable federated organizations can sometimes serve as a wall of protection from this ceaseless onslaught of requests. However, plenty of non-profits aren't connected to these umbrella organizations and they are going to continue putting a full-court press on local businesses. That's when a company will discover how useful a preprinted statement that defines its investment strategy can be. (See again Exhibit 12 in Chapter 9.)

Employee-focused and quality-of-life investments sometimes blend together when companies match employee donations to United Way or other federated campaigns, a common practice among many businesses. Although a corporation is obligated to make a payment to an organization designated by an employee through a standard company matching-gift program, which was described earlier, a business investment to a United Way campaign does not necessarily have to follow the same channel as an employee donation. Example: a worker makes what the United Way calls a "donor choice" contribution that is routed to a specific 501(c)(3) environmental organization. The corporation matches the employee's gift by making a payment to the United Way but has the option of requesting that its dollars be used for general quality-of-life purposes in the community where its headquarters are located and not be directed to the environmental nonprofit.

Regardless of whether a company relies on umbrella fund-raising organizations or makes conditional grants directly to community-based nonprofits, it needs to demonstrate how a quality-of-life investment benefits the company as well as the 501(c)(3) or exclusively public recipient. There is no shortage of investment opportunities in this conditional grant category: crime prevention, neighborhood revitalization, infrastructure improvements (traffic, utilities, and so on), schooling, youth services (if for no other reason than to curtail vandalism), arts and culture (as an enrichment for employees and customers), health care, and so on. With such an extensive menu, a company should be able to design a viable quality-of-life investment plan that meets the good-for-society and good-for-the-company test.

CUSTOMER-CENTERED INVESTMENTS

When a repeat customer asks that modest financial consideration be given to his or her pet charity, a business starts to squirm.

It may sound like an innocent appeal for help, but the company can sense an undertone of extortion. Write out a check to the designated nonprofit, and it's business as usual. Say no and the company risks having its commercial knees broken. For consumer-reliant businesses, the volume of these kinds of appeals can be staggering. For example, half of the twelve thousand requests that the BankAmerica Foundation handles each year are carried through the door by customers or employees.

It takes a manager with a deft hand to decide when to make a customer-centered investment and when to say, "Sorry." Here are a few guidelines that should help managers reach the right decision:

NOT ALL CUSTOMERS ARE ALIKE

The hard cold reality is that some customers are more equal than others. Frankly, the cost of maintaining a business relationship with an important customer may require making a corporate social investment. Big-hitting customer: "Scratch my charity's back and I'll scratch your bottom line." If a corporation concedes to that kind of offer, is it capitulating to extortion? Not really. It's one of the dynamics of customer relations that has to be weighed along with everything else that's done to keep business relations intact. If the nonprofit commitment a company makes is *reasonable in size* and can be reshaped so it is *relevant to the corporation,* then it's a conditional grant that should be paid. The judgment comes in defining who is an important customer and who might not require this kind of special handling.

IT'S ALL RIGHT TO SAY NO TO A CUSTOMER

For every one customer who gets lucky with a company, there will be scores of others who won't succeed. Even important customers have to be turned away now and then. So how does a business decline an "invitation" to help a nonprofit that's clearly important to a customer without alienating the individual? Remember once again Acme Diner and Deli. The technique used by that small business to beat back walk-in solicitors works well for any consumer-focused company. It's important to have in hand a predetermined investment position paper that explains what the company does and doesn't fund. Most customers will accept a no if they understand that they've been excluded by a previously thought-through policy. What irks people are what seem to be knee-jerk, subjective reactions: "For no particular reason that I can give you, I don't want to support your favorite charity." So a good no is one that's backed up by a good written investment policy statement.

KEEP GRANTS SMALL, IF POSSIBLE

Banks, insurance companies, and service businesses have long practiced the art of small-change philanthropy. Because they have so many customers and clients to worry about, these corporations have a reputation for sprinkling small donations over a wide field of nonprofits in hopes that these diminutive commitments will appease the masses. To some extent, that strategy has been effective. As the BankAmerica Foundation says (maybe rationalizes): "Large grants make statements; small grants solve problems." As a general rule, businesses should not put big money into customer-centered investments. The goal should be to make the lowest possible commitment needed to make the customer feel at least mildly satisfied.

RECAST THE APPEAL

It won't always be possible or practical—particularly if a customer-centered investment involves only a small amount of money—to reshape it into something that conforms to a company's highest investment priorities. Most of the requests thrown at a corporation by a customer are for the support of organizations or projects the business would not normally assist. However, a company should try to convert the sow's ear into a purse if it looks doable. Example: a customer wants a bank to spend $5,000 on a children's arts organization. The bank decides that it risks losing business if it doesn't make this commitment. The money is paid but only after arrangements are made to have the children's art exhibited in the local library along with a display panel crediting the bank for its sponsorship—and its concern for kids and the community. Result: a customer-centered investment turns into a business-generating public relations coup for the bank.

GOVERNMENT RELATIONS INVESTMENTS

A town council in an affluent suburb urges local businesses to take the lead in kicking off a capital campaign to renovate the community's public library. A governor of a mid-Atlantic state names several corporate executives to a school-to-work commission and then "encourages" the private sector to pay for an expensive statewide research project that the commission recommends. The federal government announces plans for another memorial in the nation's capital and calls on businesses to pick up the tab.

When a company's main motivation for making a social investment is its interest in staying on the good side of local, state, or federal government officials, then there's little question as to what kind of conditional grant it's making: a government relations investment. Although not without risk, these investments are sometimes inescapable.

It helps to keep in mind that elected officials and government career employees have the capacity to make life absolutely miserable for businesses. Local permits and variances, state regulations, federal agency directives—when any of these things constipate the bureaucratic system, business conditions are affected. Short of going to jail for using bribery as a laxative, what can a company do to make sure that it doesn't get lost in the government shuffle? Forging the right kind of relationships with influential public-sector decision makers is about the only option businesses have.

There's nothing like a phone call to someone you really know in government to unclog the system. This isn't about special favors or excessive pressure, it's a simple matter of getting through to the appropriate person who has a positive feeling about the company. Many times that's all it takes.

There are different ways to make friends in the public sector. Elected officeholders warm up to companies when the words political action committee (PAC) contributions are mentioned. PAC money is superpremium gas that goes into the tanks of pro-business politicians. Like it or not, the system of government in the United States encourages elected officials to be kind to the hands that feed them.

Although corporations are the prime movers when funneling PAC dollars to elected government officials, companies (technically speaking) don't put up the money. Employees contribute the funds, sometimes in response to bulldozer-like tactics of their employers. So considering the source of these PAC contributions and because they don't end up in 501 (c) (3) nonprofit or exclusively public organizations, they don't qualify as corporate social investments. Nevertheless, PACs deserve a mention because they are the carrots and sticks of the government relations field.

In contrast, those conditional grants that we call government relations investments are very different. These are dollars directed to nonprofits that provide businesses with an opportunity to demonstrate their support for a cause, program, or project that is of interest to key government decision makers. Government relations investments can graduate into high-impact grants like the heavily funded Johnson & Johnson community health care program. (See again the discussion in the section on high-impact grants earlier in this chapter.) It's all a matter of how strategically important the investment is and how large the payout gets to be. In most instances, government relations investments remain on the small side relative to the rest of a company's social investment program.

Managing government relations investments can be touchy. Fortunately, most companies are only rarely confronted with a direct social investment appeal from a government official. When such a request shows up, a business can find itself twirling on the proverbial horn of a dilemma. If an investment isn't made, there could be trouble. And if cash is given, it might be misconstrued. No company wants to be the lead in a story headlined *Corporation Gets Favors in Exchange for Funding Politico's Pet Charity*.

Corporations need to use good management judgment in awarding government relations investments. If any impropriety can be predicted as a result of making such a payment, *don't do it!* If a candidate making the appeal is in the middle of a campaign or if the company is working with (or having problems with) a government official who is instrumental in a regulatory, licensing, or some other government approval process that involves the business, *don't do it!* The risk of having to deal with a disappointed politician is better than having to cope with bad press.

HOLDING THE LINE

Conditional grants are most often *reactive* investments, smaller payments made in response to requests initiated by employees, customers, community organizations, or government officials. Quite different are high-impact grants and LBIs, which are more *proactive* business investments. As a rule, the more reactive a social investing program, the less strategic it's likely to be. Ultimately, if a corporation sacrifices too much of its strategic capability, it will be compromised in its ability to implement Step 2 in our ten-step plan, which is to obtain as much business value from social investments as is allowable and practical.

Again, remember that it's important to create the right balance between conditional grants and the rest of the social investing program. That can be a problem for many businesses because conditional grants have a tendency to grow like weeds. Corporations need to resist the temptation and attempt to hold these payments to no more than 40 percent of all cash investments.

Leveraged Business Investments (LBIs)

Consider this paradox: even though social investing is intended to replace corporate philanthropy as we've known it, both high-impact and conditional grants still qualify as charitable tax deductions. Whatever value is being pinched out of these types of social investments is still not so quid pro quo that the IRS would disallow these payments as charitable write-offs.

We need to add an addendum here. Although these payments may qualify as charitable deductions, businesses don't necessarily have to report them as such. If a corporation feels that a commitment made to a nonprofit or exclusively public organization gets just a little too close to that IRS charitable-deduction borderline, it may choose to consider it an "ordinary" business expense. Either way, for social investment reporting purposes, it really doesn't matter, does it? Charitable deduction or other business expense—each gets treated the same when summing up a company's social investment commitments.

Leveraged business investments (LBIs) are horses of a slightly different color. Yes, they are 100 percent corporate social investments, but they usually will not qualify as charitable deductions.

They are good old business expenses through and through. They show up in corporations with many different labels.

Sponsorships. From heavily publicized national campaigns to local dinners and special events, sponsorships are among the most obvious and prolific LBIs around.

Customer education. Providing funds to organizations that are then awarded in the company's name to customers, clients, or other important constituents so they can attend workshops, forums, and education programs is standard fare in a lot of industries.

Memberships. If a business pays a 501(c)(3) organization a membership fee and gets benefits such as publications, materials, meeting privileges, and so on, then the payment is an LBI.

Certain cause-related marketing expenses. Parts of some cause-based marketing campaigns are occasionally funded by using high-impact grants. However, in most cases, LBIs are what make these deals possible.

Risk-investment payments. Less frequently found among all classes of businesses, these LBIs can include certain basic research investments as well as microcredit lending and other forms of community reinvestment payments.

There's a good chance that most businesses have spent money on one or more of the LBIs listed. Yet until now, most corporations haven't viewed these expenses as having a place in the same basket as those payments taken as charitable deductions. Social investing changes the rules—LBIs get a new and improved status. They are put in the same league as high-impact and conditional grants.

To make it clear what adding LBIs to a social investment roster can mean to a company, see Exhibit 14. This is a simulated social investment disclosure statement of a medium-sized medical supply company. The same $665,000 in LBIs may have been made by the corporation in previous years, but most of that money probably was tucked away in different corners of the corporation and not acknowledged in any overview of the firm's corporate responsibility commitments. Social investing rounds up and brings together *any and all* transactions (except fee-for-service contract payments and money spent to purchase goods) that are made with nonprofits or exclusively public institutions. Expenses that may have gotten lost in the shuffle in years past are now given appropriate recognition as full-fledged social investments.

As part of our corporate social investing commitment, we made several business payments during the year to qualified nonprofit or exclusively public institutions that were outside our charitable giving. In some instances, these arrangements provided our company with services that were comparable to those that could have been obtained from other commercial vendors. In such cases, payments made to these organizations have not been included as part of our social investment total.

During the year, we also made other "leveraged business investments" (LBIs), which are shown below. Note that "service premiums" are what our company determines to be the value of our financial involvement with the nonprofit over and above any measurable, direct services provided to our business.

Organization	LBI Value
Sponsorships	
American Cancer Society Dinner	$10,000
Muscular Dystrophy Association Conference	2,500
Chamber of Commerce Foundation Forum	2,500
American Academy of Pediatricians Workshop	15,000
Cause-Related Campaign	
American Burn Prevention Foundation	$450,000
Research Awards	
ABC University	$120,000
DFG Medical College	50,000
Service Premiums	
Sheltered Workshop	15,000
Vendor/Supplier Payments	0
Total LBI Direct Investments	$665,000

Exhibit 14. XYZ Medical Supply Corporation, Leveraged Business Investments

Attention nonprofits and exclusively public institutions. Nonprofits need to understand LBIs because they represent an alternative route to the corporate pocketbook. If a company rejects a nonprofit's high-impact or conditional grant request, that doesn't necessarily mean the ball game is over. Look for LBI opportunities.

Here's a more detailed explanation of the different kinds of leveraged business investments:

LOCAL SPONSORSHIPS: DINNERS AND COMMUNITY EVENTS

Sponsorships are the most popular and often the most effective LBIs. It's easier to get one's arms around sponsorships if they are split into two piles. *Major event sponsorship* opportunities are defined mainly by their size and usually their reach; most are regional or even national in scope. We'll get to those later. Let's start with the second pile, which includes smaller activities such as annual charity dinners or other, usually repetitive fund-raisers (for example, golf or tennis outings) called *local sponsorships.*

Today, some corporation in America is getting a letter that reads something like this:

> Congratulations! Your company has been named this year's Golden Key Booster. We will be honoring your corporation at our annual dinner on [date]. We know your CEO or a member of your company's senior management will want to be on hand to accept this prestigious award. We will be calling you shortly to get a mailing list of your vendors, clients, and other business friends who we want to invite to help celebrate this important achievement. Finally, we will need to know as soon as possible how may tables your company will sponsor for what will be one of this year's most notable and high-profile events.

Throughout the nation, corporations are bombarded with invitations like this. It's the eating, meeting, and seating approach to raising money. Event planners are working overtime as companies get blitzed by one request after another to sponsor everything from dinners to turkey shoots. In spite of an overwhelming increase in the number of local fund-raising events around the country, more and more of these smaller sponsorship opportunities—they usually cost a company $10,000 or less—keep on popping up. Why? Simple. Most of the time, they work.

Organizing a special event can take colossal amounts of time and seriously divert the energy of a nonprofit. But when word gets out that an organization like Operation Smile cleared (not grossed, but *netted* after all expenses were paid) $1 million from a single New York fund-raising dinner—well, it's hard to hold back the rush of adrenaline. Most nonprofits would be better off buying lottery tickets than trying to emulate the success of Operation

Smile. Still, this is America and anything can happen. Knowing full well that hotels, golf clubs, caterers, orchestras, and other service providers will devour a hefty portion of whatever money a non-profit raises, these organizations press on for the gold.

The overpopulation of "the dinner" is most evident in the country's metropolitan centers. Perhaps no one has captured just how frenzied things can get when high society meets the nonprofit world than Bernice Kanner, whose 1983 article in *New York* magazine described the scene this way: "These good-cause rituals have become so pervasive in New York that from October through May scarcely a weeknight goes by that some muck-a-muck isn't being honored by some cause in some hotel ballroom. In peak season, every mail delivery seems to bring fourteen invitations that are really more like commands. All solicit for a worthy charity or program, but in the end, what they amount to is an incredible, genteel shakedown—reminding many recipients that it's not lonely at the top; it's black tie."

If a vote were taken, most corporations would tell you that they aren't crazy about local sponsorships, especially dinners. Partly that's because supporting these events requires more than cutting a check; it also means showing up. When the black tie dinners get booked for every weekend from fall until spring (for example, a few years ago, the Waldorf in New York City disclosed that it had booked sixty-eight fund-raising events in its Grand Ballroom during just the months of October and November!), the private sector's blood pressure begins to escalate. Corporations are also getting testy about something else. They don't like the way an increasing number of nonprofits are using local sponsorships to back them into a corner. It's called the "award attack" and here's how it works.

A local nonprofit organization designates your corporation as its Business of the Year. Check the fine print because that honor probably comes with a few obligations.

First, a high-ranking executive (preferably your CEO) is expected to attend the organization's annual dinner to accept the award. Once executive-level representation is arranged, your corporation is asked to sponsor one or more tables. "In the past, companies that have won the award usually sponsor at least two tables,"

149

says the organization (hidden message—help fill up the hall so your big cheese won't be embarrassed by a low turnout). Cost per table might vary from $2,500 to $10,000 for ten seats. Then, because the organization wants to be sure the "right people" are at the event to help celebrate your company's achievement, it asks for a list of company vendors and other key contacts. The organization mass-produces invitation letters with a lead paragraph that uses your company as a come-on to convince others to buy a table at the fund-raising event. Follow-up phone calls are made to encourage attendance.

Finally, the dinner is held, your company gets its moment in the sun, and the organization counts its cash. Are we through yet? Not quite. Tradition has it that the executive from your company who picks up the award this year will be on hand next year to present the award to another lucky CEO. Naturally, your company will want to take a table or two at that event too, so be sure to plan (and budget) accordingly.

Before this scheme ran rampant through the nonprofit world, it actually was a turn-on to many corporations. Ego-stroking goes a long way in the business community. But today, a different attitude prevails. Companies have found that it costs a lot of money to accept a $50 plaque or a piece of crystal. Yet, even having made that eye-opening discovery, businesses have trouble resisting the magnetic force emanating from these awards.

One way for companies to regain control over these kinds of events is to apply the ten management steps to local sponsorships. The corporate social investing model leaves ample room for companies to spend sponsorship dollars, but that money should be directed to business-relevant functions (Step 2). Having a social investment plan in place will permit a corporation to turn down invitations that just don't mesh with the firm's basic mission or interests.

There's one more reason why special events have been perplexing to corporations. Until now, companies have been notoriously inconsistent in the way they record these events as expenses. Tax regulations state that only a portion of these functions are allowed as charitable deductions—the amount you eat or drink shouldn't be allowed to creep into the contribution total your company reports to the IRS. However, what a company takes as a tax deduction for a dinner isn't necessarily what it reports as the value of its sponsorship to the public. An informal poll of the fifty largest corporate donors taken in 1996 found that one-third of these megabusinesses include the *full amount* spent on dinners and events in the contribution totals communicated to the public. Another third did it the IRS way and took only *partial* credit for the expenses when talking about their overall philanthropy activities. The rest of the businesses didn't think they should go public with any of the dinner or special event expenses (even if the money ended up in the charity's pocket) when talking about their corporate philanthropy activities.

Along comes corporate social investing and all of this confusion goes out the window. Regardless of how they are handled for tax purposes, 100 percent of these expenses are considered corporate social investments and are reported as such to the public. But what about the portion of a table sponsorship that is salt-and-peppered and washed down with a glass of house wine? Should food and drink consumed by those employees roped into going to these events be counted as part of a firm's social investment? Yes, because nine times out of ten the employees you find at these events are there to represent their corporations—not because they are looking for a good time. Corporate social investing makes few distinctions between donations and business expenses that end up in a 501(c)(3)'s pocket. Consequently, companies should regard the full cost of a dinner or special event as an LBI.

Although event sponsorships (whether major or local) can be annoying to businesses, some do have the ability of getting company or product exposure to well-defined audiences in a more effective way than other media. We live in an era where the average American adult is plastered with twenty-one thousand television commercials a year and where advertising expenditures have multiplied one-third faster than the world economy since 1950. Understandably, businesses are constantly trying to find different ways to get through the information clutter. Local sponsorships that influence small audiences can make a difference to a company. They can leave a powerful impression. This approach only makes sense, however, if LBIs are aimed and fired at the right target.

MAJOR SPONSORSHIPS

If you happen to be in Memphis some spring, you're bound to hear about the Ducks Unlimited Great Outdoors Sporting & Wildlife Festival. People from all over trek to Tennessee to target shoot, fish, and ogle the latest in outdoor equipment. The event is big—big enough to attract the sponsorship dollars of companies like GMC Truck, Anheuser-Busch (Budweiser), and PepsiCo. Want a piece of this action? Ducks Unlimited, the 501(c)(3) organization with over a half million members nationwide, will be happy to oblige. Depending on how much money is involved, DU can arrange television and radio coverage for your company in the greater mid-South area. Sponsorship fees can get you access to the organization's mailing list and the right to use certain logos.

You say you're not interested in Memphis. Well, DU holds five thousand events in different parts of the country that draw over seven hundred thousand attendees. The organization's office of corporate relations is ready to customize its offerings to meet most any sponsorship need you might have.

Welcome to the heady world of big special event sponsorships. It's a universe where more than $15 billion a year is spent to sponsor sports, music, arts, and other events worldwide. Just in North America, companies paid out around $5.9 billion to underwrite sponsorships in 1997, according to a consulting firm in Chicago called IEG Inc. The sponsorship phenomenon has grown at a double-digit rate nearly every year since 1984.

Although about 65 percent of North American sponsorship money ends up in the sports field, there is enough cash left over (around $2 billion a year) to make any slightly anemic nonprofit drool. Sponsorships are hot, and IEG says that one reason why is that they offer companies "a way to cut through the media clutter and replace bogus commercial messages with meaningful alliances."

A lot of huge corporate-sponsored functions don't have anything to do with 501(c)(3) organizations—many high-profile sporting events, for example. But for corporate social investing purposes, we're only interested in sponsorships that have a company check being handed over to a nonprofit or exclusively public institution. A few examples of 501(c)(3) nonprofits that have received notable corporate sponsorship support in the past are these: Philadelphia Dance Company (American Express), American Zoo & Aquarium Association (Borden), Autry Museum of Western Heritage (Chevron), Children's Miracle Network (Heinz USA), American Diabetes Association (Hershey Foods), Kids First! (Time-Life/Time Warner).

Although 501(c)(3)s are quickly realizing that sponsorships can mean big infusions of cash, they also are waking up to the reality that there is fierce competition for sponsorship dollars. Still, if the World of Outlaws car racing team can get Hooters Restaurant sponsorship or if the American Lumberjack Championships can attract LaCrosse Footwear dollars, there has to be hope for nonprofit organizations. There *is* a lot of sponsorship money to be had, but that doesn't mean it will come easily to a 501(c)(3) organization that's inexperienced in negotiating the terms of what could either be a lucrative deal or a financial bust.

With the arrival of corporate social investing and the ten management steps, corporations themselves have more of an incentive than before to come up with major sponsorship ideas that engage 501(c)(3) organizations or exclusively public organizations. Here's why.

If a corporation (a) has committed to the ten steps and is setting aside a portion of its pretax profits to meet its corporate social investment target for the year and (b) acknowledges that certain sponsorships can be counted in that total, then why not let the marketing, public relations, government affairs, and other folks in the company know that they have a shot at getting their sponsorship ideas funded using dollars from outside their own departmental budgets? In many businesses, putting this kind of financial carrot in front of their sales and marketing people will definitely get the creative juices flowing.

Corporations looking for sponsorship options should consider this guiding principle: *If a company wants a sponsorship to fit like a glove with its business interests, then in most instances it will have to take the lead in developing the plan or helping a nonprofit do the necessary design work.*

SPONSORSHIP PROPOSALS

Nonprofits generally don't know enough about a company's business needs to create a powerful sponsorship concept that will convince a corporation to write a check. Nevertheless, that isn't likely to stop most nonprofits from trying to get those sponsorship dollars. Corporations respond best to opportunities that have very clear-cut "deliverables." Look at the following elements taken from an actual proposal soliciting business sponsors for a volleyball tournament:

Official designation. The sponsor gets an "exclusive" for its class of industry (food products, pharmaceuticals, footwear, and so on).

Media benefits. Ten thirty-second radio spots for company promotions; the company name will be mentioned in twenty other thirty-second radio spots; company involvement is referenced in every event press release; and the company logo is featured in local newspaper ads.

Advertising and promotion. The company logo is printed on one thousand four-color posters; the logo also appears in one thousand full-color programs and registrations forms.

Signage. The sponsor gets four two- by ten-foot banners to promote its name at the event (center court and high-traffic food and merchandise areas).

Hospitality. Four passes to a VIP tent are put on the table along with VIP parking passes.

On-site promotion. Booth space is made available for product displays; ten public address announcements include the company name.

Advance publicity. Promotional materials are sent prior to the event to chambers of commerce, sporting goods stores, schools, local youth organizations, and other businesses.

This unusually sophisticated sponsorship design was actually developed by a for-profit marketing firm on behalf of a nonprofit organization. Frequently it takes that level of expertise to have any hope of winning corporate interest.

THE TANQUERAY AIDS RIDE

The Tanqueray AIDS Ride is a short case study of how a company took an idea proposed by a Los Angeles fund-raising organization and inflated it into a national sponsorship hit. Tanqueray was looking for ways to get the attention of the twenty-five-to-forty-year-old market in the United States. The company sponsored a bike ride in California to raise dollars for AIDS organizations. The event was an instant success. A few years later, Tanqueray started spending over $2 million a year to sponsor bike rides in major markets around the United States, which led to eleven thousand bicyclists promoting the company's name. By the way, the AIDS Rides have picked up a few hitchhikers: Banana Republic, USAir, Gatorade, Starbucks, and others are now in Tanqueray's marketing wind stream.

COCA-COLA AND BOYS & GIRLS CLUBS OF AMERICA

Sometimes sponsorships end up looking like a bouillabaisse with lots of different events and projects floating in one pot. Coca-Cola's $60 million "strategic partnership" with the Boys & Girls Clubs of America is one example (and a notable one at that since it has been tagged as the largest corporate-nonprofit affiliation ever). This ten-year alliance is mainly a sponsorship arrangement, with Coke plugging in money for concerts, sports tournaments, and other local activities (there are nineteen hundred Boys & Girls Clubs around the country). However, the company is also leveraging the deal through retail promotions including point-of-sale displays at supermarkets, which are really adjuncts to cause-related marketing LBIs (to be reviewed later in this section of the chapter). On top of all this, Coca-Cola will be giving the organization high-impact grants to help develop its youth programming over the next decade.

Let's stay with Coke for a while longer. Under the old way of doing things, a report on the company's philanthropy wouldn't express the full magnitude of its commitment to the Boys & Girls Clubs. Whatever money Coke is giving as a donation either directly or through its foundation probably will get acknowledged, but much of the $60 million investment will remain blurred since the deal is being financed in large part by marketing and promotion dollars.

Under our social investment model, Coke's annual draw on the $60 million pact with the Boys & Girls Clubs (whether it's a contribution, sponsorship, or cause-related marketing expense) gets brought into the open and credited as an LBI. *The full amount* becomes part of that firm's social investment total.

MASTERS OF SPONSORSHIP PREPARATION

Although most 501(c)(3)s will need help in preparing a sponsorship concept that will hold water, some nonprofits have become masters of this particular kind of LBI. The Smithsonian Institution, for example, got the bug for corporate sponsorship funding in the late 1980s after Orkin Pest Controls Inc. offered to help revitalize the Museum of Natural History's deteriorating insect display. Since then, the Smithsonian has been among the more aggressive solicitors of corporate sponsorship support.

Public television is another player in the nonprofit world that has learned how to attract sponsor dollars. There are still some corporations that write off major underwriting commitments for public television programming as charitable donations. Most businesses, however, look at public television underwriting as a sponsorship commitment and tap their advertising budgets to foot the costs. Of course, if a company has the ten management steps in place, it won't matter which corporate department gets stuck with the bill. As long as public television remains in the 501(c)(3) league, corporate sponsorship support counts as a social investment.

Lots of other nonprofits are out there trying to sell different prepackaged sponsorship deals to companies. Most cannot compete with the more sophisticated projects being peddled by more experienced organizations like the Smithsonian or public television. Even when a nonprofit stirs up some interest with a sponsorship idea, a company will often demand that it be refined so that it's more in line with corporate interests.

One highly publicized sponsorship marriage between a business and nonprofit became the plot line of an IRS decision back in 1991. The service declared that corporate sponsorship income received by the Cotton Bowl—a 501(c)(3) entity—was the kind of revenue stream that should be taxed as "unrelated business income." Giving up a percentage of sponsorship dollars in tax payments to Uncle Sam was not something the Cotton Bowl was eager to do. So after considerable pressure, the IRS took another look at the situation and in 1997 ruled that certain "qualified sponsorship payments" that companies made to nonprofits could be excluded from taxes. When a corporation has no expectation of a return benefit other than the use or acknowledgment of the sponsor's name, logo, or products in connection with the activities of the donee organization, then the IRS is out of luck.

The most recent Cotton Bowl ruling has gotten a warm reception from most businesses and nonprofits. And why not? Nonprofits can tempt businesses into sponsorships with a promise of name exposure to thousands and occasionally millions of people without the worry of having to take something off the top for the IRS. The ruling means that corporations will probably have a choice of more sponsorship options than ever before, and can now elect to categorize these expenses as either an LBI major sponsorship or (because these costs can be written off as charitable donations) a high-impact grant.

A LITTLE CRITICISM

Got the idea that major sponsorships are highly business-driven? You couldn't be more correct. And among some nonprofit leaders, that doesn't sit well. The head of the National Parks and Conservation recently wrote: "The national parks need money, but some believe that corporate sponsorship amounts to selling the parks' souls."

There are those who think the Smithsonian Institution sold its soul in 1991 when its policies were modified to permit companies to display their corporate logos in support of sponsored exhibitions. The museum accepted a $300,000 donation from the Alyeska Pipeline Services Company to cover the cost of installing a trans-Alaska pipeline exhibit. Some conservationists complained that the exhibition downplayed the environmental risks that were an inevitable part of the pipeline project. They cast a suspicious eye at the Smithsonian for being a little too quick in pocketing money from a company with a vested interest. Although both the museum and Alyeska defended the deal, they have learned firsthand that some sponsorships come with extra baggage.

Critics aside, major sponsorships continue to sprout. These are LBIs that usually have to demonstrate impressive returns for the sponsoring corporations. Yes, there's something in a sponsorship arrangement for the nonprofit partner as well—after all, that's what qualifies these commitments as social investments. However, the business benefits have to be clear as a bell because if they're not, a major sponsorship proposal will probably remain just that: an idea that won't see the light of day.

CUSTOMER EDUCATION

Heard about the boondoggle where important customers are whisked off to an "education conference" in Hawaii for a week, all expenses paid by an appreciative business? Two hours of instruction and seven days of fun and frolic later, the fat and happy clients are flown back home, forever indebted to the corporation that served as their magnanimous underwriter.

Fortunately, these thinly veiled excuses for vacations are not as prevalent as they once were. Businesses do continue to support seminars, professional education conferences, and workshops as a way of cementing client relationships. However, most of these education events are the real thing—programs that provide valuable information to attendees (although admittedly, these education forums are quite often conducted in splendid locations). Within some professions and industries, regulations and ethical standards put limits on what a business can do in shelling out money for these kinds of educational experiences.

If a company pays an individual (consulting fee, stipend) to attend a conference or education event, that is *not* an LBI. Remember: *only payments to 501(c)(3) or exclusively public organizations count for social investing purposes.* However, if a business provides money to a nonprofit organization that in turn offsets the costs of one or more participants, then the expense can be an LBI. How does the latter arrangement work? A 501(c)(3) professional association gets funding from a corporation to pay for a number of participants to attend a three-day conference. The association makes sure that those participants who benefit from this arrangement are aware that the company is picking up the tab. Result: a high level of participant appreciation flows back to the sponsoring company.

Customer education activities can work on an even grander scale. Modeled after a highly successful program developed by

Johnson & Johnson for hospital senior nurses, the SmithKline Beecham Executive Management Program for Directors of Pharmacy is offered at the University of Pennsylvania's Wharton School. Each year, up to forty pharmacists are given a "mini-MBA" experience at Wharton thanks to a grant from the giant pharmaceutical corporation. At the end of nine days, the program graduates walk out of Philadelphia with their Wharton certificates. Most graduates of that program will periodically look at that certificate and feel a strong sense of appreciation for the company that made it all possible.

Common sense should tell a business that if customer education is just a front for giving clients a fine old time in some fancy resort, then it's an investment that could easily backfire. In contrast, seminars, workshops, and other educational programs that are on the up-and-up should be able to withstand the scrutiny of any type of outside review. All the goodwill a company is trying to develop among customers could be destroyed if a business is accused of trying to buy or pay off clients.

Customer education is big business in the United States and increasingly in other countries. Check the bulletin board in any major hotel or resort and see how many professional association seminars and meetings are being held. Because there are a multitude of education opportunities, due diligence is the order of the day before a company cuts an LBI check. There are some bad apples in the basket of continuing-education offerings. A corporation needs to be sure the program it picks out to support isn't rotten at the core.

MEMBERSHIPS

Savvy nonprofits have learned that sometimes it's easier to get money from a business if they steer around a company's philanthropy program and look for another entryway into the corporation. Numerous organizations have found the word *membership* opens the right business doors. Companies have the impression that by being a member they'll get customized benefits in return for an annual fee. That might be true in a few cases, but often *member* is another word for *donor,* which means that whatever materials and services are extended to the business tend to be very general.

Nevertheless, perception is what counts and very often businesses will strike at a nonprofit's membership lure even after having spit out other kinds of bait the organization may have passed in front of the company.

A legitimate argument could be made that some memberships are nothing more than conditional grants in disguise and shouldn't be considered LBIs at all. Maybe so. However, a lot of businesses buy the nonprofit line that memberships are different. That has prompted corporations to account for memberships as business expenses that aren't taken as charitable deductions. Corporate social investing treats *all* memberships in 501(c)(3) organizations as LBIs. Perhaps some hairsplitting could be done in an effort to sort out "real" memberships from other kinds of grants. However, since LBIs and conditional or high-impact grants all get counted the same way when adding up a company's social investments, why bother?

Nonprofits use a pressure tactic called *layering* to encourage corporate members to increase their annual membership payments. Here's an example: the Environmental Law Institute is a Washington, D.C.–based research and education nonprofit that got about $700,000 of its nearly $6 million annual budget in 1995 from a membership program. Depending on the level of their generosity, company members were labeled differently in the organization's promotional materials:

Category	*Some Corporate Members Included*
Corporate counselors	LEXIS/NEXIS, United Technologies
Corporate partners	Dow U.S.A., Intel
Corporate associates	Eastman Kodak, Xerox
Corporate members	Tenneco, Eli Lilly

The Environmental Law Institute might contend that donors in the bottom layer are nearly as important to the organization as those businesses at the top of the stack. Sounds nice, but the fact is that by publishing the names of the low-end donors, the organization immediately puts pressure on those companies to up their membership payments so they can get out of the cellar and into a more respectable part of the Institute's house.

Step 7. The Social Investment Model: Part II, Strategic Plans

There's nothing extraordinary about the Environmental Law Institute's membership tactics—a host of other nonprofits do the same thing. However, here's a warning to nonprofits: corporate social investing might actually work against this concept. If a company has to justify its nonprofit investment, it may actually *want* to be a low-layer member. Because benefits to members are mostly identical regardless of the size of the annual payment to the organization, why spend more than the lowest possible entrance fee? Once again, remember the words in Step 2 of our management model for social investing: "Obtain as much business value from a social investment as allowable, strategically appropriate, and practical." Paying more for benefits that could be obtained for less is contrary to this principle.

Regardless of what membership commitment a company ends up making, it should:

▸ show the entire amount as an LBI and list the payment as one of the company's social investments

▸ limit membership payments just to those nonprofits or exclusively public organizations that are relevant to the business

It's easy for corporations (particularly big firms) to lose sight of membership fees. They are often relatively small—$1,000 to $5,000 is a common range for annual membership payments (although trade-related organizations can collect dues that climb into the six figures)—and as such, companies are inclined to renew memberships without a great deal of thought. As pointed out, memberships are usually paid by departments or divisions within a company and there's usually very little centralized monitoring of all membership activity throughout a business.

In the past, managers have been quick to approve an invoice for another year of membership in an association or organization that on the surface looks to be important. The ten-step plan for managing social investments will bring much more diligence to the membership renewal process. Still, memberships are viable LBIs for businesses and as such continue to represent an important funding channel for nonprofits.

Here's another message for nonprofit organizations: although social investing will make it more challenging to "sell" memberships, it's still worth the struggle. Annual membership renewals are a lot like annuities, which can turn out to be a valuable source of revenue. Of course, renewals won't materialize unless a company can be convinced to buy a membership in the first place. As social investing works its way through the corporate ranks, nonprofits are going to have to find ways of making a much more compelling case about how a membership brings value to the business.

CAUSE-RELATED MARKETING

When Paul Newman blinked those magnetic blue eyes back in 1982, he wasn't doing a movie shoot. The well-known actor was looking into the depths of the notoriously inhospitable food industry and probably wondering if his new idea really had a chance. It was during that year when, with little front-end capital, a lot of star-quality hype, and a concept called cause-related marketing, Newman's Own arrived on the scene.

NEWMAN'S OWN

The grocery trade soon got the message that this was more than just another celebrity-named food line. What made this new offering different was a slogan tagged to Newman's products. It read *All profits to charity*. These few words wormed their way into the consumer psyche and made other marketers stand up and take notice. Newman's Own has since expanded its business to fourteen products that are distributed around the country. The company has generated over $90 million for more than four hundred charities and has become a case study in how good causes can make for good sales.

AMERICAN EXPRESS COMPANY

About the same time that Paul Newman was putting a new marketing spin on salad dressing, the American Express Company was testing it own version of cause-related marketing in California. The corporation was going head-to-head with BankAmerica and other businesses in the San Francisco Bay Area, trying to get consumers to use the American Express credit card. It launched a three-month campaign promising to contribute two cents to the San Francisco Arts Festival for each American Express card purchase. The new idea worked, and the company began rolling the concept out to other parts of the country.

A short time later, American Express unleashed its cause-related scheme on a national scale when it promised big money for the Statue of Liberty/Ellis Island Foundation if consumers used the company's plastic. Timing is everything. During the early 1980s, the nation was caught up in a patriotic drive to renovate Lady Liberty and the clever campaign caught on. At the close of 1983, American Express reported a 28 percent increase in card usage and a large number of new cardholders.

Although variations of cause-related marketing had kicked around the minor leagues for years, it was the American Express experience that brought the concept to the main arena. The company showed what monetary muscle, beyond the dollars donated to a good cause, needed to be put behind this type of marketing approach to make it work. The formula American Express used back in the early eighties still holds true for most campaigns—for every dollar that goes to an appealing nonprofit organization, three or four need to be spent on promotion and advertising if the project is to meet expectations. American Express delivered $1.7 million to the Statue of Liberty/Ellis Island Foundation and spent a reported $6 million to let the public know what it was doing. It was the advertising and promotion that most accounted for the success of this near-legendary cause-related campaign.

DISTINGUISHING CHARACTERISTICS OF CAUSE-RELATED MARKETING

Today, cause-related marketing is as common as the dinner LBIs described earlier in this chapter. Below are a few past and present examples:

Visa International. Use the Visa credit card and a percentage of the transaction goes to Reading Is Fundamental (over $1 million raised for the organization in 1996 and 1997).

Campbell Soup. Return product labels to the company and Campbell sends money to schools for equipment purchases.

Master Lock. A portion of customer sales goes to the National Crime Prevention Council.

Hormel. The Hams for the Holidays cause-related campaign includes the donation of ninety-one thousand canned hams (in 1995).

FTD. Five percent of the sales receipts of certain floral arrangements sold and delivered through the FTD network goes to nonprofits.

And the list goes on.

It's not always easy to tell the difference between cause-related marketing and high-impact grants. For instance, Digital (now Compaq) and the National Center for Missing & Exploited Children collaborate on a program called Kids and Company, which gets the Digital name into schools around the country as part of a child-safety curriculum initiative. That may be cause-related marketing to some, but given the terms of the relationship between the business and the nonprofit, it would make more sense to call this a vintage high-impact grant.

Because cause-related LBIs and high-impact grants get valued the same way when adding up a company's social investments, it's not worth spending much time analyzing the differences between the two. For those who feel the need to make distinctions, however, here are a few words of explanation.

1. Companies making a high-impact grant generally get hyphenated name acknowledgment for a program or project. Example: the AmFAR/Bristol-Myers Squibb Partnership Program is a project that gets women into AIDS clinical trials. The corporation provides the American Foundation for AIDS Research (AmFAR) with $220,000 over two years for the project. The commitment qualifies as a charitable deduction (in fact, it's paid by the Bristol-Myers Squibb Foundation) and is clearly a high-impact grant.

2. Corporations that want the use of a nonprofit's name as part of a cause-related LBI relationship generally apply that name to a product or service in such a way that the deal might be challenged if taken as a charitable tax deduction. The American Heart Association, the American Diabetes Association, and the American Cancer Society have all entered into cause-related arrangements with different companies.

Offering businesses the right to use a nonprofit's name on products and services for a price is nothing new. Example: the

American Dental Association has been making its "seal of approval" available since the mid-1930s. Companies that are permitted to put that seal on their products pay $9,000 to get evaluated and a $1,500 annual maintenance fee.

When a company negotiates an exclusive use of an organization's name, the price can go considerably higher. Examples: SmithKline Beecham PLC reached an agreement with the American Cancer Society to use the prominent health care organization's name on its Nicoderm smoking-cessation patches—for $1 million a year. Schering-Plough will pay a royalty from the sales of a new Dr. Scholl's foot-care product line to the educational fund of the American Podiatric Medical Association.

Perhaps the most far-reaching and controversial cause-related LBI was an arrangement between McNeil Consumer Products Company (MCPC, a Johnson & Johnson affiliate) and the Arthritis Foundation. The company manufactured an over-the-counter line of products called Arthritis Foundation Pain Relievers. This arrangement gave the appearance to consumers that the Arthritis Foundation was now in the pharmaceutical business. In reality, the organization was only lending its name to MCPC in exchange for cash payments and royalties.

Some felt the McNeil–Arthritis Foundation deal went too far in blurring the line between the private and nonprofit sectors. A few states even accused the company of deceptive ad practices. Eventually MCPC folded the product line, noting that it had failed to meet sales expectations. Although the new concept may have fallen short of the company's business goals, the Arthritis Foundation expressed no regrets. The organization reported that the products (which included promotional inserts for the organization) had attracted thousands of new members and had given the foundation a much higher public profile.

Experiments in cause-related marketing are sure to continue as businesses search for narrow marketing channels that come with lower promotional costs. Not all of these new corporate-nonprofit marketing-based partnerships are going to be winners. However, if research conducted by Cone Communications and the Roper polling organization is correct, many cause-related deals will prove successful. The study found that three out of four consumers surveyed would favor brands that were linked to cause-related campaigns if price and quality were not barriers to making a purchase. An earlier study by Frankel & Company (a Chicago consulting firm) revealed that of over six hundred people sampled, 69 percent said they had responded to a marketing promotion because of its cause-related theme.

By the way, the American Express Company hasn't grown tired of cause-related campaigns. One of its most recent cause-based projects has been a partnership with the hunger-relief organization Share Our Strength. The marriage proved fruitful. Over a four-year period, SOS received $16 million and American Express recorded an increase in the number of merchants accepting its credit card as well as a jump in usage among its cardholders.

A CAUTIONARY NOTE

Can cause-related relationships turn sour? Sometimes. Perhaps the most talked about deal-gone-wrong was the public unraveling of an arrangement between the Sunbeam Corporation and the American Medical Association. In 1997, only a couple of weeks after Sunbeam proudly announced AMA's agreement to give the company exclusive rights to use the medical group's famous seal on several health care products (heating pads, bathroom scales, and so on), the embarrassed nonprofit organization asked to be let out of the pact. Even though the AMA probably would have reaped millions from the arrangement, its decision to lease its logo created a storm of protest among many of its more influential members. A contrite AMA chairman eventually told the world that the decision to approve the Sunbeam agreement had been "an error."

The Sunbeam-AMA saga makes the point that the business of logo marketing doesn't always culminate in jubilation. Nonprofits have to be sure that their own constituents won't revolt if they choose to sell their image to a corporation. Successful cause-related marketing usually depends on the communion of two fully consenting organizations. If one partner is perceived as being overpowered or compromised, then the whole process can be painted in some very uncomplimentary colors. A nonprofit has to think

about the possible consequences and not just the monetary plea-
sures that come from leaping into the arms of a business, and a corporation needs to weigh the pros and cons of mixing it up with a
nonprofit organization that doesn't conform to the same rules of
play that are commonplace in the business world.

For all the land mines that surround cause-related marketing,
it remains an alluring opportunity for both corporations and nonprofits. Although many skeptics predict that highly publicized failures like the attempted Sunbeam-AMA collaboration will put a
damper on other cause-related marketing projects, the benefits of
this kind of LBI are too tempting for either businesses or nonprofits to ignore.

RISK INVESTMENTS

A worrisome trend in America is the declining interest in
research that leads to the advancement of new, nonproprietary
knowledge in the science and technology fields. Unlike clinical or
applied research, which promises—although doesn't always
deliver—a lucrative commercial payoff, basic research is speculative and often requires many rolls of the dice before it comes up
with a winner. Still, this kind of gamble is important because basic
research is where many new business opportunities are hatched.

For many years, the private sector has tapped into the benefits
of long-term research without paying an arm and a leg. Uncle Sam
picks up most of the tab through grants made to universities and
research centers. Here's how the system works for a lot of companies: universities carry out basic research programs using public
dollars; corporations hover around the periphery waiting to see if
a basic discovery might be the embryo for a money-making commercial product; companies and higher education institutions
sign contracts that convert basic research projects into applied or
clinical proprietary agreements; and finally universities start collecting royalties on winners that businesses produce and distribute
to the marketplace.

In recent years, the feds have cut back on research grant
making. The lush, publicly funded basic research grazing grounds
are harder to find and now it's not unusual to find university-based
scientists turning to businesses for help. The problem, as *The New*

York Times has pointed out, is that corporations have themselves cut back their basic research budgets, choosing instead to direct their money to near-term product R&D. Many companies view basic research as too speculative and have come to the conclusion, says the *Times,* that "it should be done . . . by university scientists, paid mainly by government."

Corporate social investing is actually a stimulus for companies to spend more for basic research. Payments made to a university or some other nonprofit institutions for nonproprietary research gets counted as an LBI. That's not the case where there is a *proprietary* agreement between a corporation and university. Applied or clinical research represents a different kind of business relationship that can't be termed an LBI even under the broadest definition of social investing.

Basic research funding is an example of a risk-investment LBI. Most of the time, money paid to a university to carry out this kind of research isn't going to uncork a big win for a company. It will, however, give the business an inside look at the laboratory where investigators may be working on other projects that might have business value. Of course, where there are risks, there are rewards. Once in a while, an industry-funded basic research project will be the first step toward a successful commercial initiative.

Risk investments aren't confined just to research labs. They can also be found in the banking industry. Perhaps better termed "quasi" risk LBIs, these payments are largely the by-product of a federal initiative called the Community Reinvestment Act (CRA). Passed and signed in 1977, the CRA required lending institutions to make more funds available to inner-city and other hard-pressed neighborhoods.

Today, most financial institutions can demonstrate that they're making more low-interest loans to minority businesses and approving more mortgages to people who never before had much of a chance of owning a home. Many banks point to CRA payments as the best example of their corporate responsibility. For instance, BankAmerica has provided more than $14 billion in loans for low-income home buyers and community economic development since 1992, according to a report the bank published in 1997.

Nonprofit social service, arts, education, and health care institutions are sometimes among the borrowers in these low-income locations. Although nonprofit defaults are not that frequent, there are occasional disappointments. When an organization is unable to repay borrowed funds, it typically asks the lender to forgive the loan. In essence, the nonprofit wants the dollars it borrowed converted to a charitable gift.

When loans to high-risk 501(c)(3) or exclusively public institutions don't pan out, lenders can include those defaults as risk-investment LBIs. If banks know that these loans will ultimately count as corporate social investments if they can't be repaid, then they should be more inclined to help carefully selected nonprofits even if those organizations are on shaky ground. If that happens, more "socially responsible banking funds" may crop up like the one started in 1989 by the Vermont National Bank. That fund has been able to attract over $100 million from customers in forty-two states and sixteen countries. The bank uses its invested dollars to make loans to housing, educational, and environmental organizations, as well as to higher-risk small businesses.

A footnote: only uncollected loans to *nonprofits* should be applied to a bank's social investment program; individual or business loans that go belly up don't count. With this in mind, lenders may want to use nonprofit organizations as lending agents—in other words, call on these groups as intermediaries to do the lending and collecting of money to high-risk borrowers. This approach is the underlying concept of a trend called *microcredit funding* or community reinvesting. These nonprofit-managed pools of money have been the source of many inspiring success stories from as far away as Bangladesh to cities in the United States.

Banks aren't the only corporations that make this type of financial risk investment. Other businesses (insurance companies, securities firms, and even a few manufacturing corporations) invest in loan funds that are used to support low-income housing, enterprise zones, and the reclamation of deteriorating neighborhoods. Example: MetLife's social investing includes a $2 million commitment to the Atlanta Housing Equity Fund that has been set up to finance six hundred affordable housing units in the city.

Any company (whether it's a bank, investment firm, or a business in another industry category) that ultimately incurs bad debt as a result of having made a loan to a nonprofit can classify those lost moneys as a risk-investment LBI.

Clarification: there are nonprofit organizations that collect money as straight-out, unadulterated grants that are then used to finance revolving loan pools. In these cases, corporations pay their money without any intention of getting it back and usually claim a charitable deduction for whatever dollars are invested. It's best to log these expenses as high-impact or conditional grants. If they filter into the LBI pile, it's no big deal. However, for the sake of keeping a scorecard that makes sense to those on the outside as well as those inside the company, it's worth making an attempt to keep apples and oranges in their respective bins.

IN SUMMARY

Some companies will be agog when they ring up the total for all the LBIs they're already making. They may even be surprised to find they're making several LBI payments to a single nonprofit. For example, here's how one university can get several hooks into a business: a company pays the higher education institution for (a) one, two, or more memberships in different discipline-based associations or professional chapters sponsored by the university; (b) basic research grants; (c) two or three dinners and an annual golf outing to support various college activities; and (d) a whole series of customer education seminars and workshops throughout the year. In larger corporations, the "bill" for each of these activities is usually sent to different individuals and departments within the company, which makes it difficult for the corporation to keep a running total of how much is being paid to the university.

Effective LBI management should start with an inventory of what a company is already spending for these kinds of social investments. Once that's been done, a business can switch on the RODES system and decide whether existing LBIs should be continued or dropped and if any additional LBIs are warranted.

Final note: the suggested range of spending for cash LBIs is between 15 percent and 35 percent of all the cash a company puts into social investments. (Don't include product, equipment, and land investments when doing LBI cash projections.) (See again

Figure 11.) These percentages are only guidelines—flexibility remains the watchword. A few businesses may be able to make a case for spending a great deal more on LBIs. If a well-thought-out social investing plan has LBIs dominating a corporation's cash outlay, then so be it. Just remember—the ten-step management plan requires disclosure. For commitments made to nonprofits that a company thinks could be interpreted by the public as being too self-serving, *don't* fold them into the social investment total. When in doubt, leave them out. Write these ambiguous payments off as other types of business expenses and don't try to claim them as LBIs.

International Social Investing

This section isn't only for businesses or nonprofit organizations that have international interests. All aspects of corporate social investing—domestic and foreign—are influenced by how multinational companies handle their external affairs in locations outside the United States. Under the ten management principles, corporations can include commitments made in other countries as part of their social investment portfolios.

When Alcoa Aluminio bought a small extrusion factory in an obscure Brazilian town called Sao Cristovao, the firm got an unwelcome bonus—a workforce that was sorely lacking in health care services. People with medical problems don't make great employees, so the Aluminum Company of America (Alcoa) built a compact but functional medical and dental care unit not far from its newly purchased facility.

Dealing with health, education, and social issues that can make the difference between profit and loss in a nondomestic location is becoming standard fare for a lot of U.S. multinationals. When corporations invest dollars in foreign communities where they have plant sites, they set up the classic win-win scenario: they improve conditions that have an effect on productivity, and people living in the communities where these facilities are located (employees or not) see their standard of living improve.

What made the Alcoa transaction notable is that the company acknowledged the commitment as a part of its social responsibility activities, and the construction of the medical post was paid for by a grant from the Alcoa Foundation, the company's chari-

171

table arm located in the firm's hometown of Pittsburgh, Pennsylvania. To most corporations that provide funding for projects like the one in Sao Cristovao, the costs are necessary business expenses that don't get reflected in any statement on social responsibility.

The Alcoa Foundation's financial role in Brazil illustrates an interesting quirk in the IRS regulations. Although companies aren't allowed to take a charitable deduction for most gifts made to institutions outside the United States, a company foundation can make overseas grants. This means that a corporation can make payments to its own foundation and take a charitable deduction for the "gifts." The foundation then funds overseas organizations that the company designates. Assuming the tax deduction in the United States is more favorable than a deduction the company could have gotten by writing off a direct expense in a foreign location, the business may have just lowered the cost of this investment.

A "pass through" arrangement such as the Alcoa example doesn't work for every business, as tax experts will quickly point out. Even if a corporation has a foundation (many do not), they need to take into account all kinds of considerations (for example, a corporation's current foreign tax credit status) to determine if the foundation is the best financial spillway to use in funding non-U.S. programs or projects. However, under the provisions of corporate social investing, it doesn't matter how a company pays for an overseas social investment. Whether carried as a company foundation charge or an in-country business expense, the commitment gets counted the same way when a corporation totals its social investments for the year.

For a long time, the non-U.S. social responsibility activities of domestic multinationals have been either ignored or poorly tracked. Community improvements that Chevron has made in Africa or those that DuPont has underwritten in Asia have largely been overlooked. IBM's donation of computers in the Philippines or Exxon's environmental spending in Australia have been downplayed. The message to those corporations that use cash, product, equipment, or land in support of organizations or government agencies that equate to 501(c)(3) or public sector institutions in the United States is, *include the value of those commitments in your social investing totals.*

Many companies will have a hard time assigning a specific value to foreign investments because of confusing accounting systems, currency fluctuations, and other variances. If that's the case, a corporation should take its best shot. This is one aspect of social investing that allows for reasonable estimates. For those suspicious critics who feel that companies will have a tendency to inflate the worth of their non-U.S. social investments, remember the disclosure report. If numbers are overstated, a corporation risks producing information for public consumption that could come back and bite it on its social investment backside. It isn't worth taking that kind of chance.

This provision in the social investment model may pique a few people for an entirely different reason. There are nations where corporations are taxed more heavily than in the United States to finance a long laundry list of social programs. Proposing that companies make social investments on top of higher tax payments aggravates some business leaders. In an era when no government, regardless how democratic or socialistic it might be, seems to be able to rustle up all the public dollars needed to carry out its mandates, those protests don't get a lot of empathy. Even in the most unlikely nations, private fund-raising initiatives are popping up to fill the gaps that public funds don't cover. Who would have ever thought there would come a day when charity "walkathons" would be sponsored in the People's Republic of China?

No matter how rich or poor, every country can develop a list of unmet community needs that can be candidates for social investing. Hence, corporations have an opportunity to apply the ten-step management process in virtually any nation where they have business interests. Remember that we're dealing with social investments, not charitable gifts. Resources need to be directed to locations where Step 2 in the investment management plan has a chance of succeeding—places where a company can generate as much business value from social investments as is allowable and practical.

So what about poorer nations that are (at best) low-priority business regions for corporations? Are they cut out of the social investing picture? Certainly not any more than they already are.

Companies have never poured much money into these overlooked corners of the world, except in response to natural disasters or other cataclysmic events. There's a good chance that some of these countries actually may be better off once social investing becomes widely adopted. In Third World locations that show promise as emerging consumer markets, social investing might be the stimulus for corporations to send more products as a means of building brand and company name awareness.

THE FOREIGN FORMULA

A few years ago, The Conference Board looked at the international philanthropy practices of twenty-five U.S. multinational businesses. In a report released in 1992, the research organization found that, on average, global contributions for this small cluster of businesses represented between 15 percent and 19 percent of their total donations. However, for some businesses in the study, international donations accounted for nearly half of their overall philanthropy.

Deciding what percent of its philanthropy spending should be reserved for countries outside the United States has always been something of a crapshoot for multinationals. Corporate social investing does away with this uncertainty. There is a clear-cut guideline that a company can follow to figure out how much of its investment total should be spent overseas: A corporation's foreign social investments should mirror its international earnings profile. If a business gets 52 percent of its profits from outside the United States, then 52 percent of its social investment funds should be allocated in non-U.S. locations.

Domestic nonprofits may not leap with joy at the prospect of having corporate investments sucked out of the United States. Keeping in mind that many large multinationals get half their profits or more from operations abroad, there's good reason for native nonprofits to worry. However, this is not as adverse a problem as it first appears for several reasons:

There's a bigger pie to cut up. Corporate social investing means that many (especially large) companies will have more money in the till than in the past when corporate philanthropy was the order of the day. Even if nondomestic investments grow dramatically, the increased size of the investment pool should allow companies to continue most of their U.S. commitments.

A company's international investment scorecard can be filled (at least in part) with existing projects and programs. Many multinationals are already making social investments abroad—it becomes a matter of counting what's being done before directing more dollars or products to foreign locations.

Products become social investment "currency" that manufacturing companies use for international investing purposes. We already know that businesses get an attractive tax benefit by making products available to certain nonprofits. (See the section on manufacturing companies in Chapter 9.) That tax advantage won't mean much, however, if product that's provided free of charge to a nonprofit ends up in a marketplace where consumers could be purchasing the goods. As a way of avoiding this potential conflict, many manufacturers direct product investments to private voluntary organizations that ship the material to locations (usually outside the United States) where the product won't sidetrack sales.

By including overseas social investments in their public reporting, numerous multinationals are going to present a vastly different picture of themselves. Many of these corporations are far more involved with educational, health care, cultural, and civic activities abroad than most would assume.

THE PRACTICE IN OTHER PARTS OF THE WORLD

Corporate support for nonprofit or public institutions is not something that is exclusive to U.S. businesses. In Japan, business contributions reached $4.8 billion in 1994, according to the World Fundraising Council. However, Japanese corporate giving has been on the decline the last few years. To the admirers of *kyosei*, a concept that describes a connective relationship between businesses and society (an association that requires businesses go beyond just providing jobs and producing goods or services), the trend is distressing. The good news is that *kyosei* provides a very fertile field for corporate social investing, which may help stimulate a resurgence in business support for selected social causes and programs in Japan.

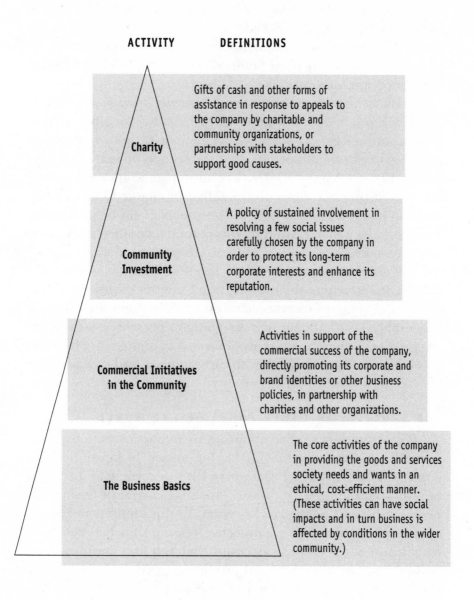

ACTIVITY   DEFINITIONS

Charity — Gifts of cash and other forms of assistance in response to appeals to the company by charitable and community organizations, or partnerships with stakeholders to support good causes.

Community Investment — A policy of sustained involvement in resolving a few social issues carefully chosen by the company in order to protect its long-term corporate interests and enhance its reputation.

Commercial Initiatives in the Community — Activities in support of the commercial success of the company, directly promoting its corporate and brand identities or other business policies, in partnership with charities and other organizations.

The Business Basics — The core activities of the company in providing the goods and services society needs and wants in an ethical, cost-efficient manner. (These activities can have social impacts and in turn business is affected by conditions in the wider community.)

Fig. 12. Template for Reporting Community Involvement

Source: "Companies in Communities: Getting the Measure"; reprinted with permission by the London Benchmarking Group

The world is filled with creative examples of partnerships between companies and private or public organizations set up to address social needs. Corporations in Western Europe, Australia and New Zealand, South Africa, Brazil, the Philippines, and other countries around the globe provide us with a long list of model programs.

In the United Kingdom, for example, a consortium of six large businesses called the London Benchmarking Group, produced a "template for reporting community involvement." (See Figure 12.) The four-layered triangle developed by the group gets very close to a full-fledged corporate social investing plan.

One member of the London Benchmarking Group deserves special acknowledgment. Grand Metropolitan (which recently merged with Guinness and is now called Diageo) produces an outstanding annual disclosure statement, a publication it calls its *Report on Corporate Citizenship*. It is a complete profile of the corporation's worldwide community activities and is worth a look by any company that's getting ready to produce a disclosure report.

The London Benchmarking Group reminds us that "private business is an integral part of all but two or three countries in the world." That translates into a tremendous number of opportunities for corporate social investing to leave its mark in virtually every corner of the globe.

What Doesn't Get Counted

A private university's ceramics department agrees to develop a new fiber optics technology for a company. The deal could mean millions in sales and profits for the corporation. The contract between the two parties requires that the university keep its work strictly confidential—whatever is discovered or produced is exclusively the property of the corporation.

The project is definitely off course for the ceramics department. The technology being developed relates only peripherally to the department's basic research activities. Nevertheless, the school is enticed into signing an agreement with the company by a fat front-end payment and the promise of lucrative royalties. This is an example of an allocation made to a nonprofit organization that does not get reported as a social investment.

RESTRICTED COMMERCIAL TRANSACTIONS

A *restricted commercial transaction* is excluded from a company's social investment total because the organization accepting the payment uses the funds for activities not consistent with its main nonprofit mission. In the case of the university doing fiber-optic research, discoveries won't enter the public domain (if they did, the company's payment might qualify as a high-impact grant or LBI). In this instance, a university plays the role of a contract research agency or a high-tech vendor that provides a proprietary service to a corporation for a price.

Whenever a business enters into an agreement with a nonprofit organization and that covenant includes words such as *confidential, proprietary, exclusive,* then some if not all the money paid to the nonprofit should not be shown as a social investment.

Note that most business-funded research projects at universities (especially public universities) are a blend of proprietary provisions and more general expenditures. Example: an agreement may state that a university will keep its work with a company confidential except for some mutually agreed-upon "intellectual properties" that the corporation has no interest in protecting. The payment that the company makes to the university is chopped up into parts that reflect this arrangement. In this case, costs that relate to research in the nonprotected intellectual domain can be counted as a social investment.

Today, universities get the majority of their research revenue from federal and state governments, not from businesses. There's a possibility that corporate social investing will trigger more business-funded research if universities and research centers can become more adept at working out ways of giving companies proprietary rights on the one hand and some social investing credit on the other.

Example: assume that a university makes a proposal to a medical device company to do clinical research. Price: $8 million. Of that amount, $5 million is for strictly proprietary work. The remaining $3 million pays for related and necessary (but not proprietary) research as well as general support services and overhead. The price is steep for the company but because it is able to deflect $3 million into its corporate social investment pool, the deal gets done. Because the corporation has implemented the ten-step management plan and will spend between 2.5 percent and 3.5 percent of its pretax earnings (based on a three-year rolling average), it has resources available that can help pay for this research agreement.

The Novartis Medical Center Alliance Program at Duke University is a good illustration of a research arrangement that *can* be counted as a social investment but also cracks open the door to future commercial contracts that *won't* qualify. Novartis—the company that grew out of a merger between the two pharmaceutical giants Sandoz and CIBA-Geigy—has committed $2.5 million to the Duke Medical Center to pay the salaries of two researchers working in the fields of psychiatry, neurology, and oncology. This basic research is quite likely to pave the way for other kinds of relationships between the company and university. If a promising discovery is made and Novartis cuts a *proprietary* deal with the Duke Clinical Research Institute, then the company needs to switch gears. The funding arrangement is no longer a corporate social investment—it is a clinical research contract with all rights restricted to the company and the university.

Although Duke has a sophisticated research arm that can lure corporations into these types of investment arrangements, many universities and nonprofit organizations don't have that built-in capacity. The company's social investment manager or management team may need to take the initiative if the corporation has a serious interest in this funding strategy. This is still another argument for finding the right people to sit on top of the social investment program within a corporation.

PRODUCT PURCHASES

Let's consider introducing the Girl Scout Cookie Dilemma. A company purchases a product from a nonprofit organization. The product gets consumed or used, but the company claims the purchase was made only because a nonprofit made the sales pitch. Like the little kid in the uniform standing on the front porch holding an order form for bakery products, the nonprofit tapped into the company's conscience and convinced the firm to do a good deed by buying something that it probably really didn't need. Is it a social investment or not?

Not.

When a business buys a product at a reasonable market rate and then uses what's been purchased, it can't claim the price paid as a social investment. It's another kind of restricted commercial transaction. If there is a heavy premium involved (the company deliberately pays way over the market rate as a means of helping out the nonprofit), just the premium might be shown as a corporate social investment. (See Exhibit 14.) However, that kind of nit-picking is usually not worth the bother.

As a general practice, forget the price paid for product purchases from nonprofits as a social investment. Those purchases don't belong on a list of social investments any more than the money that you paid for those Girl Scout cookies (or Newman's Own salad dressing) belongs on the list of charitable deductions you're taking on your own tax return.

It's important to get clarification on product purchases mainly because so many nonprofits are peddling their commercial wares in the marketplace these days. In the United States, nonprofits have a panoply of things for sale that go far beyond Thin Mints and peanut butter cookies. Greeting cards. Jewelry. Calendars. Pencils. Furniture. Clothing. Museums and other organizations have so much merchandise to sell that they've gone into the mail order catalog business.

Corporations should not try to practice social investing by buying products they don't need. There are better ways to apply corporate investment dollars. When a nonprofit offers a product that can be used by the business, a purchase decision should take into account price, quality, and competitive options. Should the corporation decide to buy something from a nonprofit, it should write it off as a general business expense—not as a social investment.

NONPROFIT SERVICE PROVIDERS

A company outsources a job to a nonprofit-sheltered workshop. The workshop employs people with disabilities to do package inserts and other labor-intensive projects. The workshop completes the assignment and bills the company for labor and materials. Should the corporation claim the money paid to the workshop as a social investment?

No.

This is another restricted commercial transaction even though the money paid to the workshop does go to advance one of its non-profit objectives—to provide training and employment opportunities for the physically and mentally challenged. In this case, the fee for service is exactly that: a payment made to get back a specified job completed.

Like product purchases, if a company were to have paid a premium to the sheltered workshop (an amount that exceeded standard market price), the firm could take social investment credit just for the dollars in excess of the customary market rate for the services provided. Trying to extrapolate those costs usually isn't worth it.

So in the absence of extraordinary circumstances, don't add fee-for-service charges to the company's list of social investments.

EMPLOYEE VOLUNTEERS

Aside from restricted commercial expenses, there's one other cost incurred by some corporations that sometimes should be excluded from the social investing total and at other times should be considered a social investment. The dollar value of the work time that employees spend volunteering for nonprofit organizations may either be in or out. To decide how to treat these costs, consider the following:

If a company keeps accurate records of the time employees are released from their jobs to do volunteer work, then calculate the value of those hours (using a median hourly rate that should be included in the company's disclosure report) and include the dollar amount in the corporation's social investment total. However, *if a company does not carefully monitor company-compensated time* for volunteer service (most companies don't), avoid trying to place a monetary value on volunteerism.

EXCEPTIONS

A lot of companies have employee volunteer programs and they range in size and format. In some corporations, the cumulative impact of employee volunteerism is awesome. IBM, for example, estimated that its employees accounted for *3.8 million hours* of volunteer time in 1995. Here are a few other examples:

United Parcel Service. UPS managers get their regular pay while on loan for three or four weeks to nonprofit community service projects. The UPS Community Internship Program has been under way for over thirty years.

Timberland Company. The company gives thirty-two hours of paid time a year to employees who get involved in community work.

Prudential Insurance Company of America. The firm holds a companywide volunteer day around the world. In 1995, its first year, over six thousand employees worked on more than two hundred local projects.

AT&T. The company gave all 127,000 employees a paid day off to do volunteering.

Charles Schwab. The company spent $1 million to bring nine hundred executives to San Francisco to build houses and renovate schools in low-income neighborhoods.

Xerox. Twenty employees at the company's print-cartridge production plant in Webster, New York, are working faster and harder each month in order to free up one day a month to teach reading to children enrolled in a Rochester elementary school.

There are hundreds and hundreds of other company-based volunteer programs going on around the country. It needs to be pointed out that although some businesses give employees time off the job to work with nonprofit organizations, this is not typical. A 1997 poll by *USA Today,* CNN, and Gallup found that 52 percent of one thousand workers surveyed said their companies wouldn't allow them to take paid time off for volunteer work even if they asked. Only 14 percent of those included in the research were employed by companies that actively sponsor programs that permit workers to volunteer on company time.

A view of the full corporate landscape also shows that relatively few businesses have the mechanisms in place to track (a) what employees are doing with their volunteer time, and (b) what that donated time is really worth. Which all leads to this conclusion: *the majority of corporations should not consider including the dollar value of employee volunteer time as a part of their social investment totals.*

What companies with organized employee volunteer programs *should* do is to acknowledge their volunteerism activities as a separate statement in their social investment disclosure reports. When presented that way, there's nothing wrong with using rough estimates of the dollar value of employee volunteer time. However, as already suggested, except in unusual cases where businesses carefully track company-compensated volunteer hours, the figures should be run alongside (not as a part of) the company's cash, product, equipment, and land social investment total.

There are corporations that point to the number of volunteer hours donated by employees as their main commitment to the nonprofit sector. In these cases, the corporation usually is taking credit for the time employees volunteer after work. The estimated value of those hours should not be used in any calculation of a company's social investing total.

Social investing may prime the pump for more after-hours, noncompensated employee volunteerism. Many nonprofit organizations that get cash or product social investments also are able to enlist company employees as volunteers. So as the ten-step management plan pushes companies to make new investments with other outside organizations, it is predictable that employee volunteerism will also grow.

11

Step 8.
When Social Investing
Should Be Postponed

I f Step 7 puts a knot in a CEO's stomach, Step 8 should help untie it. This is corporate social investing's emergency brake:

Step 8. Postpone some or all corporate social investing if projected business conditions warrant such action.

What a company budgets for social investing this year is largely a shadow of the corporation's past; it's the by-product of profits generated over the previous three years. When a corporation runs up a string of successes, everything is rosy. In the afterglow of its financial achievements, a company calculates how much it should be spending for social investing in the year ahead and plugs that amount into its budget.

But what happens if a company's sales and earnings are projected to flatten out during the next twelve months, or worse, what happens if the crystal ball says the company is headed for an even more serious tailspin? This is when senior management puts its foot on the eighth step in the social investment management model.

In the best of times, corporate social investing comes with a huge upside for nonprofit organizations—more money, more corporate involvement in nonprofit activities, more partnerships that lead to added federal and private funding, and so on. However, like most things in life, higher rewards usually mean greater risk.

Nonprofits that stand to gain from a corporation's financial accomplishments also have to be prepared to take a few body punches if a company's fiscal pulse begins to weaken. Should a dark cloud happen to park itself over a corporation, nonprofits need to be aware that a business can invoke Step 8, which gives the company some relief from the minimum investment requirements of Step 7.

If nonprofit organizations are going to find any comfort at all in the eighth step, it will be in the word *postpone.* The objective isn't to wipe out social investments that might have been planned for the year ahead but rather to delay funding them until a company's economic health has improved. Of course, if a company can't climb out of a financial sandpit, postponement is just another word for default.

Three Tips

Caution: Step 8 can be abused. Because many businesses start each fiscal year with at least some trepidation, there is a tendency to want to hold back money (and sometimes even product) for corporate social investing until there is a better feel for how sales and profits will shape up over the first couple of quarters. This is tricky business for those who manage the investment process. Here are three tips for making sure that Step 8 isn't used inappropriately to squash the life out of social investing:

THE 50-PERCENT RULE

It's smart to design a social investing budget so that at least half the spending will occur after midyear (this doesn't mean the budget is reduced at the start of the year—just that half the allocations are scheduled for payment at a later date). This should give the company a modicum of confidence that if the emergency brake had to be applied at any time during the first six months, the corporation could reduce or postpone up to 50 percent of its planned investment expenses.

If management pushes for a reduction in the social investment budget at the beginning of the year with the whispered promise that "the money can always be restored later on if the company does okay," the investment manager should strike back with this argument, "Don't decimate our budget just because you think there may be thin ice ahead. If things aren't going well six months from now, we've worked it out so that we can defer a lot of our third and fourth quarter spending to the next fiscal year."

It's a big mistake to knuckle under to those who want to shrink a social investing budget before the opening bell of a fiscal year. Step 8 shouldn't become a paring knife that's used to prematurely emasculate an investment spending plan. It is meant to be activated only when there is indisputable evidence that a corporation is hemorrhaging.

LINE ITEM

If social investing is considered a frill or an "on-the-side" expense going into the fiscal year, it's just waiting for trouble. Social investing deserves to be a specific line item in the budget.

The person assigned to handle the ten-step social investment management plan for a company should go to the mat with anyone who wants to turn those investments into a budgeting postscript. Investments are not added baggage; they are expenditures that, if managed right, return value to the business. As such, they shouldn't be allowed to dangle from the corporation's financial torso where they can too easily be lopped off.

SELL, SELL, SELL

If social investing isn't constantly sold as something that has business value, it may get an early visit from the company's cost-cutters. Gravity tends to pull management's opinion back to the old days when anything handed out to a nonprofit organization was considered plain-vanilla philanthropy. The notion that social investing is capable of pushing the business in the right direction can be lost unless that message is reinforced.

Whoever is in charge of social investments has to do whatever it takes to keep the concept in the limelight. Long before it comes time to decide the fate of social investing in next year's budget, that manager should have softened up the company with evidence of how investments have helped the business. The objective is to sell relentlessly and to enlist a squad of influential people in the company who really understand and appreciate social investing. (See Chapter 12.)

Optional Payback

There is no doubt that some companies (unfortunately) are going to find it necessary to use the emergency brake. As noted, taking that step may mean postponing part of this year's social investment agenda until a later time, or it could result in cuts that will *not* be covered in future budgets. This latter provision needs to be made very clear: *Step 8 doesn't absolutely obligate a company to pay for any social investments it defers.*

Of course, a company can increase its investments in a future year to make up for whatever reductions it chooses to make now. However, that isn't likely to happen in most cases. It's more probable that corporations will work toward reinstating their usual level of social investing, and any plans to support certain nonprofits that were swept aside in the past just won't be carried out.

"This deal smells like it just came out of the private-sector pork barrel," a nonprofit manager might conclude after being introduced to Step 8. "Companies can cut their social investments by crying wolf and then never pay any penalty for that kind of game-playing."

It's possible that some corporations may try to abuse the eighth step. However, because companies that claim to be practicing full-scale social investing have to disclose their social investments on a regular basis, this tactic will be difficult to disguise. So if a company is consistently making money and consistently rides the emergency brake, then something is wrong. Stakeholders have every reason to come down hard on that business. After all, that's not what Step 8 is about. It's a privilege that's only to be used if the corporation is in serious financial trouble.

As to the optional payback provision, it's understandable why nonprofits that are scrambling for every spare coin might think this is just too easy a way for businesses to get off the hook. But remember, social investing only works if a company is able to attain and sustain a strong profit position. The emergency brake will never need to be applied if a corporation's earnings stay even or continue to grow. The money cut from social investing during the bad times is a concession the nonprofit world has to make as a means of getting a corporation back in business. If a company chooses to restore whatever funds were cut at some later time, that's great. If not, well, that's not as important as resuscitating the company so that it can resume a stable social investing program in the future.

Step 9.
Building the
Management Team for
Social Investing

The Home Depot—the ubiquitous chain of building supply and home improvement stores—says that it directs about 45 percent of its philanthropy budget to "affordable housing" projects. This is a company that has its corporate contributions marching in step with its main business mission. What's more, Home Depot has both a CEO and a president who make no bones about the firm's concern for corporate social responsibility. Although this company may not have adopted all ten management principles, it has embraced many of the model's components.

When the Home Depot opens one of its warehouse-sized stores in a new market, the business quickly hoists its community-relations colors. The company provides money and employee time to programs such as Habitat for Humanity (the Jimmy Carter–supported home-building initiative that constructs low-income housing around the nation). In some locations, the corporation even mobilizes Team Depot squads of employees to work on community-based home-rebuilding projects.

Home Depot is not a cut-a-check-and-be-done-with-it kind of organization. Many people working for the business are up to their eyebrows in community affairs. Getting a large and growing organization to adopt this kind of get-involved behavior would be virtually impossible if there were not a group of managers at the top of the business who continually stress the need for employees to remain connected to the outside world.

Even the company's president and COO, Arthur Blank, comes on strong when talking about what he calls "the company-community connection." Blank reminds business executives that an investment in the community buys an important benefit for the corporation: leadership development. "If you want to develop managers in your company, send them into the community to build their skills," Blank says and credits management guru Peter Drucker for giving him that insight.

There's a lesson to be learned here, and it has to do with enlisting the right kind of support network for a corporate social investing program. This is so important that it is the basis for our management plan's ninth step:

Step 9. Lock in influential line and staff leaders as co-owners of the corporate social investing program.

Successful corporate social investing requires the right kind of help. Granted, there needs to be an effective day-to-day manager at the helm. (See Chapter 13.) But it also helps to have an ample number of people in the boat who have the collective muscle to pull the oars.

The Corporate Social Investment Management Team

The best way to lock in a cross section of influential individuals in the organization is to make sure they have a piece of the action. The more managers feel that they own part of the process, the more involved they will be. Getting a few handpicked managers engaged in a corporate social investment management team can work wonders for a company. Here's how to put together the right group of people:

Step 9. Building the Management Team for Social Investing

THE CEO DOES THE ASKING

"This is important to our business, and to me. It's not going to take a lot of your time and if you handle the job properly, it's going to help you and the people under you be more successful."

Nothing can do more to make things happen than a few words from the boss.

TEAM MEETINGS ARE FEW AND FAR BETWEEN

The team doesn't need to meet that often—two, three, maybe four times a year will suffice for most businesses. The most important reason for the team to get together is to debate, shape, and ultimately bless the company's annual corporate social investment plan. That may take a couple of meetings. Once the plan has been approved, day-to-day managers can take over, with the team reconvened only on occasion to make sure the plan remains on track. In general, the fewer meetings the better; any business meeting is a potential organizational bog that should be posted with this sign: *Warning! Interest and enthusiasm may get stuck or buried here! Proceed only if necessary!*

EACH TEAM MEMBER GETS AN ASSIGNMENT

This is where a company can expect a big payoff. Each team member is given responsibility for a part of the overall social investment program that's relevant to the individual's own business interests. The social investment manager and staff will handle administrative needs linked to the team member's assignment. However, the team member remains accountable for one important job: to obtain as much business value from the social investment as is allowable and practical (Step 2 of our management plan).

RECOGNITION AND CREDIT GET SPREAD AROUND

Team members who deliver the goods in the form of successful social investment projects deserve acknowledgment inside the company—and where appropriate, the CEO should do the stroking. Team members also should get top billing when social investing puts the company into a public spotlight. Press releases, photo opportunities, check presentations—they all should feature the team member as the corporate representative.

How many people should be on a team? Size will vary by company, but somewhere between five and fifteen members should work for most businesses. More important than mass, though, is composition.

Example: SmithKline Beecham convened a corporate task force in 1995 to redesign its community and charitable activities worldwide so that the corporation would be more in sync with its business interests. Ten senior executives from different segments of the company were "invited" by the CEO to participate in the project. This is the kind of executive involvement and top-down endorsement that a good social investment team needs.

Staffing for Social Investing

The corporate philanthropy world is the best place to visit when trying to benchmark staffing models that will work for corporate social investing programs. Once inside that world, however, it quickly becomes clear that there is little uniformity in the way in which companies assign people to carry out contributions responsibilities. For instance, the clothing chain The Gap has an $8 million company foundation that is administered by a staff of ten; AlliedSignal runs its $10 million program with a staff of two.

These two corporations' programs illustrate the extremes that exist in the corporate contributions field. Staffing is often a factor of (a) how much centralized control a company wants to maintain over its philanthropy and (b) how much "ownership" can be parceled out to other operating units in the corporation. Businesses that delegate specific contribution projects or programs to line and staff personnel outside the contributions office may not seem to have a large philanthropy organization, but in reality, these organizations may actually have a small army of people putting in hours and days of work that add up to several FTEs (full-time equivalents).

Exhibit 15 shows that in many companies, the number of people who spend all their time at work administering philanthropy programs is shrinking. Even taking these staff reductions into account, the exhibit makes it clear that there remains a wide variance in manpower numbers when it comes to the administration of corporate philanthropy.

Step 9. Building the Management Team for Social Investing

	Number of Employees 1991	1996
American Express	17	12
Amoco	14	9
Apple Computer	14	5
AT&T	25	15
Bell Atlantic	7	2
Chevron	15	10
Citicorp	13	8
Digital	14	4
IBM	72	19
NYNEX	18	12

Exhibit 15. Corporate Contributions Staffs, Major U.S. Corporations

Source: *Chronicle of Philanthropy,* July 11, 1996

What happens as companies convert their corporate philanthropy into social investing?

Overall, there may be a slight increase in the number of people working full-time on corporate social investing activities (compared with the head count in existing corporate philanthropy offices). There are two reasons for the increase: First, there's more to do. Social investing encompasses more territory since it includes LBIs and other nonprofit commitments that probably are not part of most corporate philanthropy programs. Second, social investing picks up the tab for administration costs—the payroll can be folded into the corporate social investment total that a company reports each year.

There may be a temptation to overstaff the social investment office when a business that adheres to the ten-step plan realizes that money can be drawn from its investment budget (which, as we now know, is equal to at least 2.5 percent to 3.5 percent of the firm's averaged PTNI) to pay the management bill. The counterforce that works against building up too large a staff is the annual disclosure report. Carrying too much administrative weight could raise a lot of questions.

Of course there are times when companies *can* justify a larger-than-normal head count. Some social investment partnerships require significant staff time if they are to return those benefits a business wants and expects. These differences in social investment strategies and programs make it impossible to present a hard and fast formula for calculating staff numbers and administrative costs that will work for every business. As a way of offering *some* guidance, however, Exhibit 16 presents what should be considered the minimum staffing numbers and administrative budgets for businesses with different size investment programs.

Annual Soc. Invst Payout (in millions)	Payout Percent for Staffing	Est. Cost	Personnel Numbers			
			Exempt	Nonexempt	Pt. Time	Consults.
Under $5	10.0% or less	Varies	—All part-time workers—			
$5	7.0	$350,000	1	1	1	$25,000
$10	6.0	600,000	2	1	2	50,000
$15	5.0	750,000	2	2	1	75,000
$20	5.0	1,000,000	3	2	2	100,000
$25	5.0	1,250,000	3	2	2	125,000
$30	5.0	1,500,000	4	3	2	150,000
$35	4.5	1,600,000	5	4	2	175,000
$40	4.5	1,800,000	6	4	3	200,000
$45	4.0	1,900,000	6	4	3	225,000
$50	4.0	2,000,000	7	5	3	250,000
$75	3.0	2,250,000	8	6	4	275,000
$100	3.0	3,000,000	9	7	5	300,000

Exhibit 16. Corporate Social Investment Programs: Minimum Staffing Recommendations

The exhibit suggests that companies with smaller annual investment payouts (under $5 million a year) don't need full-time staffs. This is a bit misleading. The programs may actually have one, two, or more of those FTEs mentioned previously who are taking time from their regular jobs to work on investment projects and activities. The part-timer who's assigned the day-to-day responsibility for the program might typically be using 50 percent to 60 percent of his or her workday or workweek on investment affairs. Some of that time should be used to prod, encourage, guide, and coordinate members of the corporate social investment management team or other employees who have taken on investment side jobs.

Businesses with larger (over $5 million) programs should have dedicated full-time people whose only responsibility is social investment administration. Even when a business has such a staff, that doesn't erase the need for FTEs—other personnel in different parts of the company (finance, tax, public relations, and so on) should be lending an occasional hand. That's the whole point of Step 9, to get as many co-owners of the social investment program and process as possible.

Location, Location, Location

Public relations, public affairs, human resources, government and community relations, general administration, finance, and even the office of the general counsel—these are all possible venues for social investing. In fact, all of these locations have been known addresses for corporate philanthropy programs in the past. So there is precedence for setting up a social investing office in any one of these departments or divisions.

Because the dynamics of no two businesses are alike, there is no one best place for the social investing management function in a corporation. It might thrive in Company A's public relations department but get stifled by the public relations office in Company B. Here are a couple of touchstones that should help a company decide where to locate social investing so it has the greatest chance of success:

THE EXECUTIVE TO WHOM THE SOCIAL INVESTING FUNCTION REPORTS IS AN ADVOCATE

Sometimes the *who* is more important than the *where*. There's nothing like a cheerleader to get social investing the internal credibility and organizational outreach it needs to be successful.

THE LOCATION GIVES SOCIAL INVESTING EXPOSURE TO LINE MANAGEMENT BUSINESS DECISION MAKING

It's tough to make social investing work for a company if it isn't consistently rubbing noses with other departments and divisions that are making day-to-day business decisions.

195

If there is such a thing as an ideal model for social investing, it would be an organization design where the function is on equal footing with other prominent staff functions like public relations and government affairs. In larger businesses, all those operations may be under the command of one senior executive (for example, the executive vice president for external or public affairs) who reports directly to the CEO or COO. (See Figure 13.) In smaller companies, organization patterns are more fluid. But regardless of how big or small a company might be, the goal should be the same: give social investing its own identity and status so that it has a shot of making the ten-step management plan work.

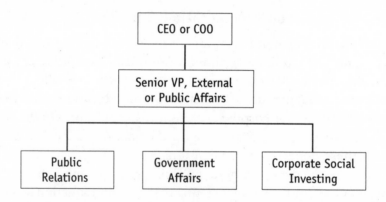

Fig. 13. "Ideal" Large-Company Organization Design

A WORD ABOUT COMPANY FOUNDATIONS

A number of businesses have corporate foundations as part of their philanthropy programs. Foundations are themselves non-profit entities that have their own officers and boards of directors. But where does the foundation sit inside the business? If it is managed by a *lower-level manager* buried three, four, or more layers from the top of the business, then it's the wrong organizational design for handling corporate social investments.

This is not a call to eliminate corporate foundations. They have a role to play even after a company makes the shift from philanthropy to corporate social investing. They are mechanisms that can be used to provide businesses with worthwhile tax benefits—particularly those corporations that have appreciated land or stock (possibly inherited as part of an acquisition) that can be quite literally donated to these self-created foundations. Multiyear donations and international contributions are often easier to manage through company foundations than if paid directly by a corporation. So these foundations are a useful tool for some (certainly not all) businesses.

What a foundation *shouldn't* be is a substitute for a strong internal corporate social investing program.

Using Consultants

Although consultants are sometimes given a jaundiced eye, they can be valuable to a company. A competent consultant can be an asset, particularly in meeting some of a company's social investing management needs.

A few places where consultants shine are project planning and administration, program measurement, and technology services. In any of these areas, a competent consultant can often stay focused on a specific task. That's something that's difficult to do for someone working in a corporate social investment department who's juggling many different balls at the same time.

If a corporation has a lean staff, consultants may be an absolute requirement in carrying out major investment programs. Because consultant costs are allowable as administrative charges, they can and should be included in a company's social investment total.

In some instances, public opinion, marketing, or public relations firms can be called on to provide consulting services. Impact assessment, for example, is not something that most companies have the capacity to tackle using internal resources. A recent study of 177 of the country's largest companies found that 56 percent made no attempt to measure the effectiveness of their philanthropic programs. It's not likely that corporate social investment programs will be measured any more frequently than philanthropic activities—unless a company budgets for some outside help.

Technology is also an area where consultants can save a business more money in false starts and bad choices than in what they charge for their time. There are software, hardware, phone, fax, and Internet experts out there by the bushel. Consultants who have helped businesses design, update, or evaluate technologies in the external affairs field, and who get good references from their clients, should be the pick of the litter.

Beware: consultants don't always come cheap. Their rates can run $300 or more per hour. Well-known management consulting companies usually charge by the project and can be very high-priced. In an attempt to save a few dollars, some businesses use retirees as external affairs consultants. The fees are much lower ($500 a day is not unusual), but corporations need to be sure that retirees have the skills needed to successfully handle consulting assignments.

Note that a few big-hitting consulting and public relations firms are beginning to dip their toes in the strategic philanthropy waters—which is an indication that there is an increasing demand for outside services in this field. The most recent organization to take the splash is Hill & Knowlton, the heavyweight public relations firm. "Consumers and investors look at a company's track record as a corporate citizen when making their purchase or buying decisions," Hill & Knowlton observes when explaining why it is mobilizing a seventeen-member team to work in this part of the business world.

Perhaps the best advice for using consultants is to start slowly and use caution. Give a consultant or agency a small-scale project and see how it flies. In time, a good social investment manager will have identified a few competent consultants who can be called upon to supplement the management requirements of the company's social investment program.

Step 10.
The Day-to-Day
Manager

Corporate social investing has little hope of meeting its expectations without competent day-to-day leadership. The difference between a sluggish, lackluster program and a highly energized, robust initiative often comes down to a single individual—the person who's holding the management reins.

It is not only essential to find the right corporate social investment manager but also critical that the individual be positioned at a level high enough in the corporation to (a) collect the information needed to make good decisions, (b) interact with other senior executives in the company, and (c) command attention and respect from those inside and outside the business. These points lead us to the tenth and final management step:

> *Step 10. Assign day-to-day management responsibility for corporate social investing to a position that is no more than one executive away from the CEO or COO.*

This is a big change from the way corporate philanthropy programs have historically been managed in many—particularly large—businesses. The point person for a corporate contributions program is often several layers down from the chief executive. With corporate social investing, that won't work. The function must be elevated to a higher executive level.

Whoever holds the top management post has responsibility for all aspects of the social investing program. In smaller businesses, managers will probably be handling this assignment along with many other tasks. As a general rule, for companies spending between $2 million and $5 million on nonprofit investing, managers should be working half-time on corporate social investment matters. When a program grows to $5 million or more, a corporation should consider assigning a full-time manager to the function.

The Right Manager

Competent day-to-day social investment managers can be recruited from just about anywhere in a company. This isn't a job limited to those who have a background in public relations or community relations—or to employees working in marketing or human resources departments. People from finance, manufacturing, law, or virtually any other part of a corporation may emerge as outstanding candidates. As of now, there is no one career path that leads to the top corporate social investing post.

When a business is searching for someone to take on the day-to-day management challenges of its investment program, it should keep an eye out for candidates who have certain characteristics.

KNOW THE BUSINESS

To date, this has been one of the big weaknesses in corporate philanthropy management. Too frequently, those charged with administering corporate contributions are disconnected from the mainstream profit-and-loss activities of their own companies. They don't have a good grasp of the corporation's finances, aren't aware of product lines, and get little or no information about new business developments.

To be really effective, a social investment manager has to be a business generalist. He or she has to be in the thick of things in order to know how and when to leverage social investment resources.

HAVE BASIC BUSINESS MANAGEMENT SKILLS

It takes a very savvy businessperson to leverage investment resources so that they benefit the company as well as the nonprofit or exclusively public institutions that receive assistance. That requires a keen awareness of strategic planning, budgeting, marketing, business development, public relations, and other functions.

The day-to-day manager position should not be a pasture for some tired executive who lacks the energy to stay current with new management practices and technologies—and it certainly shouldn't be a place for a marginal administrator who's operating on cruise control.

HAVE AN AWARENESS AND INTEREST IN THE NONPROFIT AND PUBLIC SECTORS

The management job will be difficult to do if the manager doesn't have a finger on what's happening outside the business. It's not necessary to be a Renaissance man or woman—however, the position does require some peripheral vision that enables the executive to see beyond the company gate.

There needs to be some balance in the manager's approach to external affairs. A fanatical, save-the-world type would be the wrong choice for this job. A much better manager would be an executive who has a genuine interest in social issues and problems, someone who is likely to be more creative in coming up with ways to blend a company's interests with outside opportunities.

HAVE THE RESPECT OF FELLOW EXECUTIVES

Anything that's not a profit center in a corporation runs the risk of assuming second-cousin status in the business. That's certainly the case with corporate social investing, which some may write off as a useless, pointless drag on profits.

By putting a proven business executive into the day-to-day manager's job, the image and reputation of corporate social investing immediately moves up a notch or two. Here's where the CEO can play a vital role by sending out a message that empowers the manager. With a strong endorsement from the top, the day-to-day manager will be playing on the team rather than spending time on the sidelines.

BE AN EFFECTIVE REPRESENTATIVE FOR THE CORPORATION

Next to the CEO and perhaps one or two others in the corporation, the social investment manager may emerge as one of the most visible standard-bearers for the company. This is a person who's in the face of one external constituency after another. For the sake of the company's reputation, the individual had better be knowledgeable, respectable, articulate, and good with people.

Compensation and Title

The day-to-day manager should be compensated at the same level as other staff executives who are separated by only one position from the CEO or COO. Using pay and benefits provided to corporate philanthropy and community relations executives as benchmarks, full-time compensation could range from under $75,000 in smaller businesses to over $250,000 in larger corporations (exclusive of deferred income and other perks).

The manager should be given a title commensurate with how the position fits into the company's organization chart. In larger corporations, the job will most likely be a corporate staff vice president position. In smaller companies, titles will vary widely, from director, chief, manager, to vice president. Make no mistake about it: for this job, the title *is* important—not so much for the manager's status *outside* the company, but for how the individual is regarded *inside* the business. The title needs to send a signal to other employees that this position has weight.

Training and Education

As a general rule, it is usually easier to train someone inside a company to manage a corporate social investment program than it is to import an outsider into the business, even if that individual happens to have had social investment experience elsewhere. Remember that the manager has to know the business in order to make the most of the ten-step management plan; an insider will usually prove the right choice. Of course, there are exceptions. However, it will usually be in the company's best interest to do a thorough internal search before turning to outside candidates.

Regardless of what background or experience a day-to-day social investment manager might have, a corporation will want assurance that the individual has the fundamental knowledge and skills needed to get the job done. This isn't a worry only for businesses with big investment programs. Even companies with very small corporate social investment budgets where managers spend 25 percent or less of their time on the function should have a similar concern. How does a company know if its manager has the right stuff? Or where can a corporation send a manager (or anyone else working with the firm's social investments) to be trained in the basics?

For corporations with well-run, long-established philanthropy programs, there may be management talent on the scene who can shift into corporate social investment roles without a lot of front-end learning. Many of these people already are well grounded in planning, budgeting, and program development. Converting to social investing could be a do-it-yourself exercise for some who already hold these top-end corporate philanthropy management jobs. Companies that have two or more people working full-time on contributions programs will want to think seriously about giving their junior managers basic training in corporate social investing. It's a good way to create "bench strength" within the management team.

SOME TRAINING RESOURCES

The logical next question is Where do you go to get trained?

THE CONFERENCE BOARD

The Conference Board runs two-day management seminars on corporate contributions in different parts of the country. These are not corporate social investment courses per se but still give participants a good overview of how some best-of-class corporate philanthropy programs operate. The Conference Board programs are usually taught by practitioners in the field (generally contributions administrators) and frequently take on a here's-how-we-do-it-at-our-place tone. These real-life, real-time examples can be very helpful.

The Conference Board seminars also give attendees a good look at new technologies in the field—outsourcing services for matching gift programs, new software systems for managing payments to nonprofits, and so on. The two largest vendors of these products are often on hand at the events. For more information about these seminars, contact the research organization's main office at: *The Conference Board Inc., Customer Service Dept., P.O. Box 4026, Church Street Station, New York, NY 10261-4026. Web page: www.conference-board.org. E-mail: info@conference-board.org.*

THE CENTER FOR CORPORATE COMMUNITY RELATIONS, BOSTON COLLEGE

The Center for Corporate Community Relations at Boston College offers certificate programs at the school's Alumni House in Newton, Massachusetts (with the exception of one program that's conducted during the summer in Canada). The center schedules programs around specific organizational topics that include a general orientation to corporate community relations, strategic planning, developing operational plans for community relations, program evaluation, communicating with key publics, and strategic contributions.

As the center's name implies, the programs come with a strong community relations slant. Still, the short-term training provided is timely, practical, and affordable. For more information, contact: *The Center for Corporate Community Relations at Boston College, Chestnut Hill, MA 02167-3835. Web page: http://www.bc.edu/cccr/ E-mail: CCCR@bc.edu.*

CORPORATE CONTRIBUTIONS MANAGEMENT ACADEMY

A new management education program designed for contributions, community relations, public relations, and any other managers engaged in corporate contributions or social investing is the

Corporate Contributions Management Academy. Run by Business & Nonprofit Strategies Inc., the academy offers an intensive four-day program covering the fundamentals of contributions management (strategic planning, budgeting, tax issues, staffing, outcomes measurement, and so on).

The academy does include a segment on moving from corporate philanthropy to social investing. The program is a basic-training opportunity for contributions managers (especially those fairly new to the job), company foundation directors, contributions committee members, product-giving coordinators, and special event and public relations personnel. All academy programs are conducted at a conference center in Palm Coast, Florida.

For more information about the Academy, contact: *Corporate Contributions Management Academy, 138 Palm Coast Parkway. (Suite 115), Palm Coast, FL 32137. Web site: http://www.BNSInc.com. E-mail address: Director@BNSInc.com.*

OTHER ORGANIZATIONS

Other organizations occasionally conduct management education workshops or programs for contributions and community relations staffers. The Council on Foundations, Public Affairs Council, INDEPENDENT SECTOR, and a few higher education institutions (for example, Indiana University Center on Philanthropy, Harvard, and MIT among others) periodically provide resource materials and training that might be useful to social investment managers and others. In addition, a number of professional publications can prove helpful to managers—*BSR News Monitor* (*Business for Social Responsibility*), *Corporate Philanthropy Report,* and *The Chronicle of Philanthropy* are excellent resources. Among other useful periodicals are *Corporate Community Relations Letter, Philanthropy Roundtable,* and *Foundation & Corporate Grants Alert.*

A Word about Outside Affiliations

Any external affairs job in a corporation is prone to the seduction of outside activities and organizations. The opportunities to spend time away from the office are infinite—invitations to serve on nonprofit boards or to participate in policy forums, professional or trade association events, special commissions, and so on.

As one of the main flag-bearers for a corporation, the corporate social investment manager is usually on the invitation list put together by many nonprofit associations and organizations. There are definitely occasions when the manager *should* be a player in carefully selected outside activities and functions. However, remember that first and foremost the manager has a responsibility to the company—to pinch as much business value as possible out of the social investments the corporation elects to make. In most cases, that means the manager should plan to spend a majority of time working inside a company, not outside.

Social investment managers should use discretion in accepting any type of nonprofit board position or committing to special projects or events that are not directly connected to the company's business interests. A giant force outside the business is constantly pulling on a corporate social investment manager's time. To succumb too frequently to that force will make it difficult if not impossible for the manager to deliver the maximum social investment benefits to a corporation.

Making It Work

The year was 1982.

"The major sandbag for the socially conscious executive is in the corporate world itself," Thomas Drohan observed. The speech by the president of Foremost-McKesson was not only a statement of the day but a prophecy that would hold for nearly two decades.

"It is absolutely chilling," Drohan went on to tell an executive symposium, "that fewer than 30 percent of all U.S. corporations give anything, and only 6 percent give more than $500 a year to charity."

Drohan speculated about why corporations were so miserly when it came to supporting nonprofit organizations. He pointed to a "missing ingredient" that causes businesses to come up short in their charitable giving. "Like the Purloined Letter," he said, "what's missing is right under our collective noses." Then he delivered the punch line: "That missing ingredient is very simply—a goal. No one really knows how much corporations in particular, or business in general, should be targeting."

America's private sector was mum. Drohan's call for a common goal that all companies could use to calculate their philanthropy never did materialize. However, whether because of Drohan's urging or for several other reasons, businesses began carving out a higher percentage of their profits for charitable giving, a trend that continued through the mid-1980s. Then in 1987, corporate generosity began to slide back. As we have already pointed out, by 1996 businesses were giving about 45 percent less of their profits to charity than they had been donating only ten years before.

It has been a long time coming, but Drohan's missing ingredient finally has arrived. *Corporate Social Investing* sets a clear, fair, and attainable goal for every profit-making company in America. Note: this isn't a corporate philanthropy goal. Instead, it's a target that comes bundled in a package called corporate social investing, a process that transforms a company's beneficence into a powerful business and societal resource. The words *corporate philanthropy* are gone—obliterated from the private-sector lexicon. The new model in town is corporate social investing, and it is hard to miss because it rides a ten-speed management plan that's available to any company that wants it.

Corporate social investing is a *business* concept. One of its objectives is to make a company more profitable by establishing creative, productive relationships with nonprofit and public organizations. A company's justification for making this kind of investment is to realize as much business value as is allowable and practical.

The Basic Process

A corporate social investing program doesn't have to be complex. In fact, the simpler the ten-step plan is, the more companies are likely to grasp and support it. When reduced to its rudiments, social investing is a five-part process.

COUNT

With only a few exceptions, virtually every dollar, product, piece of equipment, or parcel of land that a corporation turns over to a nonprofit or exclusively public organization counts as a social investment. It all begins with an inventory of what a company is doing now to support nonprofits or exclusively public organizations. Memberships, research, sponsorships, special events, gifts and grants—they all add up. The total dollar value will be surprising (and in a few cases, even astounding) to many companies.

PLAN

File a flight plan before taking off. Use the RODES system (see Chapter 10) to set the right course to get the most return for the business from whatever cash or noncash investment is being made.

INVEST

Spend a minimum of 2.5 percent (3.5 percent for manufacturing companies that donate product) of an average of the company's last three years of pretax net income. However, don't think of the payments as charitable gifts, even though some might qualify as charitable tax deductions. Instead, view every commitment as an investment that should be returning value to the company.

DISCLOSE

Explain in writing what your company is doing with its social investments—and why. Be liberal with facts, light on rhetoric.

MANAGE

To get a corporate social investment program to pan out, competent management is a must. The individual overseeing the responsibility should be in the upper atmosphere of the company. However, social investing is not a one-person show. A team of influential executives should be part owners of the enterprise.

Bypassing the Big Problems?

An often-heard complaint about corporate contributions and philanthropy in general is that gifts and grants too often migrate to organizations that aren't dealing with the roughest and toughest social problems. The argument goes something like this: Harvard and the Metropolitan Museum of Art get the big dollars while the local soup kitchen has trouble finding scraps.

Even volunteerism comes under that kind of criticism, and with some justification. Less than 10 percent of volunteer work in the United States has an impact on the poor; only 4 percent is directed at helping needy children. So what about corporate social investing? Being so business-driven, aren't these payments (and the employee volunteer time that often follows the money) more likely to end up benefiting organizations that aren't dealing with America's most serious human problems?

That's a possibility. However, a lot of social issues and needs make for solid social investment opportunities. Feeding the hungry, immunizing children who live in poverty, housing the homeless, educating the disadvantaged—these can be the springboards that lead to LBIs, high-impact grants, and conditional grants. Several corporations have already discovered that these issues can be translated into causes that will attract customers, make points with the media, and win new respect from legislators.

If corporate social investing is widely embraced, the level of business support for nonprofit organizations will increase. Some of that money and noncash investing will follow already-established company channels into human service agencies and institutions. Other resources may be added as companies recognize that many 501(c)(3) organizations that deal with basic human needs and quality-of-life issues can help them release the full power of their social investments.

An Easy Journey?

As long as corporations practice "philanthropy," they'll remain caught in a vise. On one side, small numbers of irked stakeholders will continue to challenge companies to justify why they are giving away corporate profits. On the other side, businesses will take flak for being inexcusably penurious when it comes to social responsibility.

Once corporations accept and implement social investing, the squeeze should ease. But will corporate social investing actually take hold? There are indications that it will. A number of companies have already made the leap from philanthropy to a different way of thinking about how to leverage resources that once were considered handouts:

> *At the Monsanto Fund . . . the word "giving" has been banned.*
>
> —John Mason, president of the Monsanto Fund

I certainly don't use the word philanthropy anymore.
      —Joe Hale, president of the Cinergy
      Foundation

*We do things for strategic endeavors—this is a weapon for
Motorola . . . our competitors are formidable.*
      —Roberta Guttmann, executive director of the
      Motorola Foundation

These statements are from executives paid to manage funding relationships between companies and nonprofits. One might wonder whether the captains of industry share these points of view. Actually, many do. Ameritech CEO Jacqueline Woods, for example, notes that there is no shortage of business potential at "the intersection of corporate and community needs." More than a few private-sector leaders are standing at that very intersection and they're looking for ways to tap that potential.

The Power of Corporate-Nonprofit Alliances

A multitude of impressive corporate-nonprofit initiatives dot the private-sector landscape:

- ▶ Aetna and U.S. Healthcare are spending $7 million to educate women about heart disease and stroke.

- ▶ Microsoft and the American Association of Retired Persons (AARP) are collaborating to run Lifetime Connection seminars to educate older adults about personal computers.

- ▶ Pfizer has a $5 million program involving several nonprofit institutions that is aimed at improving children's health.

- ▶ MCI donates a percentage of phone payments made by business owner customers to the Nature Conservancy or the Audubon Society.

Is Corporate Social Investing Necessary?

These are examples of effective corporate-nonprofit partnerships that were born and raised without the helping hand of the ten-step corporate social investing model. And that leads to the obvious question: Is social investing really necessary if businesses are already forging strategic relationships with nonprofit organizations? The answer is yes for a number of reasons.

IT BRINGS CORPORATE-NONPROFIT ALLIANCES OUT OF THE DARK

Many corporations deliberately keep their social responsibility activities in a dim light or in the closet because they aren't sure how different stakeholders will view such commitments. In contrast, corporate social investing should encourage businesses to be more open about what they are doing with nonprofit organizations. Because the ten-step model makes it clear that a company is using its nonprofit investments to enhance the value of the corporation as well as to benefit society, businesses should be less inclined to want to hide such sensible, business-enhancing expenditures.

Corporate social investing should encourage companies to take the wraps off whatever nonprofit partnerships are already in place, and then supplement those commitments with other strategic investments.

IT INVIGORATES THE NONPROFIT SECTOR

As has been mentioned before, corporate social investing could mean $3 billion or more in new funding for nonprofits each year. This could prove to be the difference between survival and collapse for many nonprofits.

Very few nonprofit organizations have a strong sense of financial security. Endowments are rare and the quest for raising money is usually never-ending. Because of the slow growth in gifts and donations, these organizations have had to rely more on fees and charges to sustain their services. Surprising to some, the government provides only about one-third of nonprofit revenues. Charitable contributions (from all sources, not just businesses) represent just 18 percent of the total nonprofit dollars raised.

Whether a nonprofit organization lives or dies may not seem that consequential in the eyes of some businesses. But a quick tutorial on the economic importance of the nonprofit sector might alter that point of view. In the United States, the operating expenditures of nonprofits account for over 7 percent of the gross national product. Nonprofits employed nearly eight million people in 1990 (latest reliable data), and those employment numbers would have been a lot higher were it not for the estimated ninety-four million-plus adult volunteers who donated an average of 4.2 hours a week to their organizations.

It comes down to this: nonprofits *are* worth keeping around. They serve as social safety nets and improve our quality of life.

IT ENCOURAGES MORE CREATIVE ALLIANCES

Corporate social investing enables companies and nonprofits to think out of what has been the traditional philanthropy box. The process should lead to bold new ventures like Campbell Soup Company's decision to team up with the American Heart Association and the American Diabetes Association to produce a line of mail-order meals to combat high cholesterol, high blood pressure, and diabetes.

Business-nonprofit thinking aimed at mutually important issues will produce a wider array of strategically focused initiatives. Expect to see more high-impact grants like State Farm Insurance Company's $8.7 million payment to the Children's Hospital of Philadelphia. The money is being used to look for different kinds of child safety seats and other devices that will reduce the risk of injury to children involved in automobile accidents—a worthy social goal and one that is obviously important to an insurance company that wants to lower its claims payments.

Warning: innovation does come with a risk of criticism. *BusinessWeek* accused the American Heart Association of "selling its soul" by lending its logo for a price ($2,400 for the first year and $650 for each year thereafter) to food companies. Even seemingly noncontroversial partnerships can come under attack. Example: in 1993, the Environmental Defense Fund joined with McDonald's restaurants to help the company reach a decision to switch Styrofoam clamshell boxes for containers made with recycled materials. Although the benefits of the partnership appeared to be above reproach, it has been held up by some critics as an example of how big business buys off nonprofit organizations.

Even in the face of a potential backlash now and again, companies and nonprofits should not be discouraged from trying new affiliations. There may be disappointments or failures along the way, but for every attempt that falls short, the corporate social investment process will generate many other successes.

IT HELPS NONPROFITS AND CORPORATIONS DO WHAT'S RIGHT

Corporate social investing makes it "right" for nonprofits to interact with businesses in ways that perhaps some organizations have considered inappropriate in the past. The ten-step model clarifies the kinds of relationships a nonprofit can have with a company (and vice versa). That clarification opens new windows of opportunity for nonprofit organizations.

Instead of relying exclusively on handouts, nonprofits can work with businesses to construct mutually rewarding programs and projects. This won't always be an easy transition for some organizations. Bill Shore, the executive who runs the nonprofit Share Our Strength, explains why: "The nonprofit sector is rich in compassion and idealism, but is entrepreneurially bankrupt, stuck in the posture of settling for that tiny margin of the financial universe that consists of leftover wealth." Corporate social investing makes it possible for nonprofit organizations to go beyond that "tiny margin" and venture into other parts of the private sector where more powerful corporate partnerships are likely to be found.

For businesses, corporate social investing defines the "right" kind of relationship that can exist between the corporate and nonprofit sectors. The ten-step model will make it possible for corporations to back up with an effective management plan the eloquent words that David Rockefeller spoke to the New York Economic Club back in 1996: "*The fact is that the implementation of well-conceived corporate responsibility turns out to be good business. It makes for good friends and good customers. There is nothing inconsistent about being socially responsible on the one hand and doing what is right for the shareholders on the other.*"

With the advent of corporate social investing, companies can now manage their way to an intelligent, productive relationship with society—and make their own businesses more successful while doing so.

References

FOREWORD BY PETER LYNCH

Articles, Reports, Books

Corporate Volunteerism: How Families Make a Difference. New York: The Conference Board, 1997.

Developing a Corporate Volunteer Program: Guidelines for Success. Washington, D.C.: Points of Light Foundation, 1993.

Gerson, Michael J. "Do Do-Gooders Do Much Good?" *U.S. News & World Report,* April 28, 1997.

Points of Light Foundation Corporate Alert. Washington, D.C.: Points of Light Foundation, February 1998.

"Summit's Good Intentions Run Against Social Trends." *USA Today,* April 28, 1997.

The Power of Volunteering. Washington, D.C.: INDEPENDENT SECTOR, 1997.

Trends in Giving and Volunteering. Washington, D.C.: INDEPENDENT SECTOR and Gallup Organization, October 9, 1996.

CHAPTER 1: THE CONFUSED STATE OF CORPORATE PHILANTHROPY

Background information for this chapter was provided by the newsletter *Business Ethics* (November/December 1997), *Corporate Philanthropy Report* (August 1997), and *New Brunswick (N.J.) Home News & Tribune* (November 13, 1996). Specific sources follow.

Articles, Reports

"Denny's Hits a Grand Slam for Save the Children." *Corporate Philanthropy Report,* January 1998.

Elliot, Stuart. "A Soft-Bodied Toy and Cause-Related Marketing." *New York Times,* November 26, 1997.

Freudenheim, Milt. "Marriage of Necessity: Nonprofit Groups and Drug Makers." *New York Times,* August 20, 1996.

Kaplan, Ann E. ed., *Giving USA.* New York: AAFRC Trust for Philanthropy, 1995, 1996, 1997.

Miller, William H. "Citizenship That's Hard to Ignore." *Industry Week,* September 2, 1996.

Piturro, Marlene C. "Creative Philanthropy." *Profiles: The Magazine of Continental Airlines,* November 1995.

Sebastian, Pamela. "Sponsorship Spending Will Grow" (news brief). *Wall Street Journal,* January 23, 1997.

CHAPTER 2: A NEW WAY OF THINKING AND ACTING

Articles, Reports, Books

Center for Corporate Community Relations. *Corporate Community Relations Letter.* Boston: Boston College, October 1996.

Corporate Contributions, 1994, 1995, 1996. New York: The Conference Board, 1995, 1996, 1997.

General Motors. *Annual Report, 1996.* Detroit: General Motors.

General Motors Caring for People, 1996. Philanthropic Annual Report. Detroit: General Motors.

Fogarty, Thomas A. "Corporations Use Causes for Effect." *USA Today,* November 10, 1997.

Friedman, Milton. "The Social Responsibility of Business Is to Increase Its Profits." *New York Times Magazine,* September 13, 1970.

John C. Whitehead Fund for Not-for-Profit Management. *Harvard Business School Social Enterprise Overview.* Boston: Harvard University, 1997.

Makower, Joel. *Beyond the Bottom Line.* New York: Simon & Schuster, 1994.

Moore, Jennifer, and Grant Williams. "Give and Tell." *Chronicle of Philanthropy,* November 13, 1997.

R. R. Donnelley & Sons. *Annual Report, 1996.* Chicago: R. R. Donnelley & Sons.

R. R. Donnelley Community Relations Report, 1996. Chicago: R. R. Donnelley & Sons.

Social Investment Forum. Web Site. [http//www.socialinvest.org/news.htm]. 1997

Stein, Herbert. "Corporate America, Mind Your Own Business." *Wall Street Journal,* July 15, 1996.

"Tax-Exempt Organizations Registered with the IRS." *Chronicle of Philanthropy,* October 3, 1996.

CHAPTER 3: MOVING FROM CORPORATE GIVING TO CORPORATE SOCIAL INVESTING

Articles

Adams, John. "Dissecting Corporate Goodness." *American Advertising,* Spring 1996.

"American Red Cross" (news brief). *Corporate Philanthropy Report,* October 1996, p. 2.

CHAPTER 4: EXTRACTING BUSINESS VALUE FROM SOCIAL INVESTMENTS

Articles, Miscellaneous

Anderson Consulting. Full-page advertisement. *The Wall Street Journal,* January 16, 1998, p. A7.

Beres, Derek. "Business: When Ice Cream Is Topped with Ethics." *New Brunswick (N.J.) Home News & Tribune,* October 11, 1996.

Enrico, Dottie. "Super Bowl Ad Roster Filled at $1.2 Million a Spot." *USA Today,* January 5, 1997.

CHAPTER 5: WHICH NONPROFITS QUALIFY—AND WHICH DON'T

Articles, Reports, Books

"The NPT 100: America's 100 Biggest Nonprofits." *Nonprofit Times,* November 1996.

"You've Got to Have Heart." *Corporate Philanthropy Report,* October 1995.

Internal Revenue Service. *Cumulative List of Organizations: Publication 78.* Washington, D.C.: Internal Revenue Service, September 1996.

Kotler, Philip, and Alan R. Andreasen. *Strategic Marketing for Nonprofit Organizations.* Englewood Cliffs, New Jersey: Prentice Hall, 1996.

CHAPTER 6: MAKING A DECLARATION FOR CORPORATE SOCIAL INVESTING

Articles, Reports, Books

Barasch, Douglas S. "God and Toothpaste." *New York Times Magazine,* December 22, 1996.

Johnson & Johnson. *Annual Report, 1997.* New Brunswick, New Jersey: Johnson & Johnson.

Makower, Joel. *Beyond the Bottom Line.* New York: Simon & Schuster, 1994.

Tom's of Maine Common Good Report, 1995. Kennebunk, Maine: Tom's of Maine.

CHAPTER 7: THE CEO ENDORSEMENT

Articles, Reports, Books

Co-Op America's National Green Pages. Washington, D.C.: Co-Op America, 1995.

Kahn, Faith Stevelman. Pandora's Box: Managerial Discretion and the Problem of Corporate Philanthropy. Unpublished doctoral dissertation, New York University, 1996.

Karson, Stanley G. "Why Corporate Executives Must Be Civic Leaders." *Chronicle of Philanthropy,* November 2, 1995.

Makower, Joel. *Beyond the Bottom Line.* New York: Simon & Schuster, 1994.

Moore, Jennifer, and Grant Williams. "Corporate Giving, the Buffet Way." *Chronicle of Philanthropy,* November 13, 1997.

Richards, Bill. "Berkshire Hathaway Pleases Shareholders by Letting Them Earmark Corporate Gifts." *Wall Street Journal,* May 11, 1983.

Rockefeller, David. "America After Downsizing: Maximizing Society's Profits." Speech to New York Economic Club, September 12, 1996.

Todd, Richard. "Looking for Andrew Carnegie." *Worth,* November 1996.

Sebastian, Pamela. "Corporate Giving" (news brief). *Wall Street Journal,* October 10, 1996.

Zorc, Anne. "Shareholder Resolutions: The Power of Ownership." In Rosemary Brown and Anne Zorc eds., *You, Your Money & the World.* Washington, D.C.: Co-Op America, 1997.

CHAPTER 8: THE ANNUAL SOCIAL INVOLVEMENT REPORT

Business Ethics (September/October 1996) provided background information for this chapter. Other sources follow.

Articles, Books

"Altruism Can Pay." *Wall Street Journal,* January 9, 1997.

"Backlash—Are CEOs Being Selfish?" *Across the Board,* July/August 1996.

Gray, Susan. "Consumers Found to Favor Goods Aiding Charities." *Chronicle of Philanthropy,* February 21, 1997.

Kahn, Faith Stevelman. Pandora's Box: Managerial Discretion and the Problem of Corporate Philanthropy. Unpublished doctoral dissertation, New York University, 1996.

Meyer, G. J. *Executive Blues: Down and Out in Corporate America.* Philadelphia: Franklin Square Press, 1995.

CHAPTER 9: COMMITTING TO THE CORPORATE SOCIAL INVESTMENT MODEL: PART I

Corporate Community Relations Letter (July/August 1997) provided background information for this chapter. Other sources follow.

Articles, Reports

Burlingame, Dwight F., and Patricia A. Frishkoff. "How Does Firm Size Affect Corporate Philanthropy?" *Corporate Philanthropy at the Crossroads.* Bloomington and Indianapolis: Indiana University Press, 1996.

Corporate Contributions, 1995. New York: The Conference Board, 1996.

Day, Michael. "Dud Drugs Dumped in Crisis Zones." *New Scientist,* January 1997.

General Electric Company. *Annual Report, 1996.* Fairfield, Connecticut: General Electric Company.

General Electric Company. *GE Fund Annual Report, 1996.* Fairfield, Connecticut: General Electric Company.

Goodman, Carla. "A Growth Industry." *Nation's Business,* January 1997.

Internal Revenue Service. *1993 Statistics of Income: Corporation Income Tax Returns.* Washington D.C.: Internal Revenue Service, 1996.

Keycorp Survey of Small Business Sentiment. Indianapolis: Wirthlin Worldwide, May 1997.

National Center for Employee Ownership. "Understanding Valuation." *Employee Ownership Report,* September/October 1997.

CHAPTER 10: COMMITTING TO THE CORPORATE SOCIAL INVESTMENT MODEL: PART II

Several publications provided background information for this chapter, including *Corporate Philanthropy Report* (October 1996, February 1997, July 1997, and August 1997), *The Wall Street Journal* (November 26, 1996, January 23, 1997, and July 29, 1997), and the *Washington Post* (May 1, 1997). Other sources follow.

Articles, Reports, Books

"A History of Leadership, Innovation, and Corporate Responsibility." *Bank American.* BankAmerica, February 3, 1997.

American Benefactor. New York: Capital Publishing LP, Winter 1997.

"BankAmerica Community Investment Programs Overview." BankAmerica Foundation presentation, February 1997.

Burton, Thomas. "AMA May Dismiss Executives Involved in Sunbeam Endorsement Pact." *Wall Street Journal,* September 18, 1997.

Cause Events. Nike SERVE 'N' SPIKE proposal. Santa Monica, California: Cause Events, 1997.

"Cause-Related Marketing Improves Customer Loyalty." *Corporate Community Relations Letter,* July/August 1996.

"Charity's Ties to Corporations Raise Questions for Some Groups." *Chronicle of Philanthropy,* May 29, 1997.

Dickey, Marilyn. "'Free Money: How Charities Can Make the Most of Matching Gifts." *Chronicle of Philanthropy,* March 6, 1997.

Environmental Law Institute Annual Report. Washington D.C.: 1995.

Freudenheim, Milt. "Marriage of Necessity: Nonprofit Groups and Drug Makers." *New York Times,* August 20, 1996.

Kaplan, Ann E. (Ed.). *Giving USA 1997.* New York: AAFRC Trust for Philanthropy, 1997.

Goodman, Ellen. "Job Creation Is the Best Display of Philanthropy." *New Brunswick (N.J.) Home News & Tribune,* September 30, 1996.

Grand Metropolitan Report on Corporate Citizenship, 1997. London: Grand Metropolitan PLC, 1997.

Harvard Business Review, November/December 1996, p. 47.

"IBM Builds on School Reform Foundation with New Grants." *Foundation & Corporate Grants Alert,* March 1997.

IEG Sponsorship Sourcebook. Chicago: IEG, Inc., 1995.

Jones, Del. "Good Works, Good Business." *USA Today,* April 25, 1997.

Kanner, Bernice. "Guilt Dinners." *New York,* December 5, 1983.

Klepper, Anne. *Global Contributions of U.S. Corporations.* New York: The Conference Board, 1993.

Koren, David C. *When Corporations Rule the World.* San Francisco: Berrett-Koehler, 1995.

Kotler, Philip, and Alan R. Andreasen. *Strategic Marketing for Nonprofit Organizations.* Englewood Cliffs, New Jersey: Prentice Hall, 1996.

LaBanca, Lisa (Ed.). "Self-Promotion: Trend or Menace?" *Corporate Community Relations Letter,* January 1997.

Logan, David. "Communications in Communities: Getting the Measure." London: The London Benchmarking Group, 1997.

Longman, Phillip J. "Endorsements for Sale." *U.S. News & World Report,* September 1, 1997.

Makower, Joel. *Beyond the Bottom Line.* New York: Simon & Schuster, 1994.

Manning, Anita. "Double-Duty Presents Also Give to Charity." *USA Today,* December 16, 1996.

Martin, Nita. "Playing with Cards." *Corporate Philanthropy Report,* February 1998.

Mescon, Timothy S., and Donn J. Tilson. "Corporate Philanthropy: A Strategic Approach to the Bottom Line." *California Management Review.* Berkeley: University of California, Winter 1987.

Metropolitan Life Insurance Company and Metropolitan Life Foundation—1996 Report of Contributions. New York: Metropolitan Life Insurance Company, 1997.

Molpus, Ann R. ed. *Philanthropy Matters.* Duke University Medical Center, October 1997.

Moore, Jennifer. "Drug Manufacturer Kills Controversial 'Arthritis Foundation' Pain Relievers." *Chronicle of Philanthropy,* October 31, 1996.

Nelton, Sharon. "Loans with Interest—and Principle." *Nation's Business,* January 1997.

"New Law Clarifies Rules on Sponsorships." *Chronicle of Philanthropy,* December 11, 1997.

"No Apologies, No Regrets: The Smithsonian's Progress." *Corporate Philanthropy Report,* January 1997.

Philanthropy Trends That Count. Alexandria, Virginia: Capitol Publications, April 1997.

"Pipeline Company's Role in Smithsonian's Alaska Exhibit Fuels Criticism." *Chronicle of Philanthropy,* September 27, 1997.

Pritchet, Paul C. "Only Congress Can Help." *USA Today,* September 19, 1997.

Sebastian, Pamela. "Sponsorship Spending Will Grow" (news brief). *Wall Street Journal,* January 23, 1997.

Smith, Craig. *Giving by Industry: A Reference Guide to the New Corporate Philanthropy.* Alexandria, Virginia: Capitol Publications, 1996.

Steele, Carolyn Odom (Ed.). "Helping Children Touch the World." *AT&T Partners,* Fall/Winter 1996.

"The AMA Isn't Feeling So Hot." *BusinessWeek,* September 1, 1997.

Uchitelle, Louis. "Basic Research Is Losing Out as Companies Stress Results." *New York Times,* October 8, 1996.

"Volunteering on Company Time" (chart). *USA Today,* April 28, 1997.

CHAPTER 12: BUILDING THE MANAGEMENT TEAM FOR SOCIAL INVESTING

Background information was provided by the September 1997 issue of *Corporate Philanthropy Report.* Other sources follow.

Articles, Reports

Business for Social Responsibility. *BSR Update.* San Francisco: Business for Social Responsibility, December 1996.

"Deciding What's Important." *Corporate Philanthropy Report,* March 1997.

Gray, Susan. "Business Are Said to Give without Measuring Effects." *Chronicle of Philanthropy,* April 3, 1997.

Gray, Susan, and Jennifer Moore. "Big Gifts from Big Businesses." *Chronicle of Philanthropy,* July 11, 1996.

Measuring Corporate Community Involvement. New York: The Conference Board, 1996.

CHAPTER 13: THE DAY-TO-DAY MANAGER

Complete names and addresses for the following organizations can be found in Chapter 13.

Catalogs

Certificate Programs in Corporate Community Relations. Boston: Center for Corporate Community Relations, 1998.

Corporate Contributions Management Academy. Palm Coast, Florida: Business & Nonprofit Strategies, 1998.

Management Seminar on Corporate Contributions. New York: The Conference Board, 1996.

CHAPTER 14: MAKING IT WORK

Articles

"Council on Foundations' Notebook: Age-Old Questions, New Ideas." *Corporate Philanthropy Report,* June 1997.

Drohan, Thomas E. "Set Specific Goal for Private-Sector Support." *Financier,* March 1982.

CHAPTER 15: THE POWER OF CORPORATE-NONPROFIT ALLIANCES

Corporate Philanthropy Report (October 1996, May 1997, October 1997, and January 1998) provided background information for this chapter. Specific sources follow.

Articles, Reports, Books

Connections: The Co-Op America Newsletter. Washington, D.C.: Co-Op America, Fall 1997.

Kotler, Philip, and Alan R. Andreasen. *Strategic Marketing for Nonprofit Organizations.* Englewood Cliffs, New Jersey: Prentice Hall, 1996.

Raeburn, Paul. "The Heart Association Is Selling Its Soul." *BusinessWeek,* November 24, 1997.

Rockefeller, David. "America After Downsizing: Maximizing Society's Profits." Speech to New York Economic Club, September 12, 1996.

Salamon, Lester M. *America's Nonprofit Sector at a Crossroads.* New York: Nathan Cummings Foundation, 1997.

"State Farm and the Children's Hospital Form Alliance" (press release). Rohnert Park, California: State Farm Insurance Company, November 6, 1997.

"The Good, the Bad, and the Ugly: Three Views of Corporate Partnerships." *Corporate Philanthropy Report,* May 1997.

Index

commitment to invest percentages
of, 92–114
explaining in annual reports, 86
private sector environmental scans,
117. *See also* strategic planning
proactive investments, 145
product donations
versus cash, 113
considerations for manufacturing
companies, 108–114
production for purpose of,
112–113
restricted commercial transactions,
179–180
as social investing "currency," 175
valuing a product, 105–108
productivity and volunteerism, xvi.
See also volunteerism
product purchases, exclusion of in
social investment totals, 179–180
professional publications, 205
profitability, 14
profit sharing, 3–4
promotion
formula for spending on, 163
for sponsors, 154
for sponsorship, 154
proposals, for sponsorship, 153–154
Publication 78, list of 501 (c) (3) status organizations, 50
publications, professional, 205
public reporting. *See* disclosure statements

qualifying nonprofit organizations,
46–53
quality-of-life analyses, 117
quality-of-life investments, 138–140
quantities, reasonable, 110
quid pro quo contracts, 10

reactive investments, 145
reasonable quantities, 110
reasons for corporate social investing, 36–45, 73–79, 212–215
recognition, 191
record keeping
for small businesses, 102
for volunteerism, 181

recruiting employees. *See* employees
reengineering, 5–6
regular business expenses, 26
versus charitable deductions, 145
rejecting contribution requests,
102–103, 141–142, 147
relationships with nonprofit organizations. *See* corporate-nonprofit
relationships
religious organizations, 501 (c) (3)
status, 50
reporting community involvement,
template for, 176f
reporting social investing. *See* disclosure statements; non-reported
contributions
reports, annual. *See* disclosure statements
research funding, as risk-investment
leveraged business investments
(LBIs), 167–168
restricted commercial transactions,
121
exclusion of in social investment
totals, 178–181
retail fair market value (FMV), of
donated products, 107–108,
110–111
returns on investment (ROI), 38–43,
xii
rightsizing, 5–6
risk investments, 146, 167–170
risks
accepting sponsorship, 157–158
cause-related relationships,
166–167
written annual social involvement
reports, 82
Rockefeller, David, 79–80
on business leadership, 65–66
implementation of corporate
social investing programs, 215
RODES planning process, 116–123.
See also strategic planning

salable products, 108–109. *See also*
product donations
scientific institutions, 501 (c) (3) status, 49

The Author

Over the past twenty years, Curt Weeden has been directly or indirectly responsible for the distribution of more than $1 billion in corporate contributions. He recently founded Business & Nonprofit Strategies, Inc. (BNS), which manages the Corporate Contributions Management Academy in Palm Coast, Florida. The academy provides management education to contributions, public affairs, public relations, and other business executives who interact with nonprofit organizations on behalf of their corporations.

For seven years, Weeden served as Johnson & Johnson's vice president for corporate contributions. Under his direction, the Johnson & Johnson multinational contributions program grew from $41 million in 1991 to $146 million in 1997.

Prior to joining Johnson & Johnson, Weeden headed a consulting firm that extended contributions management services to several of the nation's largest businesses—AlliedSignal, Merck, Xerox, BankAmerica, General Motors, and many others.

Earlier in his career, Weeden worked as vice president of The Asia Foundation (San Francisco) and AFS International Scholarships (New York). He held positions with the National Education Association and the New Jersey Education Association after completing his undergraduate and graduate degrees at Northeastern University (Boston) and New York University.

Weeden has also provided consulting services to private foundations and the J. Seward Johnson, Sr. 1963 Charitable Trust. He writes and speaks extensively on philanthropy and social responsibility issues.

Weeden can be contacted at the Corporate Contributions Management Academy or BNS at 138 Palm Coast Parkway, Suite 115, Palm Coast, Florida 32137 (E-mail: Director@BNSInc.com; Web site: http://www.BNSInc.com).

Berrett-Koehler Publishers

BERRETT-KOEHLER is an independent publisher of books, periodicals, and other publications at the leading edge of new thinking and innovative practice on work, business, management, leadership, stewardship, career development, human resources, entrepreneurship, and global sustainability.

Since the company's founding in 1992, we have been committed to supporting the movement toward a more enlightened world of work by publishing books, periodicals, and other publications that help us to integrate our values with our work and work lives, and to create more humane and effective organizations.

We have chosen to focus on the areas of work, business, and organizations, because these are central elements in many people's lives today. Furthermore, the work world is going through tumultuous changes, from the decline of job security to the rise of new structures for organizing people and work. We believe that change is needed at all levels— individual, organizational, community, and global—and our publications address each of these levels.

We seek to create new lenses for understanding organizations, to legitimize topics that people care deeply about but that current business orthodoxy censors or considers secondary to bottom-line concerns, and to uncover new meaning, means, and ends for our work and work lives.

See next page for other books from Berrett-Koehler Publishers

Other leading-edge business books from Berrett-Koehler Publishers

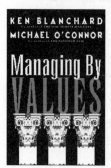

Managing By Values

Ken Blanchard and Michael O'Connor

BASED ON over twenty-five years of research and application, *Managing by Values* provides a practical game plan for defining, clarifying, and communicating an organization's values and insuring that its practices are in line with those values throughout the organization.

Hardcover, 140 pages, 1/97 • ISBN 1-57675-007-8 CIP
Item no. 50078-251 $20.00

Imaginization

New Mindsets for Seeing, Organizing, and Managing

Gareth Morgan

"IMAGINIZATION" is a way of thinking and organizing. It is a key managerial skill that will help you develop your creative potential, and find innovative solutions to difficult problems. It answers the call for more creative forms of organization and management. *Imaginization* shows how to put this approach into practice.

Paperback, 350 pages, 8/97 • ISBN 1-57675-026-4 CIP
Item no. 50264-251 $19.95

When Corporations Rule the World

David C. Korten

DAVID KORTEN offers an alarming exposé of the devastating consequences of economic globalization and a passionate message of hope in this well-reasoned, extensively researched analysis. He documents the human and environmental consequences of economic globalization, and explain why human survival depends on a community-based, people-centered alternative.

Paperback, 384 pages, 9/96 • ISBN 1-887208-01-1 CIP
Item no. 0801-251 $19.95

Hardcover, 09/95 • ISBN 1-887208-00-3 CIP
Item no. 08003-2510 $29.95

Available at your favorite bookstore, or call (800) 929-2929